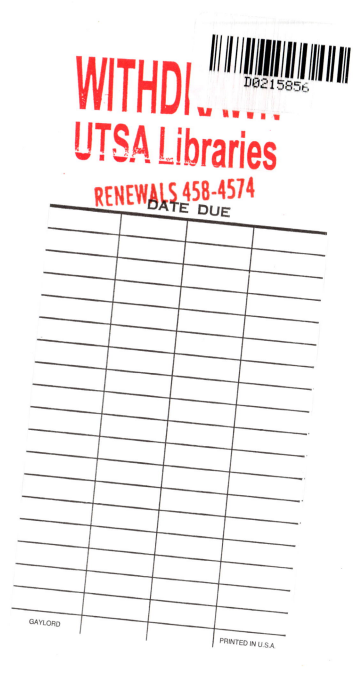

TASTING TOURISM:
TRAVELLING FOR FOOD AND DRINK

New Directions in Tourism Analysis

Series Editors: Kevin Meethan, University of Plymouth
Dimitri Ioannides, Southwest Missouri State University

Although tourism is becoming increasingly popular as both a taught subject and an area for empirical investigation, the theoretical underpinnings of many approaches have tended to be eclectic and somewhat underdeveloped. However, recent developments indicate that the field of tourism studies is beginning to develop in a more theoretically informed manner, but this has not yet been matched by current publications.

The aim of this series is to fill this gap with high quality monographs or edited collections that seek to develop tourism analysis at both theoretical and substantive levels using approaches which are broadly derived from allied social science disciplines such as Sociology, Social Anthropology, Human and Social Geography, and Cultural Studies. As tourism studies covers a wide range of activities and sub fields, certain areas such as Hospitality Management and Business, which are already well provided for, would be excluded. The series will therefore fill a gap in the current overall pattern of publication.

Suggested themes to be covered by the series, either singly or in combination, include – consumption; cultural change; development; gender; globalisation; political economy; social theory; sustainability.

Also in the series

Tourist's Experience of Place
Jaakko Suvantola
ISBN 0 7546 1830 7

Tourism and Economic Development
R.N. Ghosh, M.A.B. Siddique and R. Gabbay
ISBN 0 7546 3053 6

Tasting Tourism:
Travelling for Food and Drink

PRISCILLA BONIFACE

ASHGATE

Published by
Ashgate Publishing Limited
Gower House
Croft Road
Aldershot
Hampshire GU11 3HR
England

Ashgate Publishing Company
Suite 420
101 Cherry Street
Burlington, VT 05401-4405
USA

Ashgate website: http://www.ashgate.com

British Library Cataloguing in Publication Data
Boniface, Priscilla
    Tasting tourism : travelling for food and drink. - (New
    directions in tourism analysis)
    1.Tourism 2.Food 3.Gastronomy
    I.Title
    338.4'791

Library of Congress Cataloging-in-Publication Data
Boniface, Priscilla.
    Tasting tourism : travelling for food and drink / Priscilla Boniface.
        p. cm. -- (New directions in tourism analysis)
    Includes bibliographical references and index.
    ISBN 0-7546-3514-7 (alk. paper)
    1. Food. 2. Great Britain--Description and travel. 3. Europe--Description and travel. I.
Title. II. Series.

TX357 .B657 2003
394.1'0941--dc21

                                                                2002038377

ISBN 0 7546 3514 7

Printed and bound in Great Britain by MPG Books Ltd, Bodmin, Cornwall.

Contents

List of Illustrations

Preface

This book is about food and drink tourism, as seen especially through a cultural 'lens'. Its assumes that a culture represents the particular attitude and way of life of a person or group, and so it sees culture as conditioning what people do, how they do it, and why they do it. Therefore, it regards culture – past and present – as an invariable and inevitable part of food and drink tourism, and as necessary to the discussion of the subject.

The consideration is about what food and drink tourism consists of. It is about why food and drink provisions and information points have become tourists' destinations in their own right rather than remaining only among tourism features and components. It is about the cultural dimensions and dispositions influencing and determining, finding input and appearing, in the food and drink tourism domain.

The shape of the book is: in Chapters 1–4 introducing the subject, providing context and theory and delivering perspective on general dimensions; in Chapters 5–11 considering practical entities of efforts and visitor provisions, in Chapter 12 looking at some specific food and drinks and how they are acting as subjects of tourism activity; and finally in Chapter 13 drawing conclusions about food and drink tourism and seeing implications for its impending shape of format and style.

In span the book is international. Many parts of the world are discussed as appropriate. Quite deliberately, however, the UK forms the central geographical area of consideration. The UK is focused upon for these following reasons. It is currently at a turning point in relation to how it uses its countryside and where emphases lie between agriculture and types of diversification, tourism most particularly. Its post-industrial phase is well advanced, and so it demonstrates strongly efforts to find new ways of gaining income, deployment, and leisure for the community. It also portrays efforts of diversification for urban processing and manufacturing plants of food and drink as well as for rural growers and farmers of the raw food and drink materials. It is the location for debates and initiatives in relation to food and drink, not least because of the various 'crises' suffered such as Bovine Spongiform Encephalopathy [BSE], variant Creutzfeldt-Jakob Disease [vCJD], foot and mouth disease. It has a close concern and involvement in considerations about quality of food and drink, environmental ethics and human outcomes of industrial food and drink production practices, and so it is the location of arrival of a considerable interest in and market for, organic, 'real' and locally obtained food. Also, the UK is a modern gathering point of cultural representation and this contributes to its being a good entity to be explored. So, the UK is being treated as a case study, and which portrays currently a picture of wide significance.

The endeavour is that the book should portray all relevant dimensions. The author is aware, nonetheless, of manifesting a mildly polemical stance and flavour of idea – a perspective doubtless conditioned through events and cultural dimensions currently presiding. This shade of perspective is of being particularly approving of the individual, artisan, local and wholesome as contrasted with the commodified, large and industrial in output and proportion. The author believes that adopting a view somewhat weighted towards a 'small and from immediate area are beautiful' preference is reflecting a strain of culture and direction now key in the world.

In essence, the aims of the book are to demonstrate how food and drink tourism is being operated, to indicate the cultural issues present and having effect, to make suggestions about the future, and, so, overall, to manifest cause and composition of what is, and may become, 'Tasting Tourism'.

Acknowledgements

This book could not have been produced without the assistance of many people. Professor Mike Robinson has helped greatly in discussing the subject of the book with the author and in commenting on the draft text. He has proposed many ideas and lines of consideration that appear in the book. Mike Grover has given much support. Emeritus-Professor Peter Fowler has provided valuable comment. Valerie Rose, Pauline Beavers and all the people at Ashgate involved in the publishing of the book have been kindly efficient. Of the many other individuals and organizations that have generously helped through giving information and answering my questions, there are too many to be named separately. To all of you, a lot of thanks.

List of Abbreviations

CAMRA   Campaign for Real Ale
DCMS   Department of Culture, Media and Sport [UK]
DEFRA   Department of Food, Rural Affairs and Farming [UK]
ETC   English Tourism Council
MAFF   Ministry of Agriculture, Food and Fisheries [UK]
TICS   Tourist Information Centres
WTO   World Tourism Organization

Chapter 1

Food and Drink, From Past to Present

Introduction

Background and Intent

Along with reasons of practicality and necessity, our practices concerning food and drink are driven by context and environment, belief and convention, aspiration and want to display. In short, lifeway – culture – is an integral element of how and what we eat and drink. Similarly, culture guides how tourism is used and operates (Boniface, 1998b, pp. 746–749). Therefore, this book in looking at food and drink tourism must accommodate and view culture's role in the activity. To explore food and drink tourism is unavoidably to visit culture also. The thrust of the book is on food and drink tourism, as it is now and is likely to emerge and develop; and culture will be considered both as it makes cause and input to the endeavour now and as it might do henceforth. Nonetheless, our exploration and presentation needs some background about influences at work, formerly and currently.

The purpose of this chapter, therefore, is to offer some modest general background and comment on those various ways of using food and drink connecting and inputting to the current scene and which in particular are influencing food and drink becoming tourism destinations. The next chapter will develop the portion of discussion which concerns *how* and *why* tourism should now so noticeably be adopting food and drink as main products and foci rather than only as usual and necessary tourism by-products. While, as has been said, culture will feature throughout the book, it is in these first two chapters that relevant theoretical aspects will be mentioned mostly, and both those concerning culture and sociology. This attention is as part of producing a framework for the practical manifestations and certain main example types to be addressed as topics in the book.

It is not an aim of this chapter to deliver a history of food and drink. Such is provided thoroughly elsewhere (e.g. Fernández-Armesto, 2001; Flandrin and Montanari, 2000; Kiple and Ornelas, 2000; Tannahill, 2002; Toussaint-Samat, 1994). Its purpose is to identify certain core strains of behaviour in relation to food and drink. Such strains are both similar and different in various parts of the world, a fact that seems to encourage tourism's current adoption of food and drink as central objects. The intention is to pick upon key moments and attitudes during the historical period that seem to contribute significantly to the current food and drink tourism situation and its flavours of type.

In the Past

Travelling to Obtain Food

Food and drink connected with and used by human beings has delivered an overall entity of practice. This is that humankind gathers or cultivates food and drink materials, and prepares these for consumption. The standard process to obtain food and drink material in the past until around 8,000 BC (Harris, 1996, p. ix) was by hunting and gathering (and to certain groups it has stayed thus). It is interesting to observe that, albeit usually over a relatively small area, the process was essentially *travelling* for food and drink matter and so the action is a precursor – of kind, and in an interpretation – of food and drink tourism. The practice was, of course, however, concerned with obtaining sustenance rather than having any dimension of being leisure and pleasure activity and so a key feature that distinguishes tourism was not present. However, already heralded was an aspect, to be explored in this book, of the bridge and overlap dynamics between food and drink and its concerns being everyday entities but too matters to the leisure realm.

Agriculture's Arrival

Farming's introduction – as Harris says, around 10,000 years ago – was a massive and influential event. Only in North America did agriculture come considerably later at around the BC/AD changeover. The general shift – occurring at various individual times across the world – was momentous. Finding and collecting items of food and drink would, of course, have had its own ways – these conditioned by physical and attitudinal circumstances – but with the advent of food being farmed, a greater level of control and imposition was introduced. The experience to humankind of food being obtained from farming was in considerable contrast to the one – mainly at the mercy of externality and serendipity – which is basic to the character of hunting and gathering. What happened was that a much greater extent of possibility was offered than hitherto for humans to decide and make ways of food handling and using. Food's arrival could be planned for and known in advance; a ritual and cycle came into place for food's appearance; the very increased secure awareness that food would be manifest permitted time for more attention to be given to issues and circumstances surrounding the production and consumption of food; food's types could be chosen, though, of course, this procedure was tempered by the limitations of local soil and climate conditions. A major change was that procedures for agriculture needed to be introduced. That there was a farming cycle, and including large periods of 'wait' while crops grew and ripened, meant that a group not only operated together and did certain things at same time, but had time on its hands and at same moment. Differing climate and landscape types lent themselves to differing and particular crops and so distinct farming cultural landscapes with their associated practices arrived and were set to progress and evolve on varying trajectories. A farmer also needed to stay put by his/her farmland, seeing its good order and husbandry, rather than wander as a nomad. All these events lent a situation for the development of a community-specific way of life and attitude in which custom had milieu for developing beyond what the basic features of immediacy and necessity cause to shape. A circumstance had been reached to allow the luxury of greater attention to the ceremony and meanings and methods associated with food and drink and their production and consumption. With farming's arrival came too greater time and possibility than before to make a range of drinks and including alcoholic, mood altering, types. This lent further encouragement for food and drink being associated with, or used centrally for, celebration, festival, event and ritual (Luard, 2001). With abundance or surplus, food and drink could be chosen and used for making statements, such as those relating to politics, identity, status, gratitude, affluence and superiority, or joy at an occasion, and too for celebrating key moments in the agricultural cycle, and as have such been carried through to the present. With a definite and known cycle of production, it was possible to plan and so events orientated on food and drink could be scheduled ahead of time and their circumstances and format be positively organized.

How Culture Could Flourish and Diversify

The overall alteration just depicted was evolutionary not sudden and the phase happened at different times over the world. The generality was of a change of process from a life of subsistence and uncertainty being undergone to a life of some certainty of nourishment being experienced and with enough fallow time for leisure and developing ways of living as art. In short, the stage was set for culture in relation to food and drink to emerge as a more enriched entity and with more variety across the world due to various groups' circumstances, dispositions and wishes. Now, food and drink production and consumption had more wide and greater opportunities for showing culture and for being linked in as cultural practices. As can be seen, already, 8,000–10,000 years or so back, a platform and circumstance had been laid for culture, food and drink, *and* tourism, to feature and interact together. An association had been laid for food and drink to concern pleasure and to be allied with the non-essentials of existence additional to those daily necessity demands. So food and drink was then, and so early in time, already in occupation of the pleasure periphery.

The Beginning of Food and Drink Tourism

Fernández-Armesto proposes six revolutions in the history of food. The first is cooking; the second is 'the discovery that food is more than sustenance' (2001, p. xv); the third is domesticating and breeding certain animals to eat; the fourth is growing plants to eat; the fifth is 'the use of food as a means and index of social differentiation'; the sixth is the trade over long distance of foodstuffs and associated cultures (p. xvi); the seventh is the ecological exchange and moving happening due to European colonialization; the final one is developed world industrialization. It is clearly manifest that food and drink tourism has beginnings and impulses through time and from each of Fernández-Armesto's defined revolutions. There are two critical elements. One is food and drink emerging as more than subsistence articles and becoming items attached to ritual and way that are more complex than before as a result. The other is material and idea being transferred. This book's thesis, moreover and specially, is that a considerable counter-revolution against food industrialization has appeared and that this is a main trigger to food and drink tourism emerging. Further, the arguments are that tourism is providing a needed society outlet to these concerns and for which it is the chosen candidate due to tourism's essence being travel and since tourism allows time of adequate attention to an item that in daily life is more difficult. Perhaps, a revolution number seven can be said as in process.

Society using Tourism

In effect, a society concern and interest is being explored and new styles of approach are being attempted through tourism as the medium. Modern tourism has helped the endeavour in two ways. First, in having needed to provide – to cater to mass tourism – new types of mass arena such as theme parks, resort complexes, airports (Pascoe, 2001), which are not bound by old cultural conventions, such fresh and hyper-industrialized entities have emerged to show size and inclusivity. So exclusivity and being 'Un-tourist' is the current prize of the minority (Birkett, 2002, pp. 6–7). Second, in offering spaces distant from home, tourism has delivered areas relatively light of usual cultural and personal baggage – albeit that the basic entities of food and drink occupy any whereabouts – and so these lend themselves to experimentation and new idea without interruption and intrusion from weight of home opinion. This second dimension to tourism is what renders its importance as a matter of general interest and worthy of studying. As an activity encompassing most daily life features, but these being used and chosen by the tourist by criteria of pleasure and without unwanted distractions needing to be present, tourism can be used for experimentation. Tourism is a laboratory for 'real', everyday, life. It provides pointers to how everyday life may change and become. It should be noted for its significance, that alongside the tourist who is occupying temporary leisure space for experimentation and who is present in 'leisure time' will be the host who is residing in ongoing everyday space and keeping to norm and habit and who is located in 'everyday time'.

Influences from History

From the myriad events and happenings to food and drink items and connected with them through history, to be highlighted and discussed here below are those that seem to bear upon, herald and lead to food and drink tourism.

Environmental Connection

A first essential dimension is the connection to land, along with link to natural environment generally and relationship to climate. Until the industrialization period with the mass move to towns and cities, the sight of food and drink stuffs growing and familiarity with its processes were routine to people. To countries still developing, the intimacy with agriculture remains, but in the developed world this is not so generally. This has meant food and drink being rather distanced among modern society from being regarded as items linked to natural and agricultural processes and rather only seen in their roles of items for sustenance, and to use in link with celebration and ritual. Food and drink's associations now, therefore, are less with *effort* and more with pleasure and indulgence, and this fits food and drink to be items of focus for that contemporary ritual and matter to be enjoyable, tourism.

Agriculture's arrival brought larger groups of people together engaged in production, intensification, a propensity for states to be created, and the delivery of hot spots of strength such as the Nile Delta in contrast with others (Beardsworth and Keil, 1997, pp. 28–29). A stage was set for places of expertise, and ascendancy of some over others, to emerge. The Mediterranean basin generally was an area naturally equipped for particular development and the Egyptian, Greek and Roman civilizations are testament to the dimension. This basin is also an area naturally advantaged for relatively short distance travel and goods and information exchange. As examples are these. Due to early being invaded by Greeks and Romans, Provence in France shows to this day strong Greek and Roman cultural presences. Similarly, from occupation by Muslims, southern Spain still manifests a Moorish (Islamic) cultural flavour as part of its make-up (Drysdale, 2001).

Quality Food

Another relevant dimension to which Beardsworth and Keil draw attention (p. 30) is the need for quality food to feed the brain adequately for it to think highly. So, a link is suggested as existing between best (most nutritional) food and capacity for most advanced development.

Religion and Knowledge

With centres of activity and organization arising, a circumstance is produced for practices and ways of thought in common to emerge as consequences and necessities. Group cultures emerge. Food and drink can be deployed to make corporate statement and display, to show distinction from others, and to manifest superiority over them. Type and distinctiveness of religion is one kind of main activity for which food and drink could be adopted. This is from the fundamental feature to Christianity of the Human Sacrament of bread and wine, to the privation from food of the fast, to religious days' special feasting, and rites of fertility such as the Harvest Supper. Ground-lines of Western civilization to the present day have been much laid by Greek and Roman culture and with considerable movement across land and sea of plants and commodities of food and wine. With this, religious houses have played an enormous role in civilization's march, as communities needing to maintain themselves and who overall have put a focus on developing knowledge. In the Western world, without these foci of information existing and developing – most especially in the Anglo-Saxon and Medieval periods – many food and drink items and certain food and drink production and preparation information would have been lost or not been able to increase.

Food Locations and Travels

A large generalization about material and knowledge of food and drink transfer is that this travel – maize, chocolate (Coe and Coe, 1996) and the potato being notable exceptions – has been from the (Near, Middle and Far) East to the West/North-West. Naturally, the world's most productive growing regions have been where soil is good, water is available, and climate not extreme. Other necessary components are the presence of enough able-bodied people to produce crops and enough technological knowledge and expertise and suitable material to make implements. Animals would have been needed to provide traction for machinery – however rudimentary. This would be additional to their role as food material. For animal husbandry the circumstances needed are good feeding crops, with adequate expertise to care for animals, and – in a usual abandonment of nomadism – features to contain animals from uncontrolled roaming.

Authenticity, Individuality

Becoming delineated is the emergence of territories defined by and rooted in shared attitudes, ethics, values and procedures and so being recognizably distinct places. In full circle, these then require – for bettering survival – the presence of a same outlook and a boundary to be drawn around it and then the perspective presented to outsiders and competitors. To maintain distinctiveness and strength and to avoid copying and so danger of losing exclusivity and features for viability, a place and its community would have a vested interest in, deliberately, keeping authenticity and manifesting individuality. Conversely, without importing any idea from elsewhere or trying others' approaches, an important avenue of new improvement would be lost. So, it would seem, a culture needs distinctiveness of authenticity to show identity and to be unique and avoid superfluity; but also open-ness to bring in new notion, and dynamism and creativity to see possibilities and progress in fusion and hybridization. One side of the essential reason for trade and trade-routes, such as those for coffee (Pendergrast, 2001), tea (Pettigrew, 2001), wine (Robinson, 1999), salt (Kurlansky, 2002) and spices (Dalby, 2000), is for exotica or key important items not available domestically to be then obtained. The other side is that goods similarly seen as exotic or necessary by trading partners should be offered in return. The aim through this is of both traders undergoing the benefit of heightened identity and being very attractive to the other but neither of them having their commodity duplicated elsewhere – or at least anywhere in proximity – to lose the pulling- and selling-power.

Imbalance

So often the outcome of European and Western colonialism was that the exchange was not equal and exploitation was prevalent so to deliver imbalances that are manifest into the present day. It is interesting to observe how closely tourism pursues the trajectory now, and with The West going on increasing ascendency all the while to the disadvantage of nations where the exotic resources reside. The possibility for food and drink tourism is that – with its emphasis on quality, authenticity, and specialist types – people of 'peasant' and undeveloped cultures who have yet to relinquish small-scale, artisan, authentic and individual ways hold a strong commodity. They, therefore, possess at least some vestige of power on their side.

Preparing Food

As one large part of the cultures developing concerning food and drink, along with how raw materials are grown, and for what purpose food and drink are used, is methods of preparation and cooking as central in this. Once fire had been able to be controlled and domesticated (Fernández-Armesto, 2001, pp. 1–24), arts, ways and techniques of cooking would be able to be developed. Of all countries, France has probably made the most overt play to be, and be seen as, the home of cooking. Similarly, it has a two-millennia-long experience of growing wine. France has a courtly inheritance of haut bourgeois/bourgeois, magnificent complexity to cooking and gourmandizing. Also influenced by the general interest and attention to food in France is a peasant tradition of regional specialities rooted to a particular land, environment, and culture, and probably the most remarked manifestations of these are the many cheese varieties across the nation to which more attention will be drawn later in this book.

Power and Agglomeration

It can be realized that leaders in the political and religious fields – having been in states of leisure and/or opulence and special knowledge (gained through having travelled or else by travellers coming to them), and needing power-show, display and pageant – would give several leads in the manifesting of how food and drink should be provided and consumed, and so would influence some cultural styles. The tension to follow in to the present day is that in the exchanges and attempts at emulation of each other, and notwithstanding much display and vaunting of local specialities, these in power have contributed somewhat to a globalization of food and drink and practice and manners associated. Courts and empires, and large religions crossing national and geographical boundaries, have almost been like today's multinationals, imposing a style and culture against local types. Travel and information communications have produced this outcome too, with entities being seen and known about worldwide, and when it has no longer seemed important on grounds of survival or expediency for a cultural group to stay true to its individual food and drink. For food and drink tourists, hungry and thirsty to find and show difference, this means that their options for destinations that will be rewarding to them, having regard to access and other general suitability issues, may not actually be too many. This aspect puts those communities still able to show individuality of culture, and localness and authenticity, to their food and drink products in a strong position – if they have marketing capacities to promote this benefit and enough of a suitable infrastructure to cater for tourism.

Industrialization, Urbanization, Modernity and Standardization

A modern period can be seen as arriving from the late 17th/early18[th] century, and arriving and staying through industrialization, the installation of democratic governments and ways of life, technological developments, more, faster, travel and trade and inter-communication among places and nations, improved education, urbanization. Its outcome, that is relevant to food and drink and culture, has been a way of certain similar life and attitude and inter-connected trade and finance, and which principally emanates from the Western world and that is known as globalization. In this environment, while the individual and their views are recognized and – theoretically – treated as equal, nonetheless success is caused through the efficiency, economy and lack of conflicts from standardization. The classic 20th century example of the business preference to provide a one colour (black) Ford car provided the name to the syndrome of Fordism. Ironically, individual ownership and use of the car was an early seed of a backlash against Fordism, bringing to the traveller the joys of the open road, of discovering personally varieties of food and hospitality available away from the city and mainstream. However as the activity became more mass, and so with air travel, therefore did the style and type of many food and accommodation service become specific, same and commodified (Urry, 2000) and delivering what Augé terms 'bubbles of immanence' (1999, p. 113). Gardiner describes Lefebvre as seeing modernity as not having continual stability but changing with a phase from 1850–1950 and manifested by 'the dissociation of the everyday and specialized activities, the destruction of organic communities, and the replacement of use-value by exchange-value' (2000, p. 87). The time post-1950, Gardiner says Lefebvre saw as a 'new phase' manifested by capitalism that is 'monopolistic' and 'state-directed', 'co-option and commodification of potentially subversive creative and revolutionary energies', 'the evacuation of a sense of historicity and change' and a sense of society jammed in 'eternal present' (p. 88).

The evolution of modernity can be seen as the development of extremitization and concentration to deliver a result of mono-culturalism. This essentially – along with a recognition that portions of the world are disadvantaged by being left out from or exploited by its practice – is what has come to be known as McDonaldization (Ritzer, 2000) and is what also can be regarded as globalization. Ritzer sees much similarity between Fordism and McDonaldization (p. 183).

Homogeneity and Difference

In broad terms what has appeared and become more pronounced in recent decades has been a cultural homogeneity to what is consumed and how it is consumed in the world, and most particularly in the globe's affluent (strong capacity to spend) portions. In this context, contrasting persons to those consuming a lot, are those not able to consume sufficiently or to consume the correct products demanded whom Ritzer identifies as 'dangerous consumers' (2001a, p. 234). A development of this trajectory is to see some consumers as able to consume greatly and stereotypically but choosing not so to do. This book argues that a sector of tourists are a group to represent a society sector that chooses and aims to consume differently, selectively and to criteria of product high quality and individuality. That they can be among leaders in the culture of approach is due to having leisure to put to the pursuit. This fits the general thesis Veblen propounded in his *Theory of the Leisure Class: An Economic Study of Institutions* (1899).

Where We Are Now

Accomplished, Conforming, Consuming

The question to be asked is what has led, and is leading, to food and drink being viewed in their contemporary way? The small historical background provided above has delivered certain pointers. The general progression depicted from prehistory to modernity has been of a build up of technical accomplishment, a sharing of knowledge, the emergence of less individuality of approach, and people being distanced from nature, soil, and distinct locale and cultural 'story' and spirit through becoming more resident in cities. Some of the seeds of the current embarkation can be seen in the Situationist approach, first promulgated in the 1960s by Guy Debord (Ritzer, 2001a, p. 181). Ritzer describes Debord as having the opinion that 'everyday social life is *mediated* by consumer society' (p. 184). Situationism, and Lefebvre's request that everyday life should have a critique, Gardiner encapsulates as having the aim 'to achieve an "authentic existence" through the establishment of non-commodified social relations, thereby overcoming the alienations and passivities induced by modern consumer capitalism' (2000, p. 103).

Discussing everyday life in the modernization context, Gardiner opines that it 'is vulnerable to the effects of commodification and bureaucratic structuring, and exhibits tendencies towards passive consumerism and an inward-looking, unreflective and routinized form'. He adds the comment, 'Late capitalism seems especially prone to such phenomena as social atomism, moral nihilism and possessive individualism, wherein personal indentity is constructed increasingly through patterns of consumption rather than forms of communal and inter-personal dialogue' (p. 13). This remark suggests a bridge between the modern situation and that starting to emerge. The circumstance now seems to have developed beyond what Gardiner says, though his description fits the situation in part because clearly statements of distinction, separation and superiority are being made currently through types of food and drink chosen and consumed. However, perhaps hastened by food scares, and showing through protest for quality, non-junk, food (Bové and Dufour, 2001; Alland Jr. with Alland, 2001) and calls such as those of Naomi Klein (2000) for fair and decent practices to be demonstrated as part of the capitalist system and by multi-nationals to producers and providers in the disadvantaged world, deep ethical and society concerns appear to be being manifested along with personal statements being made.

Separation and Individuality

The approach permitting difference and fragmentation of product which followed that of 'one type for all' feature can be termed as post-Fordist (Ritzer, 2001a, p. 99;

Pascoe, 2001, p. 97), or be called De-McDonaldization (Ritzer, 2001a, pp. 46–57). Augé in stating that 'individuality [and] singularity' satisfy one of three criteria of Hyper-Modernity (1999, p. 23) provides indication that the style under discussion could be embraced in that title. Signs of the emergence have been in the certain customization of products occurring in the 1990s to cater to – becoming pronounced – niche markets. However, the background and reality was so often of a niche product being in the ownership or control, and to culture and formulation, of that single large power entity of the multi-national conglomerate. This happened in the travel trade but with the 'reaction' of real, rather than so appearing, independent small firms and operators coming into existence and managing to run successfully, despite 'big guy' competition. This they did by knowing their individual market, sticking to it, and treating it with much attention.

Leisure and Everyday

Food and drink tourism is – of course – about consumption. The type, manner and scale of the consumption are being used by some for making personal statements and show solidarity with and participation among a group of certain cultural persuasion. In this, leisure consumption may contrast with some of that of everyday, for example the purchase of the necessary and unexciting item. Gardiner describes that 'Everyday life is vulnerable to the effects of commodification and bureaucratic structuring, and exhibits tendencies towards passive consumerism and an inward-looking, unreflective and routinized form' (2000, p. 13). He speaks of 'a homogenization of the concrete particularities of the everyday lifeworld, and an "emptying out" of the richness and complexity of daily experience'.

Cultural Statements Through Consuming

Using global brands, pursuing McDonaldization, may display an *ennui*. Otherwise, in so doing maybe manifest is the wish to use these particular items for making a remark of cultural sameness to others. A reaction to fear of too much difference and to multi-culturalism becoming more prominent may be the want to show solidarity and a shared attitude. Ritzer suggests that much new consumption can be characterized as a sort of '*conspicuous inconspicuousness*' (2001a, p. 218). Also, on holiday in a strange environment, there is a factor of comfort in finding a hotel chain representative or McDonald's outlet with its signs of familiarity and whose distinctiveness to place is only an applied and superficial 'tweak'. A final aspect of sticking to regular buying style and buying usual and known items during in daily life is that time of thought is saved.

Resistance, to globalization, to unfairness of action from large (rich and powerful) providers towards small (poor and unpowerful) producers, to factory farming, to junk food, is a domain of identified cause towards a certain type of consuming. Urry notes how 'identities of resistance… are often mediated through consumer purchases' (2000, p. 43). Leisure spending and consuming offers moment and removal from everyday 'treadmill' existence for exploring and trying alternatives, and for thinking about ethical dimensions to consumption. The resistance type of motivations are among several concerning food and drink which in leisure and tourism time and everyday life relate, overlap and contrast. The 'seepage' and occurrences between these separate elapses and along their continuum is one of the matters this book is considering.

Time and Reality

Accepting that food and drink tourism in displaying some items everyday life is revealing also, what then are the features and cultural dimensions that are especially pronounced and manifested in tourism and leisure? The time element is one aspect. Leisure and holiday allow time of study, exploration and gaining food and drink knowledge, and to the extent that now a considerable feature are holidays and events which focus directly on educating and informing about food and drink and cooking. They also permit more time to be allocated both to choosing food and drink and to their consumption, and even to their preparation in the context of a self-catering holiday. In a leisure context, having time is being affluent. This contrasts with the circumstance in daily life when to be seen as having time on one's hands can be interpreted as being idle and not being gainfully or profitably employed.

Showing in tourism is the flavour of the Slow Food movement, originating in Italy and most strong in Europe (Petrini, C. with Watson, B. and Slow Food Editore, 2001; Ritzer, 2000, pp. 217–218). It is revealed mainly by implication in the attention and reverence to traditional, artisan-produced, food. In the UK a Campaign for Real Food organization has emerged, some of the objectives of which will be provided in Chapter 13. How much items revered and sought are truly authentic or rather are new cultural extension from old products and procedures can be questioned. Augé comments about the pitfall of lapse into nostalgic fantasy, saying 'There is ... always a certain danger in wishing to defend or protect cultures and the search for their lost purity is somewhat illusory. They have only ever been alive in so far as they transformed themselves' (1999, p. 17). Probably the consumer recognizes transformation and is rather appreciating a type of spirit and approach. Their current reactions are perhaps necessary escape, and able to be more pronounced on holiday which is overtly an escape-time from a difficult, culturally complex and rather frightening contemporary world. The phenomenon is perhaps not so dissimilar to those of the later 19th century in the developed world of Europe and beyond, and which celebrations and 'revivals' of old folk ways, customs and melodies characterized. An essential cause then was the distancing felt – due to urbanization – from land, small community, certain custom, and the loss of sense of identity of belonging to a particular environment and culture, and a general disconnection occurring of an item from a specific locale.

Traditional

As has been portrayed, the types of food and drink that are the focus of attention of the depicted certain sector of society and tourists are noticeably those deemed traditional (inherent to, and long featuring in, a community), old-fashioned, 'home-style' and uncommodified, and which are produced, or perceived as produced, carefully and in a way of immediacy, and on a small-scale and in a non major-industrialized way. In a dimension, these can cater, therefore, to provide comfort against society perceptions of concern in relation to quality or safety of food treated industrially, more 'anonymously', and which has been carried long distance and so is removed from place of origin and from doorstep attention.

Local and Immediate

Among its abilities to deliver assurance to the consumer due to home and identity being visible, artisanal food and drink which is prepared and then reaches its consumer quickly, manifests localness and so should show freshness. Its contrast to items carried over distance and kept through refrigeration is that this local food and drink is in more in basic state and so likely to render its basic qualities better, for giving greater all round sensory experience through sight, touch, taste, smell and even via hearing if – as examples – a crunchy new apple is consumed or a fresh nut is cracked. This is unlike the emphasis of 'great food miles' food and drink products, as characterized by much supermarket produce, which is warped towards prominence being given to eye-appeal and a long shelf-life.

Sensory

Seeking sensory pleasure is part of a holiday pleasure (Boniface, 2001). Urry considers that we have arrived at a situation of contemporary society where the visual is uppermost among the sensory types. He regards that the smell of natural things, in the past prominent, was put to the background as modernity came upon us and is only now again becoming sought out and valued (2000, pp. 100–101). He relates that those senses less manifested now of sight, sound, smell and touch 'remain important to people's sense of belonging [and] …. appear to provide a fragmented and longer-term sense of time' (p. 104). So, it can be seen that food and drink has a way to contribute in a dimension of re-discovery or re-accentuation of the sensory and with connotations of bringing experiences over and of time, and of connection and association. This, therefore, is another regressive feature to food and drink and fitting a contemporary culture to look for comfort – in certain type – from these.

Fernández-Armesto, in making his historical review, regards a complete 'globalized marketplace' as still 'a fantasy of the biggest capitalists and the fiercest anti-capitalists, but avers nonetheless that 'An artisanal reaction is already under way' (2001, p. 250). Ritzer perceives McDonaldization as having delivered some new stimulation to local cuisine, saying 'while a general threat to indigenous culture exists, there are counter-examples that demonstrate that McDonaldization has instead contributed to the revitalization of local traditions' (2001a, p. 172).

Speed, Technology and Globalization

Augé sees technological advance, globalization, and rapid alteration as present in how people are acting: he perceives change in

'how people travel, how they look at things and how they meet, [and] thus confirming the hypothesis whereby the global relationship between human beings and the real is altering under the influence of representations connected with the development of technologies, with the globalisation of certain key issues and with the acceleration of history' (1999, p. 7).

In the situation of globalization, and technology and speed in dominance in everyday life the holiday offers space for contrast. The holiday allows time and indulgence to pursue the exotic, and in the context of food and drink what is exotic can now can be what is most plain and simple. This is due to global systems bringing so much of what were exotica to permeate everyday life meals. The most strange or different, compared to what is in everyday sensible and understandable, can represent the enticing feature. Fields describes that 'A change in diet, eating patterns or the setting of a meal can ... be an important motivational stimulus' (2002, p. 38). The overall point to be made is that on holiday what is 'other' to everyday can be explored and in a situation of assurance from being short-while and fixed-term.

Back Again?

Within his context of society's McDonaldization, Ritzer sees 'disenchantment' as having occurred as process of 'the rationalization of society in general, and from the rationalization of consumption settings in particular' (2000, p. 132). He remarks, 'Enchantment has more to do with quality than with quantity' (ibid.). Speaking of sites dedicated 'to deliver large quantities of goods and services frequently and over great geographic spaces' he continues, 'The mass-production of such things is virtually guaranteed to undermine their enchanted qualities' (p. 133). Discussing Lefebvre's view of modernity, Gardiner explains that he 'believed that modernity represents the dissolution of genuine intersubjectivity, and the end of popular celebrations like the premodern festival' (2000, p. 83). It can be noted that food and drink tourism has delivered many events and festivals to the current arena, and bringing relationship anew for people to land and season and draw fresh awareness to old, or avowedly old, types and ways of food and drink production. Food and drink tourism seems to be showing the mechanism to bring important connections of cultural identity, and to reinsert through quality, and very smallness, localness and distinctiveness of character, a calibre recently missing to contemporary life. In connection, in his explanation of the current almost obsessiveness of concern among society with food, is Fernández-Armesto's opinion, 'Fussiness and "foodism" are methods of self-protection for society against the deleterious effects of the industrial era: the glut of the cheap, the degradation of the environment, the wreckage of taste' (2001, p. 251).

Reasons for Food and Drink Tourism

Causes of Past and Present

In summary of this chapter's material, it can be said that the history of food and drink to the present delivers considerable features and cultural dimensions relevant to food and drink tourism's appearance and to its particular shape and style of operation. The main foci of influence and input are:

- agriculture's emergence and development, then the general shift of people from proximity to its processes and environment;
- cultural exchanges and certain cultural dominations and emphases;
- reactions of individualism to globalization and to the standardizations of modern existence;
- concerns with food safety;
- an old and ongoing interest in other peoples and cultures and so, as part of this, the associated food and drink products being explored;
- new wish for poetic, soulful and characterful experience;
- associations to food and drink such as celebration and ritual, comfort and escape, and the manifestation of status and cultural difference;
- relationships and differences among time and need between everyday and holiday.

The Cultural Inputs

In encapsulation, the cultural impetus to food and drink being matters of direct attention to society now and to tourism is that of reaction to modernity, industrialization, largeness, and lack of power, distinctiveness and individuality, and absence of enough quality. The culture appears as showing a type of nature to address and favour forms of the old that are hyper-real and romanticized versions. In this chapter's survey of past to present attention to food and drink and aspects, and as these relate to food and drink tourism now, culture has been shown as integrated to food and drink and its activities.

Chapter 2

Food and Drink Become a Leisure Destination

What Brings Food and Drink Tourism Among Us?

In a context of giving a background to food and drink tourism, Chapter 1 described key relevant entities to food and drink and culture in the past, and those coming forward to be influential now. This chapter will pick up upon and pursue the dimensions that seem to be bringing food and drink as direct objects of leisure and to occupy a role as destination in tourism. Chapters 3 and 4 will consider food and drink tourism's arrival and causes of appearance in more detail and focus on the particular perspectives of, respectively, the tourist, and the provider with their stakeholders.

From cause of history and by present circumstances, among the essential features appearing to have input to producing food and drink tourism are:

- the developed world's attitude to, and styles of use of, the disadvantaged world, and which encompasses cultural colonization and plunder and tourist visitation
- thrusts against globalization, multi-nationals, and commodification
- a concern, essentially located in a developed world with luxury of not being hungry, about safety and quality of food and especially concerning that produced from a large industrialized processes
- urbanization, and therefore a large part of society's loss of relationship with land and countryside, and its separation from old roots, old agricultural practice, and rural culture
- food surpluses in parts of the world and so needs for agricultural and industrial diversification
- how time is used and appears, and what spaces of use are being presented, in everyday and during holiday and how food and drink fits in the situations
- the developed world's nervousness of security of existence and concern that its way of life 'has gone wrong' or is not, as once appeared, appropriate, and so this leading to need for conviviality and comradeship, wish to indulge and 'let hair down', and being disposed to re-peruse old ways and practices
- increased consumer knowledge of, and interest in, food and drink
- general curiosity about other cultures and their ways and products, and, because of their contrast to those of the Western world, especially towards matters in the pre-industrial category and now newly-regarded as exotic

- food and drink that conforms to traditional type and way, serving in the position of delivering comfort and assurance as contrast to industrialized, mass-produced, anonymous of specific source, items
- an on-going association of 'special' food and drink with special and celebratory or important occasions and so consequently a natural linkage of the type to the holiday
- consumer focus of want on experience and sensation, to offer which food and drink lend themselves
- in essential reality of most daily food and drink being standardized, industrialized, and commodified, tourism giving the opportunity of occasion to find and try a counterpoint
- food and drink are ready, varied and culturally-rich entities for deploying to show affluence and distinctiveness
- food and drink from a particular area acting to show and re-assert an individual identity
- individually- and artisan-prepared food and drink becoming deemed as 'the real thing'
- traditional food and drink and its processing becoming – due to singularity, unusualness, and potential to obsolescence – treated as heritage, as for example is indicated by wine and rice landscapes being designated as World Heritage Sites.

Crisis of Confidence

It can be noticed that of the foregoing reasons a number share a common denominator of anxiety being their main cause or constituent. Along with positive reasons – such as interest in different cultures, foods and drinks and their methods of being prepared – for food and drink to be being impelled into tourism as a main attention object, are those more negative. These latter seem founded in a developed world crisis of confidence in the way of life now come to be its routine. The food and drink tourism sector is perhaps serving too as revealing an instinct away from McDonaldization of tourism itself and cultural tourism as an area within it – as an often-Guggenheim-presence to the world's cultural attractions reveals (Boniface,1998a, pp. 28–29; Honigsbaum, 2001, p. 4). Also, simply because food and drink are items some of which still manifest localness, the relevant types can act as spearhead for displaying how tourism can focus on distinctiveness and difference. Meethan reminds of an essential *un*-sameness as part of tourism, saying 'While tourism in general must be analysed as a global phenomenon, its spatial component means that locality, or the specificity of places and cultures, is not diminished but actually reinforced' (2001, p. 114).

Fast Movement and Transportation

Tourism occupies spaces that, in the tourist's mind, are different due to its being an activity contrasting with that of the everyday, and of which a lot of these spaces –

globalization notwithstanding – show cultural distinction among each. As food and drink manifests culture so easily and readily, this is part of why food and drink are 'naturals' for deployment as one of tourism's strong product features. The 'story' delivering culture in association with a place takes time to arrive. Most recently, however, e.g. in the 20th century, transport types becoming faster and more diffuse – and also often more individualized as with the private car – led to certain associated food and drink places appearing and developing their own culture, heritage even, rather quickly. The roadhouse, motel, drive-in food provision (Witzel, 1994), and diner (Offitzer, 1997) are examples, and these were following in the vein of the coaching inn before them. Langdon, in delivering the Foreword to Witzel's book about the American Drive-In, says that 'The uniquely American experience of the drive-in restaurant reflects the twentieth-century's ascent of unprecedented mobility and informal living styles' (1994, p. 8). Augé argues, 'place becomes necessarily historical from the moment when – combining identity with relations – it is defined by a minimal stability' (1995, p. 54). Doubtless, as part of the greater acceleration of matters in contemporary society, is that it accepts a hastened moment of arrival of an acceptance and interpretation of a setting as established.

The difficulty with certain quick-arrival new type introductions is deciding their level of cultural identity in themselves – and in contrast to any individual elements contained within – as opposed to by their feature of type. De Botton found attraction and personality in a UK motorway service station, despite ostensible reasons to do otherwise saying:

'The building was architecturally miserable, it smelt of frying oil and lemon-scented floor polish, the food was glutinous and the tables were dotted with islands of dried ketchup from the meals of long-departed travellers, and yet something about the scene moved me. There was poetry in this forsaken service station'.

He then extended this purview saying, 'Its appeal made me think of certain other equally and unexpectedly poetic travelling places – airport terminals, harbours, train stations and motels' (2002, p. 32).

The airport does portray a certain culture, but to an extent only of its kind, rather than from where it is. Augé sees airports as 'non-places' along with, among others, 'aircraft, trains and road vehicles … railway stations, hotel chains, leisure parks' (1995, p. 79), and all of which non-places and including too 'high-speed roads' (p. 34) he regards as 'the real measure of our time' (p. 79). Nonetheless, concerning airports, to be noticed by any person well-travelled is how place-specific aspects can be manifested there, even through a framework of globally-ubiquitous type, and certainly in some of the food and drink on offer and its style of delivery. Pascoe says that airports 'should be treated not as the sterile transitory zones with which we are all familiar, but as "vessels of conception" for the societies passing through them' (2001, p. 10). This suggests airports not be bland and without shade of character and to offer dimensions of providing opportunity to experiment and make novel effort. This perhaps might include buying or consuming any unusual foreign foods or drinks available in duty free shop of airport café or restaurant.

Balance and Contrast

Augé regards contemporary anthropologists as needing to consider 'how to think about and situate the individual' in a globalized environment and notes the individual's liable response of 'tinkering to establish their own décor and trace their own personal itineraries' (1995, p. 38). It is perhaps this impulse of customization and to create and manifest identity that is motivating both providers' and consumers' involvement with food and drink tourism with the activity's so much emphasis on the 'special' and individualized among consumables. Tourism, a globalized industry, is providing (though maybe not deliberately so doing) in food and drink tourism a capacity to deliver contradiction, and so serving as outlet of a consumer need for contrast and balance. This is a heightened dimension of a general characteristic of contra-culturalism, alternativism and experimentation of leisure time compared to quotidian existence that Rojek finds, saying, 'because leisure belongs to the surplus [to everyday life] it stands a close relation to the gestation and expression of antistructures of behaviour' (2000, p. 7). He portrays that in modern times,

> 'Leisure and travel become means both of renewing the existing order and engaging in deviant or profane forms of behaviour which challenge established rules and practices. They are ways of diverting and absorbing surplus energy which conflict with the assigned values which are meant to govern everyday life' (p. 13).

Augé depicts in society a general 'paradoxical' inclination in which 'at the very same moment when it becomes possible to think in terms of the unity of terrestrial space, and the big multinational networks grow strong, the clamour of particularisms rises' (1995, pp. 34–35). So, it can be interpreted, tourism – with, for reasons explained, food and drink tourism able to be a key participant in this – can give a chance to act 'out of the box' and experiment, but too, and alongwhile, meeting a deep unified overall urge to show the everyone's commonality of connectedness to rurality and a place of derivation. Also shown is the separation yet some connection and overlap between leisure time and everyday life.

Quality and Assurance

To give more attention to food and drink, obtaining knowledge about it, getting assurance through finding suitable source, method of preparation, and general quality, as tourism brings time so to do, is a way for the consumer find comfort. The motivation helps make food and drink as desirable objects to give especial attention to in tourism. Of course, tourism is not an automatic area for providing food and drink of excellence, but when on holiday – 'the paradise time' – consumers do perhaps have an inbuilt high expectation of good produce and have time to give attention to obtaining it. Simply because they are on non-home territory and confronted with non-routine food and drink, their concerns about food safety are likely to be heightened, and extending beyond the standard worry about whether local water is safe to drink or not. MacLaurin reporting food safety in travel and tourism conference in the year 2000 describes its conclusion that 'Food safety is an important component of the overall travel safety and security package' (2001, pp. 332–333).

Different Times

Time and its type and use is key in food and drink tourism. Fast food we connect of course to the consumer not having much time for the comestible. It is an 'on the go' matter. This type allows, demands, in the interests of the busy consumer and the maximum-profit-aiming provider, to have a streamlined character of not much choice or too much variety of type being offered. The defects seen by some are defined by Schlosser. Explaining resistance moves against fast food, such as those of Frenchman José Bové (Alland Jr with Alland, 2001; Bové and Dufour, 2001; Jeffries, 2001, p. 22), Schlosser says 'Fast food has become a target because it is so ubiquitous and because it threatens a fundamental aspect of national identity: how, where, and what people choose to eat' (Schlosser, 2001, p. 244). Rojek sees the time within leisure as being fast or slow and with fast being very mobile and offering a superficial engagement as with a game on a computer as contrasted with novel-reading a novel which is slow (2000, pp. 23–25). It can be assumed therefore that tourism having food and drink as direct and deep foci of tourist attention is a slow type of tourism endeavour. However, Rojek warns in association, and discussing the relevance of 'flow' that 'serious leisure does not always involve engrossing, self-actualizing experience, just as casual leisure is not always meaningless and desultory'. He continues,

'The concept of flow conveys more faithfully the anti-climactic gap between aspiration and achievement that is a common feature of leisure experience. It is also better able to handle variations in intensity and tempo of experience that occur in leisure'.

Time is of important relevance to food and drink tourism and where this is most directly connecting with the agricultural round and its processes. Urry talks of 'glacial time [which] is slow-moving' in the present. He says 'Glacial time can be seen in various forms of resistance to the "placelessness" of instantaneous time', continuing to say that 'The organisation *Common Ground* seeks to remake places as sites for "strolling" and "living in", and not just for passing through "instantaneously"' (2000, p. 158). Of particular relevance to the subject of this book is that through its Apple Week promotion and general initiative in relation to orchards, Common Ground has arrived in position of leader and encourager of apple tourism in the UK (see Chapter 12).

Food and Drink Tourist Types

A general picture can be painted of what would seem the typical person to be a food and drink tourist and to favour food and drink tourism. This would likely be the well-educated, discerning sort of person, likely but not exclusively into Third Age, and who will take their tourism experience slowly and deeply and not in a milieu of frenzy and effervescence. This is manifestly one type and probably the main one. However, another and different sector whose focus can be gourmet food and lots of drink, is the 'party animal', extrovert type, or else someone wanting to exchange a measured daily life for an exuberant existence of over-indulgence while on holiday. Rojek describes 'Wild leisure patterns' which people in the developed world can adopt for contrast to 'the modern social order', and in crowds (2000, pp. 186–187), but remarking also that 'To some extent a margin for wildness is still built into the modern social order' and provides group celebrations as examples (p. 188). The concern of the exuberant will be less for speciality foods with their rural emanation strongly manifest, as for bars, pubs and nightclubs, and up-scale restaurants of lively cities and resorts. In the area between these groups is the design enthusiast and upscale lifestyle adherent whose chosen holiday destination is the coolly-designed hotel with designer food to match. Depicting these groups displays that characteristics evident or present in the consumer in everyday life 'show through' in their choice of type and experience of food and drink holiday. The time away from home brings the opportunity for heightening and developing interests and tendencies, and exploring concerns, already in presence at home, and albeit and precisely because they cannot be, or are not chosen to be, pursued as part of everyday life and during what is being done routinely.

Town and Country, at Home and Away

A pre-eminent motivation to food and drink tourism, and attached to a certain and central type of food and drink tourist, is to seek knowledge and reconnection with land and agriculture by finding and consuming traditional, artisan, individualized and produced at small-scale, food and drink. The character of action here is making the investigation as a recreational experience on holiday or day visit. The questions are: why is these being done and how? O'Hagan delivers some causes in society, which it would be reasonable to assume find reflection in tourists. He believes that 'in the world at large, GM crops are corrupting the relation of people to the land they live in' (2001, p. 53). So, again fear is suggested as the society impulse, and in this instance not only fear about food safety but fear of loss of connection to the traditional process of food production and which is based in land and different seasons. The growing to a sizeable minority of the market for organic food and drink is doubtless rooted in fear of other types and much as positive enthusiasm for organic food and drink in themselves and for their style of production and presence. A recognition and attempt to rectify it – by both general consumer and provider – of the 'a town-country schism' Harvey depicts as present in the UK. The split has delivered 'parallel cultures in one small, crowded island', and the cause he describes as being 'Enclosures and two centuries of industrialisation' (2001, p. 88). Nettleton reports a survey of *Country Life* magazine showing 'a disturbing lack of knowledge of nature and the countryside among the nation's schoolchildren' (2000, p. 11). O'Hagan visits a large London supermarket of Sainsbury's and is told that 'Real food' is what the consumer wants. Travel which views food is itself encouraging a greater speciality food interest, as O'Hagan was advised in this remark of a Sainbury's food technologist 'People go to Tuscany … and they eat Parma ham and they come back here and they want it all the time' (2001, p. 5). The presence of the magazine entitled *Food and Travel* is revealing evidence of a food and drink tourism sector of interest, as is the burgeoning number of country guides of the Lonely Planet *World Food* series.

Levels and Types of Tourist Interest

Culture

A direct aim of discovering about a culture is one aim of a tourist's interest in food. Chesser (2000, p. 232) opines firmly,

'To understand a culture, an individual must experience its food. Tourists visiting a region **experience** the culture through the goods they consume, as well as through the people and attractions. The food of a region is often a primary attraction'.

The report *Tourists' Attitudes Towards Regional and Local Foods*, produced for the MAFF and The Countryside Agency, describes the varying amount of 'perceptual links between food, drink and cultural tourism' depending on which country tourists are in. It notes that when in Scotland, France and Italy, tourists 'closely integrate experience of food and drink within their wider holiday experience' but adds 'However, in other countries or regions tourist's [sic] have little recognition of this element in the culture of the region' (Enteleca Research and Consultancy Ltd, 2001, p. 2). This delivers the outcome that building awareness in tourists about the history and culture of food and drink is a necessary task for some among countries wanting to offer food and drink tourism as a tourism product.

Local Food

Understanding the level of experience the tourist can show, or wants to show, is relevant in catering to them, and thus, according to audience, either meeting or encouraging a depth of interest or accepting that it only a superficial flicker and reacting correspondingly. The Enteleca research found 72% of its sample of UK holidaymakers to four regions that 'took an interest in local foods during their visit' (p. 3). It found five groups, ranging from 'Food Tourists' of which there were 6%-8%, 'Interested Purchasers' amounting to 30%-33%, a group of 'Un-reached' being 15%-17%, and 22%-24% as 'Un-engaged' and 28%-17% as 'Laggards'. Only the last category expressed 'no interest in local food' (pp. 3–4). The report notes 'strong contrasts in choice of venue by age' (p. 5).

An implication of the Enteleca report is of considerable existing interest in local food and drink and more that is latent and to be developed and tapped.

Perspectives of Agriculture

As part of overcoming the town-country divide featuring in so many countries may be the need for the rural provider to not – as some appear to do – hold their urban cousin in arrogant contempt, either for being tourist or for showing ignorance of rural ways. Farm stays and visits are one way to offer education as part of enjoyment, as equally are fairs and special events provided that they serve *information* alongside food and drink. After all, part of why the consumer is present is because of concern about industrialized food and drink and as a consequent strong want to discover or be reassured about artisan, local or specialist food and drink. Farmers may have resentment towards tourism because of needing to diversify from what they consider should be their only role of farming itself. Such an impulse is implied in the remark of a UK north-west upland sheep farmer O'Hagan interviewed, who – upset at being unable to make a living from farming, and of needing to maintain the landscape to an conventional aspect society expects – comments, '"The people down the road selling postcards of the Lake District are making much more than farmers who keep the land so photogenic"' (2001, p. 40). Along with a generalized resentment that tourism is rendering more income that farming, is suggested both an unwillingness to join its ranks and a low-level of expectation of the tourist. Accepting, and encouraging more, tourist interest in food and drink and its ways of production is the necessity of the provider, and also not to see the tourist in stereotypical or out-dated way. A positive, evaluative, and contemporary in outlook, observation is this of François Dufour, Secretary General of the French Farmers' Confederation, during interview, along with José Bové, by Gilles Luneau,

'The business of providing farm holidays and study trips has evolved because it meets an increasing demand from town-dwellers and non-farming country-folk. I think it's all part of the consumer's desire to acquire a better knowledge of the quality of their food. The consumer is trying to re-establish contact with nature, and with the men and women who work on the land' (Bové and Dufour, 2001, p. 128).

The necessity for the farmer and producer is accepting and welcoming tourists if they need to earn revenue from them. In Europe, for example, the Common Agricultural Policy [CAP] has brought surplus among its outcomes (O'Hagan 2001, p. 47). So, some mechanism needs to be found if society wants the countryside to 'look farmed', and also to be handled in an environmentally-friendly manner, and if the farmer wants to remain on the land and to obtain a survival income. Providing speciality food, and making it available in the domain of tourism and in a creative and interesting way, represents a possible avenue of rescue. Part of an acceptance of tourism is to absorb levels of type of interest in the visitor. There is undoubtedly a sector that is seeing the countryside and its food and drink products 'superficially', and to demand it for its picturesqueness as on a postcard. Appreciation of sheer beauty is not, however, at all a skin-deep impulse. Aesthetic quality does much in feeding the soul and spirit, and the countryside aesthetic is now so novel to so many people that its pull must be ever more strong now.

Nostalgia and Innocence

There *is* a wish among a strong sector to engage with and find out about food and drink in its history, derivation, types and methods of preparation of food. Providers do have markets to cater to. As one important facet to the general urge, focusing on food and drink and associated environments and contexts seen as traditional, is that of nostalgia. The impulse is driven in part by discomfort with modern times and ways, and so retreat for short time into some semblance of 'times gone by', but also by simple attraction of contrast with everyday. This last is the holiday's essence. It should be emphasized that old forms are frequently labour-intensive and time-consuming and so this is part of why modern society has relinquished them so much. That it is now commonplace for women to work, and outside the home, means that a lot of women's formerly routine activity – such as cake-baking and jam-making, and simply home-cooking (as opposed to home heating-up of ready-prepared meals) – is either not done at all or only infrequently. And meals such as afternoon tea and 'the cooked breakfast' have been largely lost to everyday. This renders certain types of food, and preparation, and meal, as exotic, and subject to nostalgia accruing to them, due to becoming distant from usual existence. The culture and way of life of the peasant, the traditionally-operating farmer, the country house estate, the urban working-class terrace home, the small factory operating to old ways, the old-style hotel, restaurant and eating and drinking place, become exhibits that are interesting and worthy of investigating due to their status of being past or non-routine.

In the UK, the tearoom is a particular attraction to visit, and which has a whole culture to itself surrounding teas, scones and cream and home-made cakes, and maybe other light snacks, and consumed off suitably traditional-looking china, all amid an environment denoting age, unchangelessness and gentility – usually expressed by oak beams, frilly curtains and lots of 'knick-knackery'. Alcoholic drinks rarely feature. Jane Brown describes such a refuge, The Orchard at Grantchester, a place to eat alongside the River Granta near Cambridge made famous by the poet Rupert Brooke, and which – notwithstanding needing to be 'saved, restored and reopened' at one stage in the 1980s – is an icon to visit. Brown say that 'With only a lightweight wooden pavilion added to save staff and patrons from the weather, it offers a wholly romantic and insubstantial view of life's pleasures: it has an air of unbelievable innocence (and awfully good soups and cakes – the essence of its charm)' (Brown, 2001, p. 254). Brown's mention of innocence is to convey a strong dimension to such places. Along with other non-industrial scale and style food and drink emporia and providing places, they deliver a sense of Eden uncontaminated. This feature, which whole traditional agricultural countryside can have, is of course, a special appeal in a time of concerns for food safety and other security.

Driving Forces

It is clear that there are perennial and basic items to make food and drink and their connected features of appeal. This chapter is seeking to identify those particularly pertinent now or emerging fresh now to lead to the consumer to want food and drink and appurtenances as part of their tourism experience and to see what is in current circumstances to impel providers' participation. On the consumer side, the motivations could be encapsulated as arriving from:

- anxiety
  - concerning safety of industrial, globalized and commodified food and drink
  - wanting to celebrate through food and drink on holiday and to show bravado and to share comradeship over food and drink in uncertain times
  - needing comfort and escape through traditional and non-routine foods, and with nostalgia often appearing to help
- need to show distinction, affluence and individualism
  - special food and drink acting as media; and – towards the objective of display to others – food and drink representing a 'common' and transferable language between the everyday and the holiday
- curiosity and wish for knowledge and discovery
  - stemming from fear about food and drink content, and regarding general personal circumstance
  - to display education and superiority to others
  - 'tourism time' offers enough moment to obtain information and to experiment
- a need to feel 'grounded' amid globalization
  - so visits to roots and countryside, and to see how food is derived
- requirement for sensory and tactile pleasure, and for experience
  - food and drink tourism offers these effortlessly.

Fields, asking 'What food-related motivations make people want to travel?' (2002, p. 37), sees inspiration in tourism motivators and those categories of 'physical', 'cultural', 'interpersonal' and 'status and prestige' which McIntosh, et al. proposed (1995). Other key elements to influence the consumer to engage in gastronomic tourism, Fields sees to be the offer of 'experience' and the impression portrayed of a destination by the media (2002, pp. 41–47).

In a sense, the consumer is looking for and needing a 'high'. This can be from superiority of knowledge about food and drink and in consuming and showing consumption of best quality examples. It can be due to special taste and sensation of unusual food and drink. It can be from celebration, and escaping woes, and by food and drink as the mechanisms. It can even be in patronage of a peasant, artisan or impoverished farmer and in visiting their traditional rural existence and buying wares to transport back to town.

For the immediate provider, the need for the activity is essentially on grounds of economics and due to need to diversify, whereas for their stakeholders and partners the usefulness is also in achieving political and socio-cultural objectives. Hjalager and Corigliano point to the breadth and height of needed stakeholder for food tourism to operate with success, saying that 'national economic, agricultural and food policies, rather than tourism policies, determine the standards and development of food for tourists' (2000, p. 291). Hjalager (2002, pp. 22–23) defines a process of 'four orders' to the development of 'gastronomy tourism' – 'indigenous development', 'horizontal development', 'vertical development', and finally 'diagonal development'. Chapter 5 of this book will look at some initiatives designed to encourage and promote food and drink tourism, and to help farmers diversify in the direction.

Right Moment, and Ready

As indicating that the consumer is ready to engage in food and drink tourism and that educators recognize this and so that providers and stakeholders will find relevant training available, are these two anecdotal items below.

The first is the brochure of a specialist tour operator, Andante Travels, which is newly including food tours among its offer, and with this part of explanation

> 'Part of the joy of travel is the enjoyment of unaccustomed cuisines, using different ingredients cooked in unusual ways.
> The pleasure is not just in eating food, but finding it (mushrooming), seeing it produced (parmesan, wine and truffle production) and tasting to learn (Slow Food workshops). And because to eat local food without understanding the culture is to enjoy only half the pleasure, we have tried to include the background story of the area and its people and to intersperse interesting visits and walks through the countryside which grows the ingredients. (Also in order to work up an appetite!)'
> (Andante Travels brochure, 2002, p. 52).

The other item was the announcement by the Association for Tourism and Leisure Education [ATLAS] of holding in Portugal an Expert Meeting 'Gastronomy and Tourism', along with the 1st International Gastronomy Congress at Esposende, and the 12th Gastronomy Congress of Minho – and which led to the book *Tourism and Gastronomy* (Hjalager and Richards 2002) (eds). The occasion made emphasis on food because it recognized that wine tourism is much more established as an entity, as Chapter 11 is to demonstrate.

The aim of this chapter has been to deliver a general background to how food and drink have entered the leisure and tourism domain, and why. The next chapter will give detailed discussion and reasoning of the social contexts and causes to food and drink tourism as a particular entity.

Chapter 3

Food for Thought and Visit

Change of State and Emphasis

Food and drink are the stuff of life. Therefore, they have necessarily featured in tourism. They have been elements of the everyday to be also part of tourism. There is a difference between how food and drink featured in tourism in the past, compared with how it is now coming to appear. This is that formerly eating and drinking were mainly adjuncts and sideshows in the tourism experience and now food and drink are often causes to travel and holiday in their own right. As general causes are: the burgeoning appearance and strong capacity for consuming in the developed world community from which tourists are largely drawn; an associated boredom with products for consumption and so need for new way to consume as leisure and which food and drink tourism represents in its using an integral to life activity; that a society tendency towards indulgence is fitted.

This book is seeking to explain the phenomenon of food and drink – a part of everyday – coming to feature centrally as part of the leisure, pleasure and non-routine experience that are the contemporary holiday and the day trip. The matter is particularly worth evaluating *because* it represents something of a change to the style of tourism. The alteration lies – as indicated above – in that food and drink, being so routine, commonplace and part of normal activity and therefore essentially unremarkable, are not out of the ordinary. Therefore, they stand, ostensibly at least, as features not at all to the past standard accepted template for satisfying tourism demands, which is for the tourism offer to represent escape, specialness, differentness and new sensation, and generally to render 'otherness'.

Food and drink tourism is therefore a somewhat new beast. It is an offer generated on an everyday feature rather than on one of specialness and special production for tourism. Part of the role of this book is to consider whether this arrival, food and drink tourism's appearance, means that tourism could decide and should be set to pull more from daily life and everyday into its midst, operation, and product offers, and with all the implications attendant.

A fundamental question being posed in the matter of this book in its description of food and drink tourism as a direct touristic activity is how much a change in *culture* is occurring. It appears that this would be a change in the culture of tourism, and which in modern times has become signified as a culture of separateness (Boniface, 1998b, pp. 746–749) and whose distinguishing characteristic has been seen as its differentness to that which governs everyday life. Food and drink tourism suggest that the circumstance may be altering.

Statements of Stage and Difference

Food and drink, of course, are innately about consumption. This is because they are there as items to be, respectively, eaten and drunk. They are also goods that in their type, style and packaging and by the surroundings in which they are acquired and consumed convey messages about us. Bourdieu in his well-known *Distinction* (1986) has given portrayal overall that in the way we decide to operate our lives and in the items we choose to buy we signify how we wish to be seen and which society milieu we want to be regarded as occupying. Food and drink consumption belongs among this general activity. We are making a social and cultural statement through our choices among food and drink products and the options we select from their range of contextual environments of shops and retail outlets, restaurants, bars and cafes and tearooms etc.

In food and drink tourism, it can be envisaged that there is a likely cultural dovetailing to be considered. However, in the event of the answer to the question already posed – 'whether an elision is occurring to deliver a new touristic culture that is embedded in the style and elements of everyday life?' – being 'no', then to be asked is if – in tourism's way and daily life manner becoming kept un-clearly divided – a problematic collision is being represented.

It appears that there is deeper complexity and cloudiness due to distinctions between the types and stages of the tourist and among types and stages of everyday life. What the tourist who is practised and *who believes they are discerning* is coming to consume much on holiday, in terms of food and drink, is the everyday, local, authentic food and drink of the place, or what they want to perceive as such. Meanwhile, some hosts' food and drink consuming habits may consist of relying on mass-market products from supermarket and deep freeze rather than upon items emanating from local agriculture and traditional production ways on their doorstep. Mass tourist and less long-standing traveller counterparts to discerning tourists may be in a different stage and culture of conduct in which their desire is for a universal type of food and drink or that which is 'the same' culturally and in actuality as at home. This is notwithstanding that such food may not really be quite so uniform as promulgated and believed, it being altered and rendered marginally special by local way of some kind. The chip is an example of this. Barthes depicts General de Gaulle as regarding the *frite* as 'the alimentary sign of Frenchness' (2000, p. 64); in the UK chips, in alliance with fish, would be also be regarded as a national dish (Mudd, 2002, Walton, 2000). It can be seen that different potato varieties bring variation to the entity of the chip; different ranges of growing soil generate different tastes to the potato to be brought to the arena. This is albeit in the context that McDonald's has a formula of operation to bring a chip to the consumer that is the same the world over. In, for example, nations and religions, by presences of varying cultural attitudes, a 'same' food can be viewed differently, and to the extent that one group will treat them as suitable to eat and another will see them as unsuited or prohibited to be consumed.

Global–Local

It has been seen already that the subject of food and drink tourism carries cultural input concerning 'the global' and 'the local'. Manifestations of the culture of globalization are well-known, and in the area of food and drink its most discussed feature, to become seen as one of the main icons of the overall syndrome of globalization, has been the McDonald's ubiquitous chain of hamburger outlets (Ritzer, 2000). Coca-Cola is another universal brand. It is interesting that *food and drink*, food especially, have been items to serve as a matter of focus concerning globalization. This global–local debate concerning food and drink is connected to whole issues relating to the roles, and levels of positions and prosperity, of farming and farmers in society.

The *raison d'être* of a farmer is to provide food. In certain areas of the world, such as Western Europe and North America, though lamentably not in others, their role is one of over-producing foodstuffs. Sometimes in the UK, the farmer is set now to 'set aside' land to reduce food oversupply and/or with an objective to manage and conserve landscape and for 'presenting it' for the tourist attention and admiration. When providing foodstuffs, farmers' position has increasingly become that of mass producers and who cater globally and for a global market – of those able to afford to buy their produce. Distinct, and/or poor isolated and peripheral regions, meanwhile, have often stayed producing 'their own thing'. If so, their action will be either to distribute globally one special distinctive product – Scottish whisky for example – and often at a premium price or else to serve immediate local needs and to meet local tastes and requirements. On one side there are over-producers of a routine product, and which is often universally obtainable and so cost-competitiveness is high and influential. On the other side are producers of an item rooted in a place, and which the product is desirable and a world market for it exists and – if it can travel and provided distribution facilities are adequate – can be sold at the top of the price range but which otherwise is locked to serve only its own small, and maybe impoverished, community of vicinity. This situation is, of course, before artificial mechanisms of quotas and protectionist regulations come into play.

In this general arena, a *cause célèbre* (Alland Jnr with Alland, 2001; Boniface, 2002) has been the attack on a nearby McDonald's branch by José Bové, the activist leader of a group of farmers on a plateau, the Causse du Larzac, in southern France. Their main business is raising sheep to provide milk for Roquefort cheese and which is the local and distinctive product that is out in the global marketplace. The attack on the symbol of globalization and Americanization was in response to USA tariffs imposed on imports of Roquefort – a response to the European Union [EU] banning USA beef which had been injected with hormones – and which rose to cause disruption at World Trade Organization and World Bank meetings in Seattle and Prague respectively. The saga, which attracted world attention, served to highlight global–local tensions and to show the levels of activism and concern these issues hold within them to incite. There has been a groundswell of reaction against globalization and multi-nationals and their power and influence, and of which a key feature has been locals and individual groups operating as activists in a concerted manner (Klein, 2000; Klein, 2002). Roquefort, and José Bové, will be further discussed in this book.

Arising as part of a general public thrust of concern in the overall food area are the now widespread and publicly-vented worries about GM [Genetically Modified] foods. Some heightened appreciation of local, traditionally and organically produced food and drink is a result, and with a willingness of a sector to pay premium prices for food of assured quality and 'untaintedness'.

In the EU, many farmers of its participating countries, who used to be affluent and able to earn a living from farming now victim to quotas and only very low prices being offered for their food products, are no longer in a position of financial sustainability from farming directly. Initiatives for diversification are well established and being followed, with those for farmers to provide leisure and tourism opportunities through their farms, farming property, and by their products of their farming activity as one outcome (The Heart of England Tourist Board, 2001). A motivation can immediately be seen as present from one important provider area for food and drink tourism to be an activity.

Sameness, Difference and Similarity

Albeit that ostensibly food and drink tourism may relate to everyday products and related activity, more usually concerned in food and drink tourism is food and drink of the kind that to the typical Westernized consumer will be special, hyper-real, and ultra-authentic. Therefore, albeit that food and drink appearing in tourism and acting as destinations are everyday in entity, in their individual aspects and manifestations often they represent – to the sort of person most likely to be the regular and accustomed tourist – the unusual and non-routine. Such characterful and culturally-laden types of food and drink item are not mass-taste products and they do not represent commodification. These products and their associated venues and situations, therefore, do still in certain part and individual aspect serve to represent the escape dimension which is traditionally regarded as one of the key lures to tourists to participate in tourism. So, a scene of difference is still on offer to the tourist albeit that its basis is everyday features.

Food and drink in a role as *object* of tourism, rather than as by-product of tourism, must – to be inviting enough as a main feature – be seen as being of particular significance to the tourist. These types and situations concerning food and drink do appear to represent 'otherness' and specialness rather than the standard and routinely experienced. To elect to find and go to eat and drink at an 'olde worlde tea shoppe', rather than fall into the ever-nearby branch of McDonald's or Starbucks, is likely to be a deliberate choice, and with certain attendant implications. As one difference, *time* is available to the consumer to savour the special experience, and so this of itself implies adequate leisure time and suggests, too, special food and drink experiences as being naturally attuned for tourism. The tourist, in raising food and drink to the situation of being particularly noticed and travelled to as entities, is showing that they regard these as important and significant. The process of choosing an non-standard food and drink option, or in purchasing a commonplace type but in an expensive or unusual version, or in buying food and drink in a non-routine context or location, is to render an unusual circumstance. Separateness is displayed from those who, by choice or incapacity, do not divert from mass activity concerning food and drink. Food and drink in tourism accrues different symbolism and cultural connotation that when in its always circumstance of daily life.

In a very obvious way, to treat food and drink differently from routinely and the norm is to make a statement of separateness and exclusivity. Local produce, for example, is often a type of this sort. Frequently it has high person hours and attention attached to its production (though not, of course, to its transportation), and it is probably only available in small amounts and maybe only at special times and according to season. Its cost may well be higher than its mass-market equivalent and so a level of purchasing capacity in the buyer is suggested, and with the attendant social superiority statement. Its site of production may be also be its retail outlet, or else near by, and so on view to the purchaser. The purchaser and visitor has to go to a particular place of sale or production for this type rather than merely venture for their other type to their closest-to-home supermarket. The whole experience for the purchaser, and provider, is different from when the 'supermarket process' and food distribution chain are being used. Overall, being offered is status and separation, and this feature is another of the conventional elements of tourism's invitingness to the consumer.

For the tourist to focus on food and drink and its environments as destinations of travel, *is* a sea-change in practice and culture as has been represented. However, this sea-change, of adoption of some things from everyday, can be seen as only a modified alteration because, as has been described, while generically the food and drink is the same as in daily life, the actual items and contexts appearing as objects for tourism are, significantly, not routinely, or for many people among those of the developed world, a part of daily life experience. This qualification can be weakened when other dimensions are brought it, such as concerns about GM foods. Another dimension concerns *local* food and drink. This is that, on the part of the consumer, whether tourist or resident, opting for local produce, as well as often carrying connotations of difference, may represent also a positive move against the global and for the local, and so tie in with the anti-globalization, anti-multinational organization movement.

What Does 'Local' Mean?

A question is immediately raised of what constitutes 'local' in the context of food and drink. There does not seem to be a clear accepted interpretation. For example, The National Association of Farmers' Markets [NAFM], which is the body which regulates 'official' farmers' markets, 'says local must be defined by each market in a way that is recognisable to consumers' (Green, 2001, p. 115). It appears 'local' is defined according to perception. It can be suggested that it can mean food and drink from within short distance enough for the item to stay manifestly fresh without help of refrigeration and to be consumed quickly after growing or producing. Local may be understood according to several criteria such as by soil and terrain, climate and environment, or socially and politically, and of course, culturally which can cover all the other types. In the way of cognitive geography, while we all must have impressions in our minds of what constitutes local – and doubtless these will change according to what item the word is being used to describe – probably perceptions are too different in relation to the same item. As well as having the kind of meaning of 'from nearby', it can have the extra interpretation in the sense of an item being obtainable from that locale alone, and so to mean that this item is 'distinctly' from an area as well as being from the near proximity. It is interesting to consider where *regional* sits in the interpretation and whether local can expand in some situations to mean regional; and, moreover, perhaps the region following boundaries of developmental and tourism organizations rather than 'natural' cultural perimeters. It is clear that in the realm of food and drink, and food and drink tourism, local having an additional interpretation as *distinctly* local is too defining with over-narrowness for usefulness and purpose.

Subsistence and Abundance, and Stages in Between

The type of attitude that the tourist can give to food and drink represents a cultural style. Culture is also manifest in it being able to be considered by the tourist in making their food and drink selections. In their epitome as affluent and from the developed world, tourists have the luxury of selecting food, moving to find what appeals to them most, and also choosing amongst cultural persuasion of comestible. In contrast, those from the Third World and developing countries and impoverished portions of the First World will be most likely in position of needing to accept gladly any food that is available and near at hand. Food and drink to these latter will be regarded as subsistence matter. The First World poor apart, this sector of people have yet to, and may never, pass through the stage of experiencing the commodified abundance of the supermarket. The local and impoverished will feel impelled to eat and imbibe what is immediately available, whether in a form of locally grown or locally obtainable. Ironically, often as part of the tourist's luxury of choice – when at home and on journey – will be to be able to eat and drink what is authentic, 'real' and produced on a small-scale and in a labour-intensive manner. The tourist may eat as much or more 'peasant' food than the peasant. They can afford, and are educated enough, to be this discriminating. The food and drink tourist is likely to be a sophisticated tourist who has emerged through the miasma of mass-market sangria and ubiquitous Black Forest gateaux to arrive a higher level of discernment which favours the wholesomeness and relative obscurity of local, uncommodified and distinctive dishes and drinks.

These suggestions lead to an identification of two principal sectors of tourism providers for the general developed world consumer taste. The first is First World providers. They have the experience of tourism and the consumer sensitivity and general apparatus to notice and cater to the new inclination in tourists, and also who possess a domestic market with the appetite to be appeased and so to make any venture in the direction extra viable. If traditional food and drink are to be their offer, they need to be rediscovering 'real' items and reinvigorating traditional processes which are in counterpoint to those having been the outcome of industrial scale and type activity. The second is emerging providers. These may still have retained old agricultural methods and traditional practices concerning food and drink, and now can increase markets, augment revenue and bring about socio-economic development meanwhile in catering to the tourist audience on their doorstep. They will avoid cost of export and of keeping foods and drink in shape for consumption during transit process.

Providers and Reasons

Polarities of Difference

A wander round the World Travel Market in 2000 seeing who was showing food and drink tourism products as part of their tourism offer was not in any way equivalent to obtaining a scientific sample of these across the world. Exhibitors appeared as in categories of: those who chose to be there, those who could afford and manage to be there, those who so badly required tourism that they decided they *had* to be there. Absentees, it would follow, were missing because either they were secure enough in their markets not to need to promote themselves, or the manner of promotion was unsuitable to their customer niche, or else because they were insufficiently resourced to participate or were otherwise disabled from attending. The broad categorization of types who homed in on food and drink products as items for offering to tourists was nonetheless interesting. Essentially, exhibitors providing food and drink products and giving them focus and attention were of two types. One – and much predominating in contrast to the other – was the old tourism providing countries who were using food and drink products to refresh their tourism appeal by presenting these new items, and so delivering an altered offer, and moreover providing a product of higher quality than erstwhile. The other group was developing countries, sometimes new to international tourism, and who had noticed that food and drink was something in their midst and still rurality that they had to offer and that in its very lack of industrialization, and in its traditional-ness, could have particular appeal to overseas tourists from the developed world.

The second group underlines a key dimension to tourism whose basis is food and drink. Rural areas contain the agricultural areas and are, therefore, the focus as food, and some drink, producing areas. It is these regions, exactly, who can be so often left behind in tourism initiatives and in obtaining benefits from tourism, and one major cause being lack of the products and facilities of the type traditionally deemed as necessary to attract international high-spending audiences of Westernized taste. However, with a change of taste in enough tourists, as this book suggests has occurred or is occurring, whereby they are attracted to simple, different and authentic features of a rural, and un-culturally homogenized venue, a change of scene in the map of tourism is presented. The clichéd manifestation and beginnings of such impulses may be in the tourist rushes of visitation, to Provence to see it and its peasantry as in Peter Mayle's viewpoint (Mayle, 2000), to Tuscany to regard its olive pressing and art of cuisine as in the eyes of Frances Mayes – and she actually often 'sees' a portion of the old Etruria before her (Mayes, 1998). Also, there is an urge to regard Tuscany with its vineyards as in the British perspective of that region as 'Chiantishire'. And Peter Mayle, ever acutely atuned to a public and its dreams and priority, indicates a foodie tourist sector on the increase in that a recent book from him concerns travelling around France *for food and drink* (Mayle, 2001).

Want to Go Back?

Underlying the attraction of authentic and local food and drink may also be the sense that, in a context of globalization, homogenization, commodification, mass market products and supermarkets, of factory farming, food scares arriving and GM food in view, 'the only way to go forward is to go back' and to try to reconnect with roots and items and places perceived as typified by wholesomeness. The link of food and land is alluded to by Mason with Brown (1999, p. 12) in the French phrase and concept '*le goût du terroir*'. This they depict as 'the idea that food from particular areas is somehow an expression of the land because it is produced from local ingredients which are suited to regional soil and climate and transformed through the special skills of local people'.

Causes to Provide, and Types of Providers

Tourism is a means of diversification for the farming community. For marginal, isolated and peripheral areas, it serves too as a vehicle for regeneration, and economic and social development. The overall region of France called the Causses, of which the Causse du Larzac mentioned above is a part, and which is the source of sheep from which milk is garnered for production into Roquefort cheese, is one such area in which tourism is engaged in a gentle way. Local food and drink (cheeses, pâtés and sausages, honey, a pastis), and simple accommodation among the farming community, are distinctive elements to the tourism offer.

There is a generality and special asset about food and drink tourism. This is that, in both countryside and town, food and drink tourism is naturally fitted to Small- and Medium-Sized Enterprises [SMEs]. So these types of providers, often precluded by extent of resources and capacity from other sorts of tourism, can participate readily in this type. Small caterers on the hospitality front, specialist hotels and bed and breakfast units, farm accommodation, restaurants and cafés etc, can offer a defined special item or concept to a distinct but affluent market. So, similarly, with specialist shops, farm outlets, dairies, orchards, vineyards and wineries, small breweries, and market stalls, as examples. In the country, the place of agriculture and production can be the focus, in the village or town, the place of small industrial production such as a granary and the outlet of produce such as market or shop will be more to the fore.

Imagery and Positioning

Food and drink are regularly used as key elements of tourism imagery. They are perhaps so routine features as to neither to have attracted much comment or to have been noticed for the extent they feature in the holiday forefront rather than as surrounding items. Generally the positioning is up-market or aspirational. For the young, ebullient market the imagery connects not much to food, and rather to the process and outcomes of drink*ing* than to the product of alcoholic drink. The chilled glass of rosé imbibed on the sun-dappled terrace, the straight-out-of-the-sea fish consumed at the quayside restaurant: these are items among many that tourists travel *for*. They connect them to a perceived world of tradition, authenticity, bucolic-ness and exotic and luxuriant simplicity and which travel allows them to imagine they can inhabit. Indicative is Tony Cohan's depiction, joining what was a quite crowded genre by 2000, *On Mexican Time: A New Life in San Miguel* that chronicles his and his wife's immersion in the Mexican simple life. He describes how they experience real food in contrast to commodifed fare: 'we've left behind the California taco, the enchilada combination plate and entered the domain of real *sabor*' (2000, p.10). They start having breakfast 'in the covered market, among the food and flower vendors'. Observing what the locals eat they see that 'working Mexicans ... will have soup, *menudo*, to start out the day, or steamed *tamales* and *atole*, a thick variously flavored hot corn drink, sometimes swilling a glass of powdered Nescafé in hot water at the end'. Even when a global commodity creeps in, somehow it does so picturesquely. The couple find 'a favorite stand that serves fresh fruit drinks called *licuados* in fat soda glasses, blended to order' (p. 15). Cohan describes,

'We eat everything we see on the street: strawberries and cream; corn on the cob slathered with chile, lime and mayonnaise; chicken and enchiladas from the outdoor grill under the portals off the town square. We sip fresh juices through straws from plastic bags tied with rubber bands. We munch slices of white crunchy jicama, a root vegetable, with powdered *chile* and a squeeze of fresh lime, sold from fruit carts. Every few days one of us is ill with the *turistas*; even this seems to be part of the catharsis' (p. 16).

The power of all this to bring personal rediscovery is explained, when Cohan portrays,

'With the passing days, I note the gradual departure of the frozen, strained glare in the mirror. Some vaguely human apparition stares back'.

Cohan is transported from the western world to a naïf world of purity, authenticity, tactileness, sensuality and contrast to the globalized and commodified and mundane. Food and drink are items of imagery to appeal to these notions. He reports, 'In the States my aversion to supermarkets nears the pathological. Here in open air and natural light, moving among pyramids of tomatoes and avocados and onions, brushing hands with sellers, exchanging words, I feel alive, a participant' (pp. 30–31). Tellingly, however, Cohan does not spend all this time in San Miguel, and though a house-owner there, he lives also in California. He is in prolonged way still a tourist, and displaying the tourist's want of otherness and susceptibility and need for food and drink manifesting depth, distinctiveness and difference.

Participating Elements

Food and drink tourism concerns cultural complexity, between what is quotidian and what is special, and in the natures and motivations of both tourists and providers. It has been portrayed that 'the everyday' features clearly, and this dimension featuring is especially what makes food and drink tourism interesting and 'new'. Warde outlines oppositions represented as the messages to people about what they eat which he calls 'antinomies of taste'. He says these four to condition choices are 'novelty and tradition, health and indulgence, economy and extravagance, care and convenience' (1997, p. 3). It is not difficult to identify how these would have input and 'shake down' and which would be the features most emphasized and governing and motivating to people when in role of tourist – whether seasoned or otherwise – and albeit that all elements would be present. Warde indicates most clearly that he is portraying contradictions for peoples' choice, to show prominence in favour of, and to resolve. Discussing tourism specifically, Warde portrays it as particularly susceptible to inventing tradition, saying 'probably the tourist industry is more advanced at inventing traditions than is the food industry' (p. 63). He cites the 'Taste of Scotland' campaign as 'one striking example of the way in which tourism, food and invented tradition are brought together'.

This comment underlines that an action of this book must be looking at when and whether spurious or authentic traditional food and drink is being sought by tourists and by which types and in which circumstances and by whom each of the kinds are being offered and in what situations, and what is motivating and instigating it all. A stance has already been indicated firmly that food and drink tourism, in its interpretation of a pursuit by the tourist of an object of a food and drink product of quality and authenticity, is an action of a tourist of accomplishment and discernment. A different category of food and drink tourist exists, but whose emphasis is the experience food, and especially drink produces on holiday, and its role as 'means' rather than for its direct features. In relation to the other feature, for emphasis again, that food and drink tourism is a kind of tourism that connects to everyday, it should be said that feature will only be allowed to be presented by a tourist group whose everyday life is comfortable and not at sustainability level. Barthes discussing food types, depicts a situation in which lower-class households need diverting by ornamentation to their food from their essential need for it to represent economy and frugality, whereas, a higher-class family can afford to look real food in the face as opposed to food that has been endowed with magic to render it a diversion (2000, p. 79).

Barthes' evaluation of travel fits in with an analysis that it can portray everyday life, with the inferred assumption being that those travelling are in a position of luxury sufficient to be able to regard features of everyday life in the eye. He states categorically, 'It is unquestionable that travel has become (or become again) a method of approach based on human realities rather than "culture": once again (as in the eighteenth century, perhaps) it is everyday life which is the main object of travel' (p. 76). He says (and this, it should be noticed, was stated by him in 1957), 'Notice how already, in the *Michelin Guide*, the number of bathrooms and forks indicating good restaurants is vying with that of "artistic curiosities"'. The quotes make is clear that Barthes' negation of culture as part of travel is a negation of culture in its sense of 'the arts' rather than in the meaning used in this book of 'manner of life'.

Knowledge and Interest

There are other dimensions of appeal to a tourist of food and drink featuring strongly in their holiday at a level of their being the main foci, or else being among the key motivators for selecting a destination from among others. A noticeable feature to food and drink orientated holidays is their character of delivering an educational input, whether overtly or otherwise. In the first character are holidays, as examples, to learn about wine, to gain understanding of the methods of production of another kind of drink or of a particular type of food, to find out how to cook gourmet meals, to discover how to produce meals to a particular ethnic style or cultural way. All such holidays deliver an experience of individual improvement and so are suited to a category of discerning, or would-be discerning, holidaymaker. It can be seen at once that the 'culture-vulture' tourist of old is an obvious candidate as consumer of these holidays as is the newer 'Third Ager'. However, and this is another link with everyday life, a Westernized lifestyle of affluence, in which eating and drinking out regularly are part of normal routine and common to many, lends to a taste and interest that are embedded in daily life and generated from it being carried forward to act as the basis for an experience, in special or hyper-real form, on the holiday.

Memories

A not to be underestimated facet of usefulness to the tourist in their participation in a food and drink related holiday, and which again shows an intervention of the everyday into this type of holiday, concerns the souvenir, the take-home remembrance for tourists or the gift to be taken back to those who have not left the routine milieu. Albeit that perishability needs to be considered, special foods and drinks that are of suitable longevity can represent both easily affordable and reasonably easily transportable sources of goods. For the tourist, these retain and bring some of the 'magic' of the vacation into the holiday afterlife and find use in the everyday. For the stay-at-home person, these serve as a talisman for connecting with an experience of holiday and to temporarily bridge the divide between the environment of everyday and that of the holiday. Another bridge may be the attempt to re-create the holiday ethnic meal at home.

Key Aspects

It has been shown that important aspects to the food and drink holiday are its abilities to serve as the basis for offering *education* to the tourist and to render to them qualities of *sensuality*. It, therefore, delivers benefits at a cerebral level and a sensory level. It meets needs for being taken seriously in society, being rendered 'acceptable', and requirements of aspiration, while serving meanwhile our instinctive, individual and needs, expected to be met on holiday especially, to enjoy, to indulge, and to be hedonistic. As will be demonstrated, a contrasting consumer to the older connoisseur type of tourist is the young, fun loving, easy-going and 'in a crowd', kind of visitor.

Food and drink tourism has a propensity to meet today's tourist's needs. It has the suitability to be used by an especially broad spectrum of providers. It has the capacity to cater also to wider societal needs such as those of stimulating and regenerating rural, disadvantaged and peripheral areas, and preserving and revivifying cultural methods and practices. It can be seen as a socio-cultural and economic development mechanism overall, and with the flexibility and special propensity to be adopted and used by small-scale suppliers in the tourism field. That food and drink are, in generic form, everyday items means that nobody, neither any tourist or tourism provider, is excluded from a basic connection and familiarity with them. Food and drink tourism is a field of tourism endeavour that fits the general style of the WTO's Global Code of Ethics and Articles 4 and 5 most particularly. The Code advises that attention should be given to allowing 'cultural products ... and folklore to survive and flourish' (WTO, 1999, Article 4, 4). It calls for attention to tourism policies acting towards improving local conditions and integration with the 'the local economic and social fabric' (Article 5, 2). It suggests that 'Special attention should be paid to ... vulnerable rural and mountain regions, for which tourism often represents a rare opportunity for development in the face of the decline of traditional economic activities' (Article 5, 3).

This chapter has portrayed the difference of food and drink tourism to many kinds of predecessors and other current types. The heightening of difference is occasioned because of food and drink and their related venues becoming *goals* of travel as opposed to being trip side-components. Through these necessities of everyday life being brought so centrally into tourism as the prime offer, delivers a somewhat fresh dimension to the tourism arena. This is of holiday life and quotidian life being connected and over-lapping rather than being seen as needed by those concerned – tourist and tourism provider – to be separate and 'other'. As has been indicated the merging, and cultural change to the attitude to the holiday represented, is a modified rather than massive alteration and it relates so far to but one style of tourism, that with food and drink at centre stage. The movement is nonetheless interesting, significant and an alteration and so is worth charting and considering. The subject of food and drink tourism is specially and additionally worth attention and analysis for the aspects to which it links, which condition its circumstance and which provide its context. In this arena, as has been suggested in outline, such components feature as authenticity, globalization and local-global connections, advantaged and disadvantaged communities' polarities, activism, diversification, commodification, food concerns, and mass versus individual and alternative voices. Already through the outline depiction so far, it can be seen how importantly these issues impinge and relate to initiatives concerning food and drink tourism. They allude to what is happening and why. A move will be made to draw conclusions at this book's end. Before that, coming chapters will show and consider the detail, beginning with taking a closer look at the provider and supply side dimensions to food and drink tourism and the attendant overall culture and individual culture inputs.

Chapter 4

Ripe Time for Providers

In Chapters 1–3 the aim was to display the general arena that is bringing food and drink tourism to arrive. The overall environment, social context and general cultural currents participating in the scene and causing to deliver food and drink as an object of tourism were presented. In the initial effort of Chapter 1 to depict food and drink tourism and its emergence, and developed in Chapters 2 and 3, there was some portrayal of why the appearance is now. Certain suggestions have been made of reasons in tourism and the tourism industry for encouraging suppliers now to adopt food and drink tourism as among their tourism offer. So, some first attention has been given to considering why providers and stakeholders would make food and drink tourism their provision. Also, it has been observed to which sectors among these the type is suited particularly and among this was included noting characteristics in food and drink tourism to render it as especially able for use by SMEs. In Chapter 3, from a perspective that saw the consumer as starting point, more attention, than upon the supplier and their environment and stakeholders, was turned upon the consumer and their motivations and how these bring about and connect to food and drink tourism. Now, in Chapter 4, providers and their context, concerns and aspects as linking and relevant to the subject under discussion will be the central consideration.

Causes for Food and Drink Tourism's Emergence

Reacting to Consumer Taste

We have seen some of the reasons for appeal of food and drink tourism for the consumer. To *react* to these is the first and core motivation for the provider, and it is, of course, a basic imperative – the fundamental of a marketing approach – that the tourist's desires and wants should be reflected in the supplier's provision. So, a simple core reason for a provider to offer food and drink tourism is because a taste for this type of holiday experience now exists in the tourist.

Regarding wishes that originate in the provider, a best situation is when these wants meet effortlessly with those of the consumer. The next and perhaps more customary instance, given that tourist and producer are arriving in the arena due to distinctively different impellents, is when a situation of mutually beneficial exchange – as is the mainstay of marketing – is produced. In outcome the essential exchange is represented by the traditional holiday aspirations of pleasure, thrill and satisfaction being present for the tourist and for the supplier one or several among the fundamental motivants of profit, status, and advancement being in place. As will be seen, the provider wishes sub-divide and are more diverse than those mentioned, but their core is these three.

Questions for Asking

Discussion of food and drink tourism, and especially in relation to providers, needs to look at

- what is special or different about it for it to be regarded as a distinct activity among tourism overall
- why it should ought to be seen and deployed as a provider mechanism now
- which types of providers it fits
- which particular needs it meets, or whether these themselves differ or are unusual from those of the mainstream
- the kinds of outcomes in terms of types of products that can be delivered, and to which providers and needs these best correspond.

Society Reasons

The 'why now?' question about food and drink tourism should perhaps be looked at more first. Some causes from the consumer to produce the emergence of food and drink as being a tourism main subject have already been considered. Certain general reasons of impetus among society have been given or implied, such as movements of anti-globalization, anti-commodification, anti-GM foods, trends to urbanization and so towards rural depopulation, rises in environmental concerns, recognitions of needs for biodiversity and to try to achieve sustainability, changes of balance in types and whereabouts of farming activity and alterations of agricultural practices, increased attention upon ethnicity aspects and distinctiveness features, searches for roots and authenticity. Impacting the realm of tourism very directly is speed and accessibility of communications – in information and travel – for a large sector of society. In the developed and affluent world, from which tourists are largely drawn, food and drink are assured as items of subsistence. So, they can be looked at in a leisured, deep and thoughtful interested way for their other dimensions such as differences of type, variations of style of production and manner of preparation. Also, they can represent cultural currency to be used by individuals and groups for making social statements and for indicating separation and distinctiveness from among others.

In the spring of 2001, a pronounced connection between food production and tourism was to the fore, with the UK as the hub and centre of impact but with wider emanations and implications. This was with the appearance of foot and mouth disease in sheep and cattle. Farmers whose herds were afflicted, or which were located in zones where the disease was in appearance or judged potentially likely to appear, lost their creatures and sources of livelihood. Those linked to the cattle and sheep industry suffered hardship as a result. The greater impact, though, than upon the industry of agriculture was upon the larger industry for the UK of tourism. Visitors were banned from certain parts of the countryside, but the impact rippled more widely with overseas tourists turning away from the UK, and not only from the direct cause of foot and mouth disease and thus certain parts of the UK countryside near livestock being out of bounds. A more generalized lack of confidence existed and which had, as a key focus, fear about the safeness of UK beef in relation to capacity for delivering 'mad cow disease'/BSE [Bovine Spongiform Encephalopathy] in humans. Each recent food scare, from those about the safety of GM foods, about BSE and vCJD [variant Creutzfeldt-Jakob Disease], about foot and mouth disease in sheep, cattle, pigs, goats, wild deer, and, very rarely, in humans, can be seen as encouraging society to become wary about food production by industrial means and on a globally-interlinked way and basis. The hot-line on the everyday matter of food straight into tourism is easily seen. This is first because consuming food and drink is a regular necessity and so it and its dimensions occupy tourism and daily life as one, and so any worry among people is revealed as not only in daily activity but in tourism activity. Additionally, the general beam focused (see, for example, Humphrys, 2001) gives food and drink a higher profile in consumers' minds and encourages more consumer interest in the entities and their production and environment and so the opportunity is provided for food and drink tourism to attract more attention. Due to the general context as has been described, extra appeal will be likely to attach to the sites and locations of food and drink that can be shown as authentic, traditional, local and rooted and avoiding global processes and most advanced technology in consumables. A particular climate of timeliness is in presence for food and drink tourism to be emerging strongly.

So, food and drink issues are 'in the air' to reinforce everyone's necessary attention upon food and drink. But why should *tourism* adopt these items to be used as direct object to entice tourists? How do food and drink serve tourism providers and what is especial and distinctive to food and drink tourism to cater especially to tourism providers and to what sectors and in what ways?

Affluent and Disposed Consumers

Apart from the food concerns elucidated, an interest in food and drink and their features among consumers has been long emerging. Probably its prerequisite has been a situation's arrival of the consumer being beyond subsistence level and therefore the time appearing for the consumer of their possessing adequate affluence to be able to look for interest and enjoyability in food and drink and their circumstances. Writing in the year 2000, Warde and Martens (2000, p. 23), for example, describe the preceding hundred years in England as the time of 'the gradual evolution of eating out into a leisure activity'. Their 'survey of English urban populations' finds 'the great sense of pleasure and satisfaction that people claim to derive from eating out' (p. 215). This contrasts with the puritanism Scruton articulates as formerly intrinsic to the English and which he opines extends to the viewpoint on choice and attitude on food (Scruton, 2000, p. 51). An impulse to improvement in standards, and change and more open-ness to other cuisines, Paxman attributes as caused by immigrants to England (1999, p. 259). Commenting on Bryson's 1996 observations in *The American Social Review* of a diminution of cultural separation, Warde and Martens make the observation, 'One explanation is that there is now so much variety of choice that it is impossible to connect people's tastes to their social position. Thus taste becomes socially unimportant, distinction obsolete' (2000, p. 226). A reaction to this comment would be to suggest that tourism in objectifying food and drink offers a new arena for consumers living in variety and affluence to show discretion and exclusivity in the items and so allowing distinctions still to be drawn. It should be highlighted that Warde and Martens are speaking of the English, and so discussing people from the developed Westernized group rather than talking about communities living at subsistence level or in remote or peripheral places.

City, Countryside and Agriculture

An aspect to be emphasized is that those among the developed world, the sector generating most tourists, are increasingly urban dwelling. It may act both to lend a viewpoint of romanticization of the countryside and its agricultural activities, and/ or, as is often suggested by the agricultural community, an ignorance about its farming practices and the rural way of life. Bayley sees a cultural input to our contemporary view in the domain, and class as still prevalent as a dimension, saying 'Our present view of landscape is distorted by class and cultural prejudice' adding in no-nonsense vein, 'The countryside is a factory' (2000, p. 10). The urban community is, meanwhile, developing eating out habits near to home in the city itself. A café and restaurant society has emerged, and as arrival is 'third spaces' such as Starbucks and Internet cafés. The European Task Force on Culture and Development projects cybercafés – 'any establishment that sells food and drink as well as providing access for customers to computers and the Internet' (1997, p. 360) – over the world as developing their own culture and to serve as models for *fora* for meeting and for generating ideas. Destination accommodation, meanwhile, has a wide – city, countryside and seaside – physical distribution but a main clientele that – whether their object is a designer hotel or pseudo-pauvre stilted hut over sea or eco-yurt among wilderness – is essentially from the educated, discerning and sophisticated urban sector.

How much our growing urbanity of habit and attitude is impelling food and drink tourism to the fore is to be borne in mind. The country and town polarization which is occurring generally, may be lending to the rural end of the food chain being seen by urbanites as quaint and other worldly and therefore fitting the recognized tourism product template of being other, usual and 'different'. (In the UK, the Countryside Alliance – formed to highlight and vaunt the concerns of the countryside which the Countryside Alliance believes city dwellers are either ignorant of, or else fail to understand or give adequate attention to the matters – interestingly has now accepted that correspondingly the countryside has not tried to 'read' the city, and it perceives that each 'side' ought to see that their connection and inter-dependency.) Tourism visits to the countryside are able to take on the leisured, unreal and romanticized vein of Marie Antoinette escaping duty, reality and courtly life to play at milkmaid in the picturesque *hameau* at Versailles.

The ground has in a sense always been there for occupying because of a fundamental divergence always in existence. This is what Ronald Blythe depicts as 'the great division which separates growers from the mere consumers of food the world over' and in saying that former persons are linked by 'the internationalism of the planted earth which makes them, in common with the rice-harvesters of Vietnam or the wine-makers of Burgundy, people who are committed to certain basic ideas and actions' (1972, p. 15). A world-wide fraternity exists also focused on the consuming sector, as Chesser describes saying, 'food is the global language' (2000, p. 232).

Inglis reminds us how the term holidays, derives in England, 'taking its magical charge, ... from the "holy days" of the agricultural year on which heavy collective labour was replaced in brief respite by collective recreation'. The connection between holidays and agriculture is shown, therefore, to be basic and old. Inglis also portrays the food and drink link in describing that holy day revelry and unconstraint 'were given their usual lead in the pleasures of food and wine' along with 'sex and talking dirty, extravagant display and indecorous attire' (2000, p. 6). Focusing on the present day holiday, Inglis depicts its key features. Encapsulating one aspect, he opines that

'the holiday must be plentiful and it must be licentious. The end of every good holiday is a vast meal. Every holiday lives on the liminal .... I shall eat what I like and drink more than I can.... I will buy food such as I would never buy at home and cook dishes never attempted there either. I will drink gin at midday and Chardonnay at three' (p. 12).

Travelling and Transport

Travelling of itself – tourism, emigration and immigration – lends to exchanges and adoptions of gastronomic tastes, style and habits. Media articles and programmes on food and drink and foreign cuisines and lifestyles, along with those on tourism, reinforce and encourage the syndrome and interest more. The vehicle of travel too (the plane, train, ship), so often essentially the same among its type – but because it is operating in a competitive situation needs to try to manifest distinction – has food and drink as strong among its battery of items to use to entice the traveller. So, for the tourist, in travel to a destination, a destination en route may be the gourmet meal aboard the transport vehicle. In the long-haul flight's essential boredom to the tourist, the meal and its amount of desirability can feature as their highest aspect of attention. Lovegrove describes that, 'Now, the award-winning "cheferati" command healthy consultancy fees for planning in-flight menus and vintners suggest suitable bottles of Chardonnay with which to wash down the ragout and roasted root vegetables' (2000, p. 53). He draws attention that types of airlines use food and drink differently: one type following the gourmet avenue, while others – in tune with their style and length of route – may serve basic no-frills items for eating and drinking. Special trains and train trips often feature the food and drink they provide as keynotes to their offer along with aura and ambience and the passing view, and so with the eventual destination as only part of the attraction. The point of emphasis is that in providing a journey, food and drink can be the items used as selling points to render the journey special to the traveller and to render it a tourism product.

De Botton sees that simply eating in the air gives extra thrill, saying 'Food that, if sampled in a kitchen, would have been banal or even offensive, acquires a new taste and interest in the presence of the clouds (like a picnic of bread and cheese that delights us when eaten on a cliff-top above a pounding sea)' (2002, p. 45). He is portraying that *surroundings* influence impressions of food eaten. This makes the important suggestion – and which if true is asset to the provider of holiday food and drink – that food and drink consumed away from base in interesting places may seem more appealing to consumer than when they have its exact equivalent at table at home.

What Should Providers Do?

The critical things for providers considering engaging in tourism by delivering food and drink and hospitality as the main or only product offer are these:

- to identify themselves and their product clearly
- to see if a market taste and tourist niche is there to fit with, and to an extent to offer viability
- to decide whether diversion, and alteration of products, is necessary to cater to a target market's disposition, and whether the change is financially possible and worth making
- to assess whether and how the necessary dialogue and connection can be made with the consumer, and at affordable cost.

Provider Categories and Styles

Most of the major likely categories of suppliers for food and drink tourism have already been suggested in outline. In looking back over recent times to which styles of providers were 'first off the block' to make tourism offers whose focus was food and drink, some further foundation of indication can probably be delivered of those types most suited, equipped and needing to deliver products of this kind of emphasis.

The catering and accommodation sectors have, of course, always been integral to travelling. Any tourism activity occupying more than an hour or so will call in a need for a pause for relaxation, refreshment and diversion, and which requirements eating and/or drinking serve extra to their direct role of giving sustenance. Similarly, tourism confers a basic need for lodging into the need for an interesting and 'other to home' experience in terms of where to decide to reside for the night. A feature from the early 19th century was travel to good and supposedly beneficial water and which delivered the phenomenon of the spa resort. Now the water is more likely to travel to us in a bottle to be placed on the meal table or for the water to be consumed 'on the go'. Tourist sightseeing has long included observing agriculture and food production as part of viewing the countryside. Markets have been visited as 'local colour' and for their distinct food and drink products. In Austria, the long custom has been to been for visits out from the capital of Vienna to surrounding village *heurigen* (wine taverns) to sample the local wine. Industrial food and drink production and processing centres and outlets for particular items have joined the attractions being visited once industrial features have become accepted as interesting.

The *distance* of much of Western society from agriculture and industry, by lack of participation in them, to emerge in the post-industrial phase has encouraged a transfer among many people to see these things as now related to their realm of leisure rather than of work. Obtaining strawberries, for example, became a Sunday afternoon relaxation activity of driving from town to countryside to a 'Pick your Own' rather than being the individual's prolonged and involved matter of growing, tilling and gardening. Whisky Trails linking distilleries in Scotland were established (see Brown, 2000). Cadbury World near Birmingham in the UK is a theme park type of attraction using matter from among food and drink – chocolate of the manufacturer Cadbury – as a its topic: this albeit that the central subject was Cadbury and its operation and realm. At Eugénie-les-Bains in France, a leading chef, Michel Guérard, established a hotel with spa to extend the promotion through books of his Cuisine Minceur and Cuisine Gourmand. In the UK, outings to teashops are traditionally a favoured pursuit, and which was driven by the appearance of the private car and so the activity of car-touring. These tea shops/tea rooms can be regarded as the more enticing to consumers and increasingly overt as a matter of tourism in the contemporary climate of women as well as men working, of watching-weight being routine, and so neither time and lifestyle of everyday permitting the indulgence of the meal of afternoon tea except as the treat of tourism. As greater travelling/tourism, and affluence, have happened, more knowledge and interest in the world's many various foodstuffs and types of drink have developed. The more knowledge gained and the more commonplace a general strong attention to gastronomy there is occurring, the more a stage is set to need to display elitism in some way through such as extra fine knowledge or having discovered something special or obscure. A stage is set for leisure educational provisions such as holiday cookery schools, attractions with an overt educational dimension such as Vinopolis in London (Boniface, 2001) and Copia: the American Center for Food, Wine and the Arts, a charity organization located in California's Napa Valley wine-growing area (Goldstein, 2001). Copia is self-described as 'The World's leading cultural center dedicated to the discovery, understanding and celebration of wine, food and the arts' (Copia Press Release 19 December 2000). Such provisions fit a current culture of lifelong learning. They add to old existing and weighty agricultural and science museums with their displays and information and on food and drink matters. In museums themselves, the recognition has occurred – as the much alluded-to advertisement for the V&A Museum in London which focused on the café and portrayed the Museum as merely the side-show was an early indication – that not only is food and drink integral to the museum or other tourist venue visit, but for some attendees these represent *the* attraction. The covered courtyard restaurant of the Wallace Collection in London is indicative of the sort of type of glamorous café/ restaurant that museums and art galleries round the world are now providing and which serve as distinct and separate objects of lure.

Gradually through these background and causes described, an area for greater tourism occupation and provider exploitation has developed, showing food and drink as reasons of themselves for a trip.

Links and Elisions

The elisions of items to cater to supposedly busy lifestyles – such as holiday cooking schools represent – are emerging features. As indications of this, there are guides not only to teashops but to teashop walks (see Patefield, 1999; Anderton, 1998) and similarly to pub (inn) walks. Here travelling for food and drink is an object but it is being allied to another aim or aims, and beyond that of making a tour, in these instances physical exercise and fitness and/or moving about on foot among country, village and town. Meanwhile, gardens and teas are an already well-established link, and set in the visitor mind. Picnics and concerts became embedded as a link in the UK much through the Glyndebourne opera concerts in the Sussex countryside, a prominent part of which is the long break for having supper picnics in the grounds (though meals are available indoors as an alternative). Offering two experiences together gives *added value* to the consumer.

Prevailing Environment

The general answer to the 'why now?' question about food and drink tourism is that is suits current circumstances overall. A key situation to which food and drink tourism are able to offer amelioration or salvation, as has been depicted already, is to offer a route of diversification for a farming community undergoing hardship or penury in its primary role. The wider context is that food and drink tourism is an activity which is capable for supplier adoption in marginal and peripheral areas, providing that the tourist can be encouraged either to reach the relevant areas or else can be brought to an outlet for the supplier's produce. It has been described that food and drink tourism is suitable for SMEs' adoption. Modest operators and operations at both production and purveying ends can engage in the activity. They can look for a viable niche to serve that equates to their size and type.

Towards Social, Economic, and Political Objectives

The capacity of food and drink tourism to be beneficial endeavour to rural areas and economies and to help regenerate these, brings it to government and development agencies' particular attention and into the political domain. Similarly, large rural land-owning organizations or others with countryside involvement, and who have charitable and philanthropic and social aims, will see usefulness in the activity. In the UK, The Countryside Agency, the Heart of England Tourist Board, The National Trust, and Tastes of Anglia Ltd are among those engaged in projects or initiatives. The Countryside Agency promotes a scheme 'Eat the view' (The Countryside Agency, July 2000; The Countryside Agency, August 2001) to increase awareness and purchase of local produce, for local benefit and sustainability and to 'help maintain the environmental quality and diversity of the countryside' (p. 1). In partnership with The Countryside Agency, among others, the Heart of England tourist Board in 2000 initiated a three-year research, development and marketing Project 'to develop the distinctiveness of the region through its food and drink culture' and which 'will be "rolled out" as a model which can be applied throughout the country [England]'. One of its aims is to 'Strengthen the links between tourism and the food and drink sectors' (ETC, 2000, p. 3). The National Trust has published a brochure *Farm Food and Crafts from National Trust Tenants* (The National Trust, 2000; National Trust, 2002a) as part of helping its tenants of farms and renters of land and towards the Trust's conservation objective. In summer 2000, it up-scaled its already strong leaning to provide traditional English cooking, local cuisine and regional produce at restaurants/cafés/ tea shops at its country house and other properties for which chefs were given a seminar at one of the Trust's leading properties and restaurants at Sissinghurst Castle in Kent. In 2002, it opened its first own-run farm shop at one of its visitor properties, Wallington Hall in Northumberland, and which was seen by the Trust as a pilot project (The National Trust, 2002b, p. 91). Tastes of Anglia Ltd Trail is a group sponsored by the Rural Development Commission (Suffolk), MAFF [now DEFRA] and the relevant country and district councils which promote the Tastes of Anglia Trail of speciality food and drink suppliers, outlets and eating and drinking places (Tastes of Anglia Ltd leaflet, undated but probably 1998). Initiatives using food and drink towards development aims and which focus on or include tourism will be discussed in full in Chapter 5. To be noted here is the sheer range of interest, knowledge and representation that needs to meet together towards food and drink tourism serving general social, economic and political goals. This calls for more wide cooperation than merely the sectors of tourism and gastronomy understanding one another and working together for which Fields calls (2002, p. 36), and, crucially, the demand is that the farming community should accommodate diversification and accept a shifting emphasis.

Being Reached

Part of the motivation to so strongly promote agricultural producers and farm or other rural lodgings, and other food and drink sites and places of accommodation in the periphery, is their being vulnerable to not getting noticed or travelled so far out to. Also, these can need to be avoided – as was the instance for part of the UK countryside during the foot and mouth disease epidemic. By their nature, rural areas' general overall character is of being peripheral and away from crowd and 'off the beaten track'. Promotion generally, and special initiatives, and routes (Moulin and Boniface, 2001, pp. 237–248), trails, walks and so on, offer the way of drawing places to the tourist attention and to bring tourists to sites they would otherwise have passed by. Linkages being made by theme and across area serve through the subject interest or in encapsulation of a region to make an incentive for travelling around and about from one place to another.

More Than the Home Site

Any cessation of tourist visits to countryside and periphery, after all the essential sites of growth and production of food and drink and so where their main tourism sites can be expected to be, exposes a fragility of these types of, essentially small, tourism operators. Many will be changing or diversifying from a full farming focus due to direct and dire economic need and so will suffer any tourist withdrawal keenly. The foot and mouth disease outbreak in the UK in 2001 underlined the aspect. Noticing the dimension emphasizes that food and drink tourism venues need not to be seen as only rural features. Even the smallest farmer, grower and supplier needs to consider whether the food and drink source and home venue needs to be augmented and extended in terms of tourism. Having a presence in some manner in town or suburbia offers another and alternative option from earning money from the tourist and consumer. It delivers an extra income source and offers the insurance of some income should one outlet be temporally removed to the tourist. Also one site can 'feed' off another, connecting with it to build a larger and more lucrative and beneficial overall entity. Products in town act as income generators, and also serve as standard-bearers and to generate consumer curiosity to visit the production site elsewhere. Of course, it should not be lost sight of that certain sites of production or processing, usually those of the more industrialized nature and larger-scale can be in or near cities, for example a brewery, bakery or sweet factory. The broad generalization, however, is that growth of raw materials and small-scale processing belongs to rural areas, whereas major processing occurs, and produce outlets and food and drink venues most exist, among wider communities and where people most gather and congregate.

A food and drink centre serves as more than an alternative and extension to a visit to a site of production. It can serve as a gathering point for small suppliers to group and act in cooperation – informal or formal – and to save the visitor needing to travel to each production site, and so offering, for certain circumstances such as where time is short, a value-added entity to the visitors. The old market and the newer concept of the farmers' market meet the criteria. They offer a relatively easy and immediate way for a newcomer to bring their existence and produce to the public's eye. The centre often acts in role as a first contact point of introduction, information, and direction for touring, and so serves in mode of visitor centre. It can operate to explain an overall entity e.g. wine, or wine of a region, as in Bordeaux's Vinorama. Food fairs and festivals serve to collect numbers of producers and interested parties under a general theme of food and/or drink or to be focused on a particular type e.g. beer or to serve a more detailed speciality.

The extra and key and transforming site the food and drink provider now has to cater to the consumer, and for engaging in productive dialogue with them, is the Internet. Use of the Internet solely by the consumer to visit, see and buy food and drink can be regarded as sedentary tourism. The Internet being deployed for use by the tourist as part of making a real visit for food and drink, to gain information for planning a trip, to make follow up purchases after a venue has been visited, and to pursue an on-going relationship with a provider, lends the further and more central dimension of using the Internet concerning food and drink tourism. Since a Web site is essentially easy and inexpensive to set up and run, the Internet represents a strong element for overall provider use and is especially helpful and suited for small scale or newcomer operations to be able to sustain a presence in the marketplace.

Specialness and Difference

That food and drink tourism offers an area in which SMEs can readily participate has already been well emphasized. In addition to that the various kinds of *sizes* of providers can participate in food and drink tourism, the discussion so far has also made plain the variety of *types* of providers able to join in the arena, and that their *locations range across urban, rural, and cyber domains.* The overall provider stage of participation is therefore, large, diverse and open to certain fluidity. The provider objects of focus are in their essential form everyday features. Tourism offers providers the use to build on this fact but in so doing they must recognize a critical need to deliver a dimension of specialness and difference to their product and/or its associated visitor experience in order to render it in the realm of tourism. By food and drink tourism, tourism itself is offered a branch of change and rejuvenation at a time when the activity can be regarded as of longevity and of now familiarity of product and approach to many consumers. A sense in established tourists needs to be countered of less excitement in tourism, and of déjà vu. So, in its different product and practice associated, food and drink tourism offers an avenue for rendering new life to the somewhat tired industry of tourism, to provide an extra dimension, and to also serve to imply other products and altering ways of provider approach. A change to relate to tourists as they are now and in their contemporary context is needed of tourism (Boniface, 2001).

Within the general alteration, it needs to be decided by providers what types of markets food and drink tourism can best cater to. That food and drink can be used for social statement and differentiation means that the dimension requires quite careful consideration by providers. With mass tourism active, and affluence, consumerism, and interest in food and drink on the menu and prevalent among the developed world sector from which most tourists are drawn, a certain and 'fused' style of food and drink tourism product can be regarded as for the general travelling public. Peckham said in 1998, discussing nations that consume, 'Today, it could be argued, commodified foreignness in the form of world cooking is served up by a mainstream culture and consumed in a feast that feeds the muscles of the ravenous nation, incorporating and finally annihilating all difference' (1998, p. 181). The more the wide audience adopts an interest in gastronomy and levens food and drink of various cultures into a globalized 'Mc-cuisine', the more an opportunity is created for consumers seeing themselves as apart from the throng to find ways of showing their distinction by way of food and drink. The food and drink tourist who regards themselves as distinguished, apart, trend-setting will need to search for and pursue the more obscure, specialist, and less-easily to mass taste, entities for pronouncing their difference and higher level capacity of discernment. For the provider, part of their tourist awareness will be to know, when they are presenting an item that is esoteric or very culturally distinct, whether it will suit the tourist culturally and satisfy their ethics – for example concerning which animals, if any, they are willing to countenance as food, and of how they expect to see animals treated at rearing, butchery, and cooking stages.

Whom to Cater To?

There are perhaps three main kinds of food and drink tourist. The first type has been around for a long time: their predilections follow a certain path of tradition and modesty, and so they travel for a tea shop, a special hostelry or particular glass of beer, or to visit an orchard or an apple occasion. Many of food and drink tourism's day-visiting group are drawn from their number. The second type is the aspirational person, the now long-distance and affluent traveller and who is a strong attendee of the mass-media's contemporary rampant attention upon gastronomy and travel, and who is the candidate for new and large tourism entities concerning food and drink such as festivals and centres devoted to subjects such as wine. That Lonely Planet, a large travel guide publisher, is providing World Food Guides for many countries – generally those most widely known and perceived as having distinct foods and cultures – must be indicative that this tourism industry provider believes a big enough market exists of food tourists to be worth specifically addressing. The presence and general title of these Guides are perhaps somewhat signalling a cultural commonality and globality of treatment, and a sameness of attitude to the cuisines being featured, and albeit that there is a variety of authors and that each cuisine in itself is, and is described as, distinctive. These Guides maybe, therefore, confirm Peckham's depiction, provided above. Similarly, there are specialist guides in wide circulation and set for a large audiences, such as to best curry restaurants (Chapman, 2000). The final type is the tourist of discernment who represents a niche market for which small and specialist food and drink suppliers and accommodaters such as designer hotels are suited to cater, and with always the potential for such providers to become – by some such method such as producing extensions or branches or developing as a chain or group – as part of the large main channel as a taste for a special product spreads to be adopted by the aspirational group.

Types of Operation and Circumstance

Main tourism types of providers in the food and drink domain are:

*   farms
*   farm shops
*   fruit-picking sites
*   cheese manufacturers
*   honey producers
*   processors and manufacturers of individual food types, e.g. jam and chocolate
*   regional produce outlets
*   food markets
*   vineyards
*   breweries
*   restaurants
*   bars
*   cafés and teashops/tearooms

- farm cottages, *gîtes* and campsites
- hotels
- museums
- information centres
- festivals
- routes
- tours
- events.

This group of kinds at once reveals that food and drink tourism venues occupy both rural, urban and suburban space, that they may represent Small-, Medium-, or Large-sized Enterprises, and that they can be stand-alone or cooperative entities, depending on their type and what they provide. Since food and drink have as their basis growing and/or farmed entities, places of land and agriculture, and therefore rural areas, will serve as the domain of focus. This produces the general situation of items available as a tourism provision having the countryside as its natural centre. This provides an asset to be used in initiatives towards halting rural desertification, offering farmers extended and diversified ways of livelihood, to providing socio-economic development, and to maintaining local cultures as manifest in ways of food and drink growing, harvesting and preparation. The crop-cycle and the 'farming year' lend the further help of being perennial and ongoing so that at all times of the year something is happening in relation to growing food and drink matter, and with many features peaking usefully in what, in tourism terms, is traditionally a shoulder season.

Within the overall arena of food and drink tourism there are differences. One general one of these is between the tourist consumer and the rural inhabitant provider. A poor, isolated local resident is brought into contact with an affluent and worldly visitor. The contrast, and potential for culture clash, can be stark. Burns comments,

> 'for vast parts of the world, including many that are only just engaging in the global tourism nexus, consumerism and commoditisation have no relevance for day to day existence which is dominated by survival and coping. Even so, given that most tourists come from richer countries of the West (or North), both consumerism and commoditisation collides with the lives of destination residents' (1999, p. 62).

Once a mass tourist has an interest in travelling for food and drink, an opportunity exists for the provider to cater to the tourist looking to find items of these with which to show their difference from the crowd. This context puts attention upon the most remote and poor farmer who is engaging in a most old and obscure method of food and drink production, and/or who has a product yet un-rediscovered by the mass-market food industry and the consumer society. In the instance, unusually, and as has been discussed already, the poor, disadvantaged, and 'behind' has something to offer. Indeed, they can be in a positively privileged position, provided they have a context to be able to make use of this through financial help and training in how to cater to this discerning tourist from such as a rural development agency. In a matrix of conservation and sustainability, the rural farmers have on offer a tool of livelihood and viability in focusing on meeting the desires of the gastronome. They have too an opportunity for leaving industrial production behind and to focus on meeting the needs of the sectors of the tourist, organic food eater or gourmet. (It will be interesting how much in the now post era to the foot and mouth disease outbreak of 2001, UK farmers assume this direction.)

It has been shown that food and drink tourism, while a specialist portion of tourism overall, embraces many provider types and which vary in size, activity and location. Several consumer bases are served: a sector of modest aspiration and which has stayed faithful to old manifestations; a large group which is aspirational, well-travelled and increasingly well-informed; a final smaller congregation that is using its travel consumption as part of an effort to show distinctness from fellows and connoisseurship.

Chapter 5

Initiative and Opinion

The preceding four chapters have provided a background to food and drink tourism and have suggested the causes for it to be emerging strongly now. They have shown that some of the main reasons for food and drink tourism appearing are for it to act as a vehicle for helping 'save' rural areas. Food and drink tourism is seen as having use and benefit towards retaining the countryside's traditional aspect, keeping it looking cared for and farmed, and towards the rural community having economic livelihood and a vibrant socio-cultural milieu – and with outsiders and visitors bringing new refreshment to this. The wider dimension is of projects and initiatives being for the development not only of the countryside but of any disadvantaged places and which have an existing function or potential ability of delivering food, drink and hospitality, and associated products, to the tourist and visitor.

The matters to be considered in this chapter, and using the UK as the main example of focus, are what initiatives, projects and promotions are under way and in which tourism is a feature, what opinion informs them, who is doing the activity, towards what objectives, whether these aims are being/are likely to be met, and if there is appearance of un-envisaged outcomes – of good or bad kind. A further idea of this chapter is that it should act to bridge the general discussion of earlier chapters and the ensuing consideration in Chapters 6–11 of specific features of food and drink tourism.

Context to Initiative

The Example of the UK Farming Crisis

In the UK, there is a 'crisis in farming'. Its general heritage is in the post-Second World War impulse of governmental support, later replicated in action from the EU, of farmers to create some surplus and which chemical biology has caused to be too great. This has been later replicated in EU impositions upon the UK. Also, some laziness in farmers has been brought by subsidy to them and thus lack of innovation been delivered in farmers. There have been imports from overseas at a price less than in the UK. The UK consumer has traditionally and generally been reluctant to pay most for ensuring best quality. Food scares have changed what many consumers want, meaning that some industrially farmed or traditionally-desired items are in the reduced favour of some consumers. The public, and tourists strong among it, wants picturesque old farming – not featureless prairie-farming – rural areas. The outcome is of a countryside over-farmed, in too industrial manner, and with farmers finding that what they have been producing, and in the level of amount delivered, now has not public approbation and value enough for giving them a livelihood.

O'Hagan gives a vivid description of what the current situation is and its causes,

'The strong pound, the payment of subsidy cheques in euros, the BSE crisis, swine fever, and now foot and mouth disease, together with overproduction in the rest of the world's markets – these are the reasons for the worsened situation. But they are not the cause of the longer-term crisis in British farming: local overproduction is behind that, and it is behind the destruction of the countryside too. For all the savage reductions of recent times, farming still employs too many and produces too much' (2001, p. 12).

Changes in Lifestyle

Public taste and culture and lifestyle are strong reasons for the situation present now. This is in an everyday life preference to one-stop shopping in a supermarket rather than in the more time consuming way of visiting a series of small shops and specialist suppliers, and to select commodified ready-prepared food items. This main cause must be in demography, of so many families having both male and female partners in employment outside the home, often working long hours and so each with limited time for shopping, meal preparation and cooking, and their wanting too to 'free-up' as much time as possible from domestic tasks towards leisure activity – and of which tourism and day outings are a dimension. The general move to purchasing commodities from large suppliers is part of the general globalization trend. Large operations render economies of scale, giving power to the retailer to make a deal with suppliers which lowers the cost the retailer pays per unit, and so benefiting the retailer and the low cost being passed on to the customer to their benefit and approbation. The provider of the basic product, or the specialist outlet, however, can be losing out, if they are not big enough to make economies of scale themselves, and through the public's transfer of patronage away from them directly and to the supermarket instead. Also, as is thoroughly familiar, shops in towns and cities are victim to the rise of the out-of-town shopping centre and shopping mall as well as to the ex-urban supermarket. So, although the farmer is suffering from a particular situation, the small provider and processor anywhere, and so in town or on urban edge as well as in country, is at risk from some same current syndromes. Therefore, encompassed, and possibly suffering, are, as examples, the independent brewery or pub, the family-run hotel, restaurant or café, the specialist food shop of fruiterer, butcher and fishmonger. These are all at the mercy of overall changes of public habit and all are affected by changes of culture to way of shopping style (Chung et al., 2001).

It is clear from the foregoing that there is a prerequisite background for initiatives concerning food and drink. Farmers and small-scale providers need help to ameliorate hard times along with impetus to be creative and new in outlook. Society wants countryside and farmland to look good and to be conserved and rendered as sustainable and environmentally rich as possible and to have strong recreational use. A consumer sector is showing trend of having positive interest in traditional local, speciality and organic food and drinks and actual wish to consume them at least at times and on occasion, and among important of which is the leisure and holiday moment. At least partly, the group's inclination is away from the globalized and homogenized way in food and drink purchase and consumption. National government, development and support agencies and organizations, some regional, district and city and town authorities, are primed and in place with aim of offering help towards all these objectives. They are doing so by means of providing research and reports, offering comments, ideas and suggestions, giving funding and marketing assistance, and offering, establishing, or encouraging particular projects and promotions. Some activities are too the preserve of business and trade groups, either those relating to a particular type of food, drink, or hospitality venue, or to a certain area. This chapter's intention is to offer a selection, from relevant initiatives to the area of food and drink tourism, to act to be indicative of the sort of types of processes and measures in use. It should be emphasized again here that tourism can offer a leading role and impetus towards a generally-useful change in consuming culture in society overall. This is because tourism offers unusual time and opportunity for the consumer to gain more awareness and understanding about kinds and processes of food and drink production and provision and concerning benefits of consumption of highest quality food and drink.

Activity in the UK, and in Relation to the UK

The situation in the UK is of farming generally in poor heart and economic state. That 400,000 marchers joined the September 2002 march of 'country to capital' for Liberty and Livelihood, and – albeit that that fox-hunting was under threat of ban or heavy regulation was the clear main issue – showed the sense of suffering and concern felt about their circumstances of those inhabiting the countryside and trying to earn a livelihood from it. Tourism in the countryside had had a setback in 2001 to recover from because in the first part of the year access to some portions were denied because of foot and mouth disease. Some overseas potential tourists have shown reluctance to visit the UK because of fear about safety of food due to a sequence of food scares, and of course during the foot and mouth disease epidemic overseas tourists, like their domestic UK counterparts, could not go to parts of rural areas. The circumstance produced an understandable heightening and quickening of agencies' and bodies' reports and initiatives concerning rural welfare and livelihood. Tourism, now having shown itself as more economically important in the UK countryside than farming itself, attracted much effort and attention to bring its revival there and much emphasis was placed on getting back fast to a situation of a countryside reopened for visiting. For political, economic and tourism reasons, attention was upon encouraging the public to visit the countryside and support its businesses and buy its food and drink products.

A key player in the UK in connection with food and drink is the Government Department DEFRA. In reaction to the foot and mouth outbreak, the UK Government established a Rural Task Force chaired by the Minister for Rural Affairs and with reopening the countryside and helping businesses as key aims. DEFRA had in its formation inherited relevant endeavours of MAFF. For example, in 1999 with the organization Food from Britain, the speciality food and drink sector had been studied and including how it linked with regional economic development. Food from Britain assists marketing of the products overseas, and in the UK in liaison with local food groups whom it helps support in their business and marketing advice activities. It has set up an Internet site (www.speciality-foods.com), which acts as a 'virtual shopping mall' that promotes speciality foods by area – nine in England (Anglia, Hampshire, Heart, Kent, Middle, North West, South East, West, Yorkshire) and then Scotland, Wales and Ulster. DEFRA supports FoodUK.com that is 'an Internet portal for special food producers'. With the Countryside Agency, MAFF had commissioned in 2000 the already referred to Enteleca Research and Consultancy Ltd Report *'Tourists' Attitudes Towards Regional and Local Foods'* (2001). Also in 2000, the seven-year-long England Rural Development Programme was launched with UK Government and EU funding. This Programme involved ten schemes, towards helping community and economic development and environmental conservation and improvement. The farmed trout industry was helped through DEFRA holding a March 2000 seminar that, among other conclusions, noted a need for more consumer responsiveness. In 1998, before vanishing for its function to be subsumed within DEFRA, MAFF published a booklet *Success with a small food business* (MAFF, 1998) which aimed, the Foreword by Lord Donoughue says, to help 'small rural producers and those interested in joining them' and who want

> 'practical guidance on the everyday but vital aspects of producing and selling food. How to maintain quality. How to market. How to develop the business and how to keep in touch with legal and technical requirements in a fast changing world'
> (Donoughue 1998, p. 1).

The English Tourism Council joined with The Countryside Agency in 2001 to produce a strategy (ETC and The Countryside Agency, 2001) which recognized that 'Increasingly, tourism is seen as part of the answer to supporting the rural economy and communities' (p. 5) and which put emphasis on need to deliver a quality experience to the visitor. It sought to promote local produce and gastronomy and made these comments,

> 'For too long, food has been a neglected area in rural tourism. The promotion of locally produced food and traditional dishes identifies the visitor more closely with the area; supports the local economy by retaining spending in the community; gives enterprises a marketing edge; reduces "food miles"; and can have a beneficial effect on the landscape through sustaining traditional agriculture. The seasonality of local produce can also be useful in influencing the time of visits' (p. 28).

The strategy contains recommendations for the future revolving around the delivery of pilot studies of best practice in promotion of local produce; performance benchmarking; improving advice, and increasing support, funding, and training to providers; encouraging quality; and 'close identification of certain rural destinations with specific icon food products or dishes' (p. 29).

As was mentioned in Chapter 4, The Countryside Agency began a Programme called 'Eat the view' in 2000. It seeks to utilize 'a growing interest in alternative forms of retailing, as shown by consumers [sic] willingness to buy on the doorstep, at farmers' markets, at the farm gate' (The Countryside Agency, July 2000, p. 2; The Countryside Agency, August 2001, p. 2). It also looks 'to promote the development of markets for products which … may strengthen the sense of place of the area in which they are produced – products which are strongly identified with a particular locality' (p. 3). Among the goals of the Programme are 'cutting out the "middlemen" and bringing consumers closer to producers .... local marketing and branding initiatives which utilise unique features ... an increase in the number of local and community-led food initiatives which will create stronger markets for produce and strengthen the links between producers and consumers' (p. 4). By a year after instigation the Programme was being manifest in funding of The National Association of Farmers' Markets, and by work with the Farm Retail Association and England's regional food groups (through Food from Britain), and with an Area of Outstanding Natural Beauty and a National Park. A typical project was that of mainly funding farmers' markets in the north-eastern Dales of England and with the Rural Development Programme, a District Council, and the Northern Dales Meat Initiative as other funders in partnership (The Countryside Agency, 2001a, pp. 4–5). By the early autumn of 2001, the Programme had its own Internet site (www.eat-the-view-org.uk). In the North East of England, an 'Eat the view' project which has the strong participation of the University of Newcastle upon Tyne's Centre for Rural Economy [CRE], led to, at the latter's suggestion, a Northumbria Food Fair held over the 2002 Easter weekend and which was so successful and with 'people ... queuing to take part in the consumer research' (University of Newcastle upon Tyne, 2002, p. 2), to lead to more CRE plans for research and activity of the kind along with its partners.

Both The Countryside Agency and The ETC are partners, with various others such as DEFRA, Regional Development Agencies, The Royal Agricultural Society of England, Farm Stay UK and Heart of England Fine Foods in The Heart of England Tourist Board Project that was mentioned in Chapter 4. The Project's aim is to 'strengthen the links between tourism and the food and drink sectors; encourage local sourcing; create locally distinctive cuisine; create added value for leisure and business visitors' (ETC, 2000). Its culmination in the Project third year is a regional strategy with case studies of best practice. The complexity of network and involvement in such endeavours can be indicated by the supporters of one of the partners, Heart of England Fine Foods which is itself a business member promotional organization and which publishes a member guide. The direct supporters in the instance are Advantage West Midlands, Birmingham City Council, The Countryside Agency, The European Rural Development Programme, Food From Britain, the National Farmers' Union, and the County Councils of Herefordshire, Shropshire, Staffordshire, and Warwickshire. Of equivalent complexity of support and alliance are, as examples, the partnerships which represent the Anglia Region brochure *Tastes of Anglia Trail: Gourmet Discoveries*, as depicted in Chapter 4, and the brochure for direct suppliers of South Somerset and West Dorset called *All in Good Taste: A Guide to Wholesome Foods in South Somerset and Sherborne*. This latter publication makes the points,

'Buying local produce helps to support the local businesses – farmers, smallholders, producers and retailers – and those whose work in them and supply them and service them. It puts into practice the Local Agenda 21 objective of sustainable development. It boosts the local economy at the same time as providing the pleasure that comes from eating delicious fresh food'.

The Heart of England Project soon recognized a need for profile raising and awareness building about regional/local food and drink among tourists. It found from a workshop on food tourism market segments that 'a brand image was needed to represent the concept of "locally produced and supplied food and drink"' and with the 'associations/attributes' of

'Identification with the Food and Drink Tourism project regionally, with potential for national application
A food and drink that is fresh, locally produced and sourced
Distinctive, high-quality cuisine with seasonal emphasis
Beneficial to the local economy and environment'
(The Heart of England Tourist Board, 2001).

Heart of England Food and Drink Excellence Awards were launched at the 2001 Ludlow Marches Food and Drink Festival by Raymond Blanc, the renowned French chef who has restaurants and a hotel in England. In his launching address, Blanc made the key points of emphasis that food has now become part of the lifestyle in England, that a market of quality must be the aim, and that training was crucially necessary and important.

The first chosen case studies as part of the Heart of England Tourist Board Food and Drink in Tourism Project were: 'Maturing the Flavour – Herefordshire' (emphasis on skills, quality, distinctive local products and exceeding the expectations of customers); 'Big on Apples – Herefordshire' (programme during autumn for 'local pubs, catering establishments and accommodation providers' to focus on apple-related products); 'Asia Town – Leicester' ('research into local sourcing of food and drink'); 'Farmshop.net – Leicestershire' (developing sales of local and regional produce to the Leicestershire hospitality market). And among endorsed projects was the 'Peak District Environment Quality Mark' that overtly drew in environmental stewardship, aiming at

'the development of new products linking environmental management with quality that can be promoted as "environmentally beneficial" providing distinctive local supplies for catering outlets'
(The Heart of England Tourist Board, 2001).

Research and activity concerning training, and giving business advice and guidance; helping business start ups; collecting a data base of 'local'/specialist suppliers for DEFRA to hold; are other key facets to the overall Heart of England Tourist Board Project. It has acted to trigger the arrival of a completely new UK food festival in 2002, the East Midland Food Festival.

In January 2002, DEFRA received the Report of the Policy Commission on the Future of Food and Farming. The Commission's Chairperson, Sir Donald Curry, himself a farmer, depicted UK farming as having taken knocks of which foot and mouth was but one, and to be in need of 'radical measures'. The Curry Report saw as the cure for this 'reconnection' of threefold type,

'Reconnecting farmers with their market with the rest of the food chain.
Reconnecting the food chain with a healthy and attractive countryside.

Reconnecting consumers with what they eat and where it comes from'
(Press Release, 29 January 2002).

By July of 2002, Sir Donald was launching a The Countryside Agency and Soil Association partnership project for local food to be promoted. Also by July of 2002, DEFRA had received an Action Plan 'to help the home-grown organic food and farming sector achieve sustainability' (DEFRA News Release, 29 July 2002) which was produced by a Group of whom the Chairperson was the Organic Farming Minister. Two months on, in September, the National Farmers' Union [NFU] produced a farmers' markets survey (*Farmers' Markets: A Business Survey*) that noted a burgeoning number of customers. Of the total customers, the largest number were 'retired persons', and with 'families' next – though some large way behind (NFU Press Release). Customers' main reason for shopping at markets was stated to be that of obtaining 'local, fresh food'.

The safety dimension has been referred to frequently. Consumers in the UK have been made worried about food and its styles of production, due to concern of possibility of illnesses, such as listeria and vCJD, from consuming certain contaminated foodstuffs. The *Get real about food and farming* Report from the environment campaigning organization Friends of the Earth describes that 'Public confidence in the ability of the current farming system to produce safe high-quality food has been severely damaged' and adds that 'the huge increase in demand for organic food highlights the desire for an alternative approach' (2001, p. 26). One of the schemes of the England Rural Development Programme is The Organic Farming Scheme which 'is to encourage the expansion of organic production' (MAFF, 2000, p. 12). The UK Government Organic Action Plan has been referred to above. The main recommendation of a study in the UK on behalf of the Joint Food Safety and Standards Group to the Food Standards Agency [FSA] was of 'a need for the Agency to develop a specialist function to examine food safety and standards issues in depth' throughout the whole food chain from 'farm to fork', not just 'on the farm'. Certain specialist providers and other farmers are concerned about over-regulation, especially concerning traditional food and farming practices that are now not generally seen as acceptable and sanitary enough and in a climate of consumer concern are being stipulated against. One such concerned body is The Specialist Cheesemakers' Association. Highlighted overall is a general difficulty with some traditional and specialist foodstuffs. The new and strongly campaigning organization The Countryside Alliance which came into being as a rural – and supporters thereof – uprising against their impression of Government and urban-dwellers' lack of understanding and support of country people and their ways (such as fox-hunting), has an organization within – with its roots as a former group called Save Our Foods – called Honest Food. This particular Campaign has the objectives of enquiry into European and British regulatory structure concerning food and to encourage caterers, supermarkets and consumers to obtain local and seasonal food. Honest Food, with a stance that sensible regulation rather than exemption or subsidy is the way forward in the UK, responded disbelievingly to the FSA Task Force's assertion, from looking at regulations on small food businesses, 'that food regulations are not perceived to be a burden by the small producers' (Countryside Alliance Honest Food response of 8 November 2001 to the Task Force Report).

The Countryside Alliance was an instigator with the Guild of Fine Food Retailers and the Campaign for Real Food of a British Food Fortnight, held in autumn 2002. The Fortnight was the autumn promotion of the 'Your Countryside You're Welcome' campaign (by DEFRA, The Countryside Agency, the DCMS and the ETC). Among the events and occasions were a Food Lovers' Fair, a Farmers' Market (in the tourist mecca of Covent Garden, London), a British Beer Day, a celebrity chefs' breakfast 'fry up', and the World Cheese Awards Final (www.britishfoodfortnight.co.uk/main.htm).

A major private body, and like Friends of the Earth a charity and membership organization, is the National Trust. It was founded in the late 19th century with a social mission. The National Trust Director-General's Review of the Year 2000/ 2001 describes (The National Trust 2001a, p. 7) on one of the three founders, Octavia Hill, believed in 1875 – twenty years before the Trust was formed by herself and two others – that society wanted/needed four items of 'Places to sit in, places to play in, places to stroll in, and places to spend a day in'. The National Trust is now a major landowner. While its essential role is preservation of its inalienable property for posterity, it is involved both in much of its territories being for current leisure recreation and tourism, and in needing to see all its tenants able to have livelihoods so they can persist in their caretaking role. It has been put into a role of campaign and special initiative in relation to farming and farming prosperity because so much of its holdings are the countryside (245,000 hectares) and so that these are kept and can be publicly seen, visited and understood. Some of its efforts in relation of food produce from farm and locale were discussed in Chapter 4. For example, National Trust restaurants and tearooms put emphasis on using food and drink from the vicinity of the property. The Trust's has a 2020 Vision for Sustainable Farming. To be aimed for, The Trust avows, is 'A local food economy'. It says that 'A much greater focus on producing, processing, marketing and consuming food locally and seasonally is needed to underpin the move towards sustainable farming' (The National Trust, 2001b). As has been described, at one of The National Trust country house properties, Wallington Hall – interestingly with a radical tradition through its former owners the Trevelyan family – a Farm Shop was opened in 2002. At two other National Trust country houses open to the public, Mount Stewart in Northern Ireland, and Ightham Mote in Kent, were opened new restaurants in 2002 whose emphasis is locally-sourced, fresh food and which are open in the evening for dinner and so which can cater to a 'different' type of visitor. These are seen by the National Trust as pilot projects (The National Trust 2002, p. 10).

As has been shown and explained, many initiatives are led or given background by the public sector. Particular places produce identities for marketing and using based on local cuisine, food or drink. For example, Ireland – the country which, unlike Northern Ireland, is not part of the UK – was promoted in 2001 by The Irish Tourist Board 2001 autumn break brochure entitled 'A Taste of Ireland' and which in presenting a full range of types of breaks brought into the overall presentation Irish food and drink recipes. Within the UK, Bradford is an example of a place with a culture that has become more colourful and distinctive through hybridization. Against a UK (Yorkshire) background and to cater to a UK market, it has found and used through Asian immigrant arrival – largely in the 1950s – such a strong identity of association with curry to lead to Bradford's self-designation as the 'Curry Capital of Britain'. Curry is so favoured in the UK overall for it to earn itself a special consumer guide (Chapman, 2000). The Isle of Wight is off the south coast of England and relatively poor (Boyd, 2001, pp. 31–32). It operates a Project named Island 2000 with biodiversity running through it and which is made up of five initiatives. One of these uses a logo and name 'Sunshine Fare' and sees 'biodiversity as a source of premium value'. The action 'will allow Island 2000 to release the brand label effectively backed up by particular criteria for Island authenticity, provenance and local distinctiveness'. Testing of the branded products is to be at 'the Island's Farmer's [sic] Market'.

As examples of initiatives from the private sector is the major one of 2000 by the Heritage Hotels group. This was displayed through a particular festival of food events over a month entitled 'Taste of Britain – a festival of food and drink' and represented also by a book *Heritage: A Taste of Britain* (Heritage Hotels, 2000). This latter, in extension of the main object and event, but nonetheless as clever support to them and so actually rather central, described a vast range of other food and drink venues and occasions across Britain.

While vaunting the name of a company directly connected with road travel, but nonetheless appearing objective of view, is the Michelin series of travel guides, called *The Green Guide*. At the time of writing *The Green Guide* series has only one regional *Guide* for the UK, the others being for London and for England, Great Britain, Scotland and Wales. There is one too for Ireland. The regional *Guide* is for the west of England with the Channel Islands included. While as part of their attention to matters cultural, the series routinely covers food and drink for the place it is depicting, worth noting is how much attention is given to food and drink in this the only UK regional *Guide* of the series. Trailed on the back cover are 'Cream teas and fish suppers' (Michelin, 2000) and within is a section on 'Regional specialities' and which include cider, wine, beer, cheese, Cornish pasties and saffron cake (pp. 62–69).

Relating to Consumers and Their Preferences

Consumer pre-existing notions and ideas, their reactions even to initiatives, or possible reactions to impending initiatives, are, of course, what providers and stakeholders are seeking to relate to, shape and tap into. It can be said that *The Green Guide* overall, with its strong consumer following in the travelling world, through its content is both reacting to market taste and helping in shaping its style. By giving its attention to food and drink it is expressing the importance of these alongside more usual cultural products such as architecture. The Enteleca Research and Consultancy Ltd Report mentioned in this chapter and Chapter 2 shows the propensity and potential of the market among UK tourists for regional and local food and drink products. It makes the general overall remark that for the market for local food, 'Local produce is associated with images of freshness, and personal rather than mass-produced processes', and continues with the comment 'These qualities link well with rural tourist themes of; rest, relaxation, good scenery and discovery'. The Report recommends that 'General motivational messages should include references reinforcing the value of local production to the local economy and local environment' (Enteleca Research and Consultancy Ltd, 2001, p. 7). From this Report and other aspects mentioned in the book so far, it is clear that 'local' is a key word. Freshness and the associated connotation of quality are important. Artisan production invites fine regard. Showing benefit to local economy and environment seems to attract good reception.

Example and argument in this book so far have demonstrated the strong likelihood that associating the food and drink with the auras expected of a holiday and giving the dimensions that the holiday allows such as time for experience, experiment and learning are also facets to appeal. Food characterized by time of preparation fits naturally to the holiday, as has been said. Understanding concerns and propensities carried over from everyday life, such as worries about food safety and so, as in the UK, putting increasing favour on organically produced food, is also necessary to the provider. Concerns about globalization and industrial scale and style production are other items to be suited to being especially shown in the time – and moment to reflect – that is permitted by the holiday. Bauman says that 'some of us become fully and truly "global"; some are fixed in their "locality" – a predicament neither pleasurable nor endurable in the world in which the "globals" set the tone and compose the rules of the life-game. Being local in a globalized world is a sign of social deprivation and degradation' (1998, p. 2). He sees '*degree of mobility* ... freedom to choose where to be' as distinguishing those in society '"high up" and those "low down"' (p. 86). Perhaps consumers are sensing and now feeling uncomfortable in inequality and feel need to patronize, and help in delivering income and benefit to, the local, as the rural farmer and provider so obviously exemplify. It is clear that the local is the thrust and so much of the association of so many food and drink tourism endeavours that are subject of initiatives.

The Slow Food movement (Petrini et al., 2001) is the McDonaldization antithesis, this having had its inception in activist Carlo Petrini's horror at the intention to place a McDonald's branch at the base of Rome's famous tourist site The Spanish Steps in the Piazza di Spagna. Ritzer in comparing 'Slow Food versus McDonald's' sees an anti-McDonald's market, saying 'There is a population throughout the world that is repulsed by McDonaldization and craves leisurely produced, high-quality goods and services' (Ritzer, 2001b, p. 20).

Important is recognizing and catering to an interest present in everyday already, and which tourism gives time and opportunity to indulge, such as curiosity about different food and drink and cuisines. As example of the alteration of circumstance is the remark of Raymond Blanc quoted above about a change in English culture of now incorporating a food interest as compared with a flavour of situation Scruton stipulates of the English of the past. Scruton describes the English as having been in relation to their pleasures 'anxious not to care more than they should', and so which 'led to one of their least celebrated triumphs – a cuisine in which ingredients were systematically deprived of the flavour, so that everything tasted roughly the same and manly stoicism prevailed over sensory enjoyment' (Scruton, 2000. p. 51).

Comment and Reminder

In describing initiatives, the focus of this chapter – because it has been discussing the UK as an example, and since the UK farming industry is 'in crisis' and rural areas are often now disadvantaged – has been on country areas and actions for these to survive and prosper. It should be remembered, of course, that the countryside is not the only place for and object of endeavour or solely the place where it is needed. The permeation of the discussion is that:

- the essence of food and drink tourism is that it can and should have a focus on the local, distinctive, high quality and good;
- varied and relevant initiatives are around and to have capacity to deliver products and environment the tourist is disposed to want and for benefiting and highlighting the specialist and small and medium scale producer, wherever located – country, suburb, town or city.

Given that the thrust of this chapter's discussion on initiatives has been to render the definition of providers of food and drink having arrived in their occupation through poverty, disadvantage and need to diversify, it should be mentioned here that there is a quite other category in the food and drink tourism 'world' which is of rather different circumstance and style and not really needing help or initiatives. This is the sector emblemized by small boutique hotels of city, seaside or country, by trendy restaurants and bars, and which has a high-level of design profile and quotient and often with a celebrity chef connection. Its markets are the affluent, and while it may have aggressive and expensive marketing and publicity campaigns, these are likely to be established individually, or by commercial sector alliance, and without public sector agency help or initiative.

The examples deployed from the UK are a selection and not exhaustive. They have been used to be indicative and for showing various characters of operation, and for relevance and potential to other places and nations. They intend to give the flavour of initiatives and to indicate cause, reason, and opinion underlying them. Finally, and continuing the use of the UK as example, perhaps one initiative the UK is still needing is one of 'pulling together'. This is for bringing all initiatives and projects into awareness of each other and to be completely complementary and without overlap and to avoid bringing over-complexity to producers. It is also to deliver to the tourist and visitor a one-stop place and point of focus which gives access and information to the whole scene available, and initiative underway, in food and drink tourism – and as the Copia Center in the USA, mentioned in Chapter 4, appears to be serving somewhat in the role. Further initiatives will be mentioned in Chapter 10 that is considering events.

Chapter 6

Production and Display Centres and Venues

This chapter will look at production places such as farm outlets and other close-by-production entities.

Making Contact

A provider or manufacturer of food or drink who wants to diversify by catering to tourists needs to make contact with them. Information about products needs to be provided, and an easy opportunity for purchase requires to be made available. The connections can be direct between grower or maker and the tourist, or else a middle-person may be needed for rendering the link. The situation of an outlet for products being required away from a site of production will be considered in Chapter 7. Here the focus is on the direct method.

Adequate Information

The advantage of being in direct encounter with the tourist, of course, is that a layer of intervention is avoided, and so costs can be less and an immediate impression and understanding can be gained of tourists' tastes and preferences. What the initial supplier needs to assess, as part of finding familiarity with their market is whether the latter can make access to the production location, and if so, how much pre-information is needed and whether a suitable direct medium to provide this exists. Therefore, to establish person-to-person contact may need nonetheless an intervention. This is the task of an information provider. As examples of these are: an outlet for leaflets such as a Tourist Information Centre [TIC] or a hotel; an Internet server or Web page provider for making information available to consumers' personal computers. As other ways for the tourist to become aware of a product are mentions in the newspaper and television travel media and in travel books and guides. The provider advantage of food and drink being everyday items is that the halfway point of awareness and appreciation of a product may be already installed in the tourist. So, only the other half of information needs to be divested in the tourist, which is that a production site (or else off-site sales outlet) is open to be visited.

Linking Up

A theme of this book is that there are inter-relationships and productive links possible among types of supply and supplier, for example between a production place or outlet or attraction and an accommodation provider. Available too to the provider is the option of forming clearly horizontal links of publicity and recommendation with compatible fellow similar providers. This, in representing a shared input and outlay, is efficient of an individual supplier's marketing resources. So, it is especially useful to the very small or specialist provider. Also, in other attractions being suggested to the tourist – and perhaps in the form of a formal route – critical mass is delivered and help is provided in rendering one geographical area a large enough and adequately time-filling proposition to the holidaymaker. A manifest disadvantage to the process is that with a theme of certain type being used, such as vineyards, similar and competing suppliers are being vaunted. Another disadvantage for a producer, in allowing their product or facility to be marketed among others, is the loss of control. Other externally-supplied partners may not be suitable and sympathetic to an individual provider's eyes, in terms of sharing the same level of quality or else being similar or complementary. The compromises of shared marketing are accepted, therefore, towards bringing reductions in costs of promotion, for probably gaining professional marketing help, and in achieving better and wider circulation of information to the consumer through shared and connected effort.

Being Inviting

The food and drink site, whether it is the production place or another place used to be a sales and display centre or domain, to act in a role as a tourism attraction and to bring revenue and benefit at that location, needs to be inviting to tourists. An appetite, therefore, needs to be created in the visitor encouraging them *to journey* for a food and drink item or something in association with it. So, a feature particular and extra demand to be made available beyond what is either found on-line or at a supermarket or shop immediate to the consumer's home. Something special needs to be provided, either in way of product itself, or through provision of one or both of an additional dimension or a more pleasurable opportunity than in purchasing on the home patch. In occupying the realm of tourism the food and drink product needs to become a focus to provide *experience* and *enjoyment* rather than only sustenance. If the product itself is the cause to visit, it is likely to represent in some way not an option that is routine or easily found. Hence that 'speciality', short run or short supply, distinctive local, or especially fresh, or untreated due to lack of need to travel long distances to reach consumers, food and drink is frequently the type to form the matter for bringing tourists. Otherwise, the added value is given in way of showing or informing how the item is produced, or in other elements being attached to the offer – such as a café, or something specific for the amusement of children.

Work and Play

The dimensions that actual production centres have to marry is being places of growing, making or processing, and therefore serving as *work*places, while catering well and healthily and safely as sites available to tourists, and so acting too as *display* and *recreation* sites. Certain segregation and restricting of access can be required and necessary, but it may be anyway that the tourist only desires limited sight of production itself and would be bored by seeing overmuch. A portion of a vineyard or orchard, for example, can have being visited as its prime role while other sectors are left to operate in their prime role in peace and without having any possible taint or damage from visitor-presence.

Showing Method and Process

The essential thing that a production site is offering, above an outlet, is the chance to see *how* an item is grown or made and how it is rendered ready for the consumers. Concerning agriculture and growing elements for food and drink, for the urban constituency (and which is increasing in the world), sight of these processes and sites of origin is unusual and non-routine. This audience rarely encounters the starting point in the food and drink cycle. As has been explained already, this renders to the urban audience, farms, dairies, vineyards, orchards, hopfields and other locations of producing food and drink as in a category of exotic features. Such elements are not the stuff or everyday, as are supermarkets, and so take the stage to be foci of time used in a discretionary way and for pleasure, and so to be destinations for the holiday. Factories for processing food are unfamiliar also to the consumer in terms of them not having sight inside them, and so they join the category. However, as overtly industrial in nature and often located in or near urban centres and where many people reside, they do not have, for the town dweller, such a high dimension of strangeness, and are not imbued with the overlay of romanticism probable to rural and small-scale sites of farming and production.

Specialness and Experience

It can be argued that, while the site of production of any type of food and drink is potentially a venue for tourism, probably those most inviting and interesting to the tourist are those related to food and drink that are seen as special, which the consumer does not buy routinely, 'on auto-pilot', and which they like to choose personally. These products are, therefore, exactly the reverse types to those which supermarkets expect most to sell by on-line ordering; these latter being necessary, but rather boring, to the consumer, and are bought by them on a regular basis. Nonetheless, the home supermarket does serve as a front-line stimulator to the impending food and drink tourist to visit production sites. This is in a positive way of displaying and 'trailing' certain goods themselves and so putting them before the consumer's eye and starting off inquiry about them in the consumer's mind. In a negative way it is through showing commodified and hackneyed goods and so setting off a desire in the mind of the 'alternative' shopper for goods not available, such as those particularly esoteric and distinctive and which can only be obtained by immediate way at their local production places or local produce centres or outlets. As has been said, certain of these special items can be bought directly from a supplier on the Internet or by mail order, but missing to the purchaser is the associated *experience* obtainable from visiting a provider.

What Attracts the Tourist?

The products most likely to lend themselves to be causes to the tourist to see their production sites or local outlets, and as a holiday experience, are these:

- those linked with a particular area
- those whose landscape of production is distinctive and appealing
- those showing especially the human and individual dimension in their style of growth or manufacture
- those displayed as especially natural or close to nature
- those that manifest recognizably more freshness and tastiness at their home base
- those lending themselves to visitor involvement in their gathering process, e.g. picking of fruit. Such products and their sites of production or centres of explanation lend themselves to representing *extra value* in various ways. They require the extra effort of finding or knowing about them and frequently the products only have limited availability. Also, merely through being seen and obtained by the visitor at a production site itself and in their native locale, these products become special.

Price and Characteristic

Holidays, as we know, represent an optional activity that can be entertained if basic needs are already satisfied. The food and drink obtainable on holiday bearing the characteristics just outlined show the match. The forms of products visited contrast in style with those types used routinely and in developed world situations of necessity. They are items to portray affluence, distinction and discernment to the consumer. Therefore, and importantly for the provider, as, to the tourist, non-everyday representatives and to be used for displaying difference, they can be set at premium price. As has been described already, these food and drink goods, when not perishable, can serve to the tourist as souvenirs and presents to make impression after returning home and to show status from those who have not made the journey. Perhaps the essential feature to food and drink visited in tourism and for displaying a separation from the mainstream is their emphasis on the time and amount of human intervention characterizing their production. They are likely to be more labour intensive than their commodified counterparts in the supermarket and fast-food restaurant. This may well account for their premium price, but for a provider to place a high price on a good may be also so that the consumer, in paying it, is able to communicate to others the status of being able to afford the high sum being asked.

Contrast and Discernment

There is of course an irony. This is in that those goods made in the developed world through intensive human labour and which are produced and crafted by hand are the most expensive of all and are bought and used for showing distinction. In the Third World, by contrast, comparable items are the matter of basic-ness and necessity and they are produced at a low cost through the low financial rate that is put on the human activity that is involved in producing them. Of course, the use and exploitation of these contrasts among costs of labour over the world is what has produced the mass-market commodified products typifying globalization and which has led to activism. This is both to remove exploitation of the Third World by global institutions and multi-national organizations (Klein, 2000) and to render appreciation of the distinctive, and presented by proponents as higher quality, products of the small individual farmer.

The capacity to purchase, find and use special, short-run, and not easily available food and drink items is a way to show discernment. What food and drink we buy and the manner of its consumption is always relatively easy way of making a lifestyle statement. A holiday, with its free-time available and constituency of providing a journey to another place than home and so delivering new opportunities and items for purchase, renders an especially good and pronounced opportunity for pursuing food and drink.

Local and Distinctive?

This book provides countless examples of types of food and drink and their provision being used in tourism. Much of this deployed bears the style of being 'local'. As Tregear describes 'the differentiation of products by territorial origin has become a highly popular means of addressing socio-economic development objectives in the agrifood sector and in rural areas' (2001, p. 1). Clearly, tourism serves among this general initiative. She discusses various types of endeavours in Europe, and who is leading and participating. She considers distinctions between the 'local' and what, in recognizing that 'there is a strong socio-cultural dimension to the associations between food and territory', she terms 'typicity' in food and which she defines as 'the territorially distinctive attributes of food products.' Concerning tourism and food the question is whether the tourist sees this distinction and if so whether it matters to them and if any preference is shown between one and the other. Examples abound of initiatives and promotional leaflets to visitors to an area whereby enrollees and participants are presented together or present themselves together. Some of these show the suspicion that, for the objective of forwarding the initiative, the emphasis has been placed on providers being local rather than necessarily that they have products distinctive only to a locale. Pragmatism seems to recognize that if, solely and always, only products confined in their nature to a region are presented, too few providers would 'get through the net'. By the criteria important to the usual tourist that have been set out earlier in this chapter, the indication would be that distinctiveness to a locale is only one among attractive dimensions to the tourist of food and drink obtained only in an area. Probably the *immediacy* to the product and its preparation, and so rendering different taste to a commodified and long-travelled version, and the freshness to correspond are the features to be most important to the tourist. Though enjoying uniqueness to an area where it is present, the tourist is probably realistic and informed enough to know that few products fall within the category and so they are quite content with the other dimensions. Of course, where a product distinct to an area exists, there is the extra marketing dimension for use and maximization by providers of the Unique Selling Proposition [USP]. This carries the nice imperative, therefore, on the tourist that they *must* venture to the specific area to find this particular food and drink and with all the connoisseurship they are able to manifest and make much of to others for impressing them.

Cultural Correlation

With the tourist's selection of the food and drink destination bound up with features of making a personal statement, and along with a holiday representing a time of doing what is most appealing, then clearly that which they visit is going to show their individual preference. Though other constraints and factors come into play, such as wishes of other party members, nonetheless a choice is likely to manifest a person's feeling of *cultural empathy* with it. The feeling of comfort this will imbue is part of the experience of relaxation wanted of a holiday and the factor of feeling-good. The cultural match may superficially be a linking of opposites – for example, an artisan-cheese production in a small rural dairy being visited by a company director or global financier – but this ignores deeper dimensions. These are, firstly, that a holiday provides an opportunity to explore personality features that are left ignored during everyday life, and, secondly, the aspect already explained of the cachet obtainable among peers in seeking out unusual and esoteric goods. Patronage of peasantry while on holiday, provided they are delivering food and drink that tastes and displays well at a dinner party later back at home, and if the story of the food and drink production will repeat well at the gathering too, *does* actually represent a cultural match.

To an extent, the more *outré* is the food and drink, or the more inaccessible it is in terms of location or quantity of amount, the more status the holidaymaker can earn from having got it, seen its production, and having found out about it. The organic farm in North Zealand, Denmark, run by 'a type of intellectual farmers' (Flyvbjerg, 2001, p. 86) seems a natural cultural correspondent and partner – and without strain – for the connoisseur tourist and whom in daily life spends well to obtain food of quality and manifest goodness and for presenting it among their peers. This farm, Fuglejerggård, is intended as 'a living show room giving the public first hand experience of organic farming'. A special objective 'is to heighten the sense of quality … for something as basic as bread'. Towards this, old types of cereal are grown such as kamut. At the farm in summer can be found a tea garden and there is a gardening school, and in winter a cooking school and other seminars. The missionary zeal of the two owners is apparent in the remark of one of them that 'We have a food culture that is breaking up' (p. 89). Yet, they communicate their message winningly. In their farm, 'ecology becomes edible and delicious – a trendy enterprise and a politically correct statement for affluent, politically conscious urban consumers' (p. 91).

For Earning and Diversification

The types of presentation and message manifest at production places and displayed at information centres depends, of course, on their aims and objectives, on whether their main purposes are to earn revenue, or to educate, and whether they are commercial or non-profit making enterprises. The mass of operations is in the private sector, and many are such small enterprises as to consist of one or two persons only. In which instance the characteristic provider is the farmer seeking some diversification through offering farm visits, and selling his/her one special product, or his/her excess crop supply. Frequently simple accommodation and meals may be offered too. The matter of appeal these last have to offer the tourist, as with all such on-site provisions, is of being a product of directness with the countryside and of authenticity that can be verified directly. The supply chain between supplier and consumer being direct, it offers each the chance to know and understand each other's concerns and perspectives.

Core, or More Too?

It is noticeable how many production centres offer a range of attractions. Production sites' necessity is to decide whether their core entity is appeal enough to draw visitors, and importantly for those aiming to attain income, whether it can generate this or whether another item is needed to partner it for earning purposes. Maybe the main item will be the lure to visitors, and the other is only needed for bringing in revenue. Otherwise, it may be the add-ons that provide equal or even most appeal and so the core product is only the entity for the provider to show differentiation from among attractions competing for the visitor's attention. The judgement for all types of providers is a difficult one, of whether they should stay with their main feature or whether they need to deliver a number of mini-attractions as part of their main entity in order to appeal. Part of the decision revolves around who they perceive their market to be. If a provider is catering for groups composed of different types, e.g. a family, then they could well need to offer different things to be inviting to the different group elements. If a clear market niche is identified as the customer, and it is shown as only interested in the core product without adjuncts, then unless income-earning requirements demand it, there is no requirement for diversification. If the need is to encourage repeat visits from a market – day visitors from a region, for example – then extra and passing attractions, and such as special events (see Chapter 10) may need to be put on the menu. The danger of diversifying is in dissipation of a message and watering down the core product's own strength. A criticism to be levelled at food and drink attractions is that too few show the courage of their convictions in concentrating on their essential entity, and ensuring the quality and specialness of immediate experience in relation to it. Rather, they appear to be 'hedging their bets' and offering an all-round experience and the extras in which are somewhat mediocre, inappropriate and serving to dilute by association the thrust of message of the food and drink item of excellence which they are there to support and enhance.

Quality and Training

Quality is an issue. With so many providers being small-scale, and/or their first concern is not catering to visitors, often they fail to show enough visitor understanding. They need to recognize the standard the visitor expects, and to accept that a holiday experience is a high-expectation experience and in which the visitor will not put up with lapses and lacks of perfection to their expected concept that in everyday life they might be willing to tolerate. So, the matters of developing awareness in producers and in training them for their task as tourism attraction operators are raised. The intruding dimensions upon the correct offer being made to the tourist are these: that suppliers are often small in scale of operation; that their prime duty may not be, or else may not be in their categorization, tourism; that their time is over-committed; that they are usually in rural areas without easy access to centres of training and advice. To a certain extent, tourism advisers do perhaps need to be so proactive as to go to providers to help them, and as is the culture and norm in the domain of agriculture.

Diversify or Direct Focus?

Of course, making a mixed and diverse provision may be engaged in deliberately and as the best option. A situation could be where income-earning and promotion of a certain food or drink brand is not the necessity, and rather of prime importance is serving an educational, cultural or social role and the best way of bringing in an audience is a variety of activity. Sowing seeds of consideration of information among an audience may require a diversified approach, and to reach one sector of an audience may require their travelling companions to be at least content and diverted alongside and meanwhile. This method is of course equally valid for the overtly product-promotional and income-generating sector. For a family or group choosing a holiday visit or an outing, the focus of the attraction may be almost irrelevant. The main concern may be the level and range of facilities or entertainment available and whether these are adequate to occupy and make happy a family's or group's various members over a reasonable amount of time. Nonetheless, some distinguishing feature needs to be offered as means for a market to select one attraction among competitors, and a particular food and drink is an obvious method for so doing. Here, a known brand, familiar on the supermarket shelves has the advantage, as the product has been quietly pronouncing its existence and selling itself, where the consumer is located, all the while. Therefore, all that is needed of the producer – albeit this may not be easy to achieve – is to act on the consumer's brand awareness for converting them to be curious to go to a product's home site to see how it is grown or made.

Interest or Experience?

Providers need to know whether strong interest in a product is their audience's disposition and strong inquiry their aim, or whether their main objective is a generalized enjoyable experience and in which the product is acting as lure enough for the market for their arrival at the producer's door rather than that of a competitor. Their other assessment needs to be whether income is needed from the attraction and if so if their essential product delivers this or whether other extra facilities need installing to produce the outcome. So, both knowing their market's preferences and their way of spending, and being very conscious of their own aims and objectives, are very salient for providers in deciding the type and character of the provision they will offer.

Dynamic Entity

A crop-growing site is 'live', as so also is a site of crop-processing. As has been mentioned already, the blessing to the provider in terms of tourism is that food and drink core entities grow to reach their time of harvest in an off-high-peak visiting season of early autumn. The compulsive and affluent food and drink tourist has two different peak seasons to travel to and enjoy, those of the northern and southern hemispheres. To each provider, however, this is unlikely to represent benefit, unless they are in the position of being a large player with sites north and south across the world. There are other farming cycles with their own peaks, of course, such as the processes of dairy or meat farming. The general point of emphasis is that when a provider's offer is linked to an item whose production is dynamic and to an essentially fixed pattern, the provider, in planning the operation of their tourism dimension and venue, needs to decide how to maintain visitor interest and gain revenue at off peak times of the product. Obvious ways to handle this are to make a shop as well as a site tour main focuses, to have a range of products with different natural cycles, to operate with items whose shelf-life is long, to provide a presentation about production in the form a film, information boards etc. A café can be the perennial. The usual essential aim should be to *keep in theme*. There can be reasons for non-adherence such as need to diversify to cater to different audiences, but the overall integrity, strength of identity, and thrust of communication and emphasis, of a venue can easily appear as, or become, lost or dissipated, through a provision showing too many disassociated parts. The optimum objective should be to 'keep on message' and show obvious connection between all parts.

Prolonging and Enhancing the Visit

In the UK, the herb garden is the item that seems to be delivered most routinely as part of trying to keep visitors entertained and to extend their visit. These are not always of very good upkeep, range and explanation and frequently bear no relation to the main product item. Their ubiquity help reduce the specificity of an attraction, and infrequently so they have any relation to its core item other than perhaps general and un-focused associations in the visitor's mind with 'countryness', 'traditionalness' and 'wholesomeness'. Most on-site cafés and restaurants, while usually delivering something to consume of their immediate product, nonetheless betray the syndrome of not keeping enough integrity and to theme adequately. So, often these lose the line and impetus in some dimensions, whether it is in providing mass-market drinks, poor quality and inappropriate to overall theme crockery, or offering plastic chairs and table cloths. Often their lapse is simply, but centrally, one of absence of both general high standard and recognition of what experience the visitor is seeking. The general prerequisite of tourism, that it should represent an experience of escape and 'otherness' advises the circumstance. Precisely that, for example, homemade food, craft pottery, rough-hewn wood furniture, and consumption of comestibles in a barn, are not the usual daily experience is the reason it is fun, enticing and a contrast for a person when on holiday.

Because its essential product being offered is viewing 'a self-sufficient lifestyle' of the family – the Kemps – who own it, Gifford's Hall, in Suffolk in the UK, is able to promote elements which otherwise would not all be very closely connected. They are displaying 'otherness'. Their essential offer is 'to join us for an afternoon in the country savouring the delights of our way of life'. The features include vineyards, wild flower meadows, St Kilda sheep, Black Berkshire pigs, chickens, sweet peas, rides on the Grape Express, a children's play area, a rose garden, a vegetable garden, countryside walks, a winery, a farm shop selling eggs, honey and vegetables, tearooms, and a picnic area. Nonetheless, the Gifford's Hall leaflet from which this information is gained shows a difficulty. This is in that Gifford Hall's is vaunted centrally as a Vineyard and Sweet Pea Centre; and these two elements are not natural partners. If the main promotion had been, alternatively, of 'a self-sufficient smallholding' at least coherence would have been shown, albeit probably not adequate focus, differentiation, or cause for visitor excitement and interest, being manifested.

Keeping it Together

An off-production or processing site venue serves as a display or information centre about a specific product will not have access to the real thing growing or being processed but will still be concerned with a brand. An information centre can also be about a general process such as cheese-making or brewing beer. An away-from-production or processing centre has the greater option of pulling in different elements because the promotion can be of the centre itself rather than its content or subject. An example of this last is Snape Maltings, also in Suffolk, whose publicly-accessible portion, though it was part of a processing centre, is now promoted by its name and with the line 'a unique experience in the Suffolk countryside'. The world-renowned Concert Hall apart (from its Benjamin Britten and Aldeburgh Festival connections), the Maltings' essential lure is as a picturesquely-located, visually-appealing and unusual, complex providing a 'shopping experience' of 'traditional' types of items such as crafts, countrywear, paintings, and the Granary Tea Shop. A pub offers country cuisine and available are self-catering cottage accommodation, craft and painting courses, and river trips. At Snape, no particular emphasis is on food and drink, despite the heritage of the place, and quality among the contributing and different ownership elements is variable, with the general standard of appropriateness to environment and potential market being really rather low. The Maltings complex manifests the difficulties of a centre containing different participants – essentially all from the private and commercial sector and so at heart in competition – and of different type and objective, and shows involvees' need to accept helpfulness to their individual aims of showing overall coherence of theme and common high standard.

The gardens open to the public in the UK of the Henry Doubleday Research Association [HDRA], 'the organic organisation', show an agenda for education, campaigning and conversion as would be expected. It is a membership body whose Patron is The Prince of Wales. It portrays partnerships of types with organizations naturally companionable such as Brogdale – Britain's Heritage of Fruit (see Chapter 12), the Royal Horticultural Society, the Royal Society for the Protection of Birds. Clearly HDRA recognizes that visitors to its Gardens want enjoyment, but while this experience of enjoyment is provided, the educational aim is manifest. Its Yalding Organic Gardens in Kent offers a 'A Great Day Out in the Garden of England' (Yalding Organic Gardens leaflet) which is represented by a historical tour to the present delivered by individual gardens and leading to organic fruit and vegetable gardens, a garden which can survive on low water, a recycling area, and contemporary, wildlife garden, and childrens' gardens. There is a shop, and an organic café. HDRA's Ryton Organic Gardens in Warwickshire are presented as '*the* place to find out about organic gardening, farming and food' and courses include 'vegetarian cookery, making real bread, planning a vegetable garden' (Ryton Organic Gardens leaflet). It has a restaurant, and a shop with 'the widest selections of organic food and wine in the Midlands' and which offers enrolment to a 'veggie box scheme'. The last two are accessible without visiting the Gardens. The HDRA Gardens are held together by integrity, and each shows a coherence of theme and presentation.

Demanding Occupation

Food and drink production sites and venues and display and information centres that engage in tourism vary in type and manifest different priorities and levels of offer. The situation of production sites wishing to entertain and accommodate visitors is a distinct one. These face the very challenging demand of this kind of diversification, that of trying to marry being a site of work and leisure simultaneously. Frequently too, these types represent the most small and geographically remote operations, with the difficult demands to these of finding enough time to dedicate to the new function and to gaining access to adequate tourism knowledge and expertise for running visitor appealing concerns and which are lucrative. The need for help in this dimension has been highlighted in this chapter. An essential matter for decision by the provider, of whatever among the kinds of site under discussion in this chapter, is where they want, or need, to 'sit' on the continuum between commercial enterprise and educational resource.

Another key, and associated, consideration is who their type of market is and what are its kind of expectation and requirement. A criticism is that not always is enough high standard shown by providers to suit today's markets of any kind, and for winning visits by them from among their competitors in the leisure field overall, and in the tourism arena in particular. There seems a generalized recognition among providers of need to offer an experience but a failure to note that the forcefulness and appealingness of such is not likely to be of the optimum without a manifestation of coherence and focused message. A medley of items strung together can deliver a dissipated, unenergized, and so uncompelling, item of no distinctive visitor appeal. Income generation – where needed – may need to be through an add-on feature, such as shop or café, and these can be set up to serve as attractions which can be visited independently from the main feature, but all elements must show same semblance and aura. This is to keep a concept, which maintains throughout, of delivering something special and different and of stimulation and which offers the period of 'time out' from everydayness needed of the tourism attraction.

Dimensions of Being Away a Little

The off-production site venue provides the benefits of being able to be drawn up from scratch and to be entirely focused on the objective of catering to visitors, this is both in facilities and in location. Its site can be entirely to attract and encounter the visitor to the maximum. Frequently the centre of information and presentation can serve as a themed point of introduction to an area and it may act as a promoter of individual providers as part of a group. The advantages of this sort of cooperation are savings in individual promotional resources, critical mass being provided, and mention being obtained in a place to which the visitor is drawn. The loss is in amount of capacity of individual statement. Sometimes, too, the disadvantage to participating individuals may be that the information provider's agenda or criteria may need to be present. So, brought together would be elements that do not have 'natural' linkage of type or area activity, e.g. the portion of country from where a certain cheese is obtained, or else any equality among their level of standard, e.g. good and poor quality attractions being presented together and as similar. As presenter examples of this are: agencies' presentations made by political or legislative boundary basis e.g. a county: a professional area basis, e.g. a tourist board region.

Finding Suitability and Resolution

Two concluding comments for this chapter are these. For the visitor, the essential appeal of visiting a site of food and drink production seems to be in its delivery of a local, rather than necessarily, locally-distinct, item. Among the types of facility being here discussed, perhaps the paramount difficulty rests with those providers who have the dual roles of trying to reach an acceptable resolution and, at one site, in meeting necessary requirements of the two domains of food and drink production and visitor attraction operation.

Chapter 7

Outlets and Markets

Away from Site of Growth, Production or Processing

This chapter is looking at the places and installations for purveying food and drink produce that are away from the site where the raw item is grown, produced or processed. They exist to enable connection between goods and consumers, and when that link can occur best apart from the site of production and especially can be a means most easy and accessible to the consumer.

A Disadvantage

The off-site outlet, unless it is established by a sole and core producer him/herself, differs in an essential way to the home produce facility. This is that it is selling and promoting items that are disconnected from their own story of production, and from their particular environment and culture. It can be recognized that this is a loss to be compensated for.

The Advantages

Of advantages to sites of show and retail that are not located where production occurs are that providers can choose them in regard to having best characteristics of consumer access and optimum ability of displaying wares. Another advantage is that a congregation of separate food and drink items can be created, and so to deliver critical mass for bringing enhanced lure to consumers. Further advantages are that goods can be placed in theme for heightening and focusing their appeal, and that if necessary other appropriate supporting attractions can be brought in. Finally, the need is avoided to meet successfully the demands of visitor access, enjoyment and health and safety, while continuing maintenance of safety, quality and integrity of the food and drink product.

The tourist, of course, has time, propensity, and likely heightened attitude, of being prepared and wanting to see a food and drink item on site and in its context. Nonetheless, even for this consumer category as whole, or else certain sections of it, it can be that off-site centres are more worthwhile propositions to them either entirely or sometimes. This is because of convenience of location, by ability of seeing more in less time than by visits to sites on an individual basis, and through promise of more 'colour' and greater and larger experience from entities which are pulling together products in group and with special focus. Also to be considered is that at the off-site place with a collection of goods, there is the capacity to the consumer of certain anonymity and being lost in crowd. They may thus be feeling less pressure to buy than at the on-site, one-product, place where a consumer or the unit of consumers may feel somewhat trapped and vulnerable to needing to buy something. A consequence of the relaxed, less intense mood of the extensive, multi-product, type of venue can be more actual sales to consumers as their reaction from not feeling particularly strongly impelled to make a purchase. The market is the obvious example of presenting an impression of no imperative to buy and being available for merely wandering, looking, and soaking up its particular style of experience. The market, in usually allowing goods to be touched and handled, too offers some substitute for absence of those experiences sometimes available to the visitor to a crop-growing site. At this latter type, on occasions, the visitor can pick items and move among them while they are still in growing circumstance and so obtain tactile pleasure and sensory joy of their particular aromas.

Aura and Cultural Empathy

The generated aura to making produce available is important. The provider needs to see that this is conducive to sale of the product, in tune with the style and type of product, and perpetrating an image the visitor wants, expects and is suitably stimulated by. The difficulty of the product being displayed and sold by an intermediary and away from the producer's sight is to ensure that the environment of presentation and sale are appropriate for their product and complementary for it. Choice of presenter and retailer is crucial. It should be remembered that an outlet's way of display will be subject to needs and priorities of the retailer and in relation to which among suppliers is providing products most desirable and selling to the consumer. In giving up power of place and style of presentation, for greater visibility and access of their product to the consumer, or for other reasons, the supplier is making a judgement of trade off. As an example, Thursday Cottage Ltd recognizes the need to be offering its produce through a retailer that is culturally sympathetic to it and appropriate to its products. The firm makes jams and marmalade in Devon. Its Managing Director says the following in the *Success with a small food business* brochure (MAFF, 1998, p. 3),

'To us the relationship with our retail customers is all important. That is why we endeavour to sell to shops which we feel are suitable and with which we are comfortable. The taste and quality of the products then guarantees repeat business'.

Shades and Varieties of Option

There are shades between being on the one side an on-site provider and visitor receiver and on the other side an agent and outsider having been allocated a role of consumer greeting, presentation and supply. Between directness and indirectness of connection between producer and consumer are varieties of degree. Giving as an example the farm shop in its type of being an on-the-farm entity and selling only the produce of the home supplier; often its position to receive visitors and effect sale of product is on the edge of, rather than in the midst of, farming, or other producing activity. This is so for reasons of safety and practicality and for keeping visitors from interrupting or spoiling the working activity. The overall matter for looking at by the provider is how much loss of visitor link with production needs to be accepted for various reasons such as health, safety and practicality, and how much any loss of immediacy affects sales and visitor interest. It may well be that, even for the small producer, an overall and interlinked programme of publicity, offer and sale needs to be established, and in which notice and invitation are set in one place, information about the general food or drink type laid out in another, certain sales are made through an intermediary, and with visits to producers at their home location serving its distinctive and special part. Public sector agencies are noticeable in the role of delivering a context of consumer awareness about products and in delivering umbrella marketing of assistance to small suppliers, and the activity probably with either focus by region or particular category of kind. In presenting a type of food and drink, or else produce from a region, as opposed to a food or drink brand, the way is particularly available to those resources dedicated to objectives of information, education and entertainment rather than those of straightforward selling. A presentation on wine could be in the category. Vinopolis in London (Boniface, 2001), for example, is a visitor attraction whose focus is wine but is nonetheless a commercial operation and it has individual selling portions and businesses such as Majestic Wine among its complex and with restaurants included in the venue.

The farm shop has several shades and variations. It can be on- or off-production site and the location of the produce of one provider or several. The on-production site farm shop which sells solely home produce is in direct communication with the customer, but any providers from outside who join in are not and so they are in a disadvantaged, indirect communication, position. The off-site outlet or information place of a single producer, say a shop located in a village or town street, and which the producer runs him/herself, has direct connection with the customer. It has been chosen as off-site for being placed where the customer is to be found and as a place of good access and more visibility than the production site. To obtain staff for the facility may be easier at such a site. The off-site venue of promotion and information of a range of products, and whether or not sales occur there also, is chosen by similar criteria. When the location is the premises of one among the group, that person has the advantage compared to the other participants of being in direct communication with their public, whereas for all other producers not on their own territory, the communication is indirect. When no producer is at the off-site sales or promotion venue the location is neutral and fair among them all, and it represents for them all indirect contact with the client. Also the matter being promoted at a location where no producer is present may be a type of food and drink, or the food and drink or a particular region, rather than providers – as such. This entity's role is to be as intermediary between producer and consumer and so its style is to be indirect. As an example with strong tourism dimensions is the Gourmet Pavilion sited high in the gardens alongside the Papal Palace in Avignon, France, the historic area of which is a World Heritage Site. Designed by the Italian architect-designer Gaetano Pesce, the Gourmet Pavilion, made up of four small pavilions, was scheduled to open in July 2000 while Avignon was one among several millennial Cultural Capitals of Europe but its construction was behind time. It is to be a permanent display and tasting opportunity for visitors of 'Provençal culinary specialities' (Connaissance des Arts, 2000, p. 56).

Fairs

Fairs are among special occasions to act to link consumer and producer and their food and drink produce, and these have a heightened aura from being temporary and non-routine. Since these are particular occasions they will be discussed further in Chapter 10 whose subject is events. Another main method of sale and information is the Internet. This may be used by the provider as their direct way of communication and making sales. Also, the Internet can operate in many of the other options of ways that non-electronic and tangible methods present and so it can serve to act as an entry-portal to a variety of products or as a virtual market of them. British farm shops have a dedicated Internet site, www.farmshop.net and which welcomes the visitor with the invitation to 'Wander around the vast UK Rural Market Place in the comfort of your own home'. In terms of tourism, the benefit of the Internet is as displaying and informing about options and opening up and interest and knowledge. While sales can be on-line, curiosity can be engendered and appetite be whetted for then making a visit to a 'real' site of purchase or to a site of growing or production.

Mail Order

Of course, mail order sales directly to the customer are a method of establishing contact with the customer without an intermediary. Overtly, they would not have any connection to tourism and food and drink, but, as with other examples and types this book describes, so often links are constructed of more than one method being used toward an objective. Mail order too is a way to generate interest to see production, buy at a shop or market stall etc. Facets used in combination offer the possibility to link everyday practice to that when tourism is being engaged in. By provision of connected elements, different demands such as that of wanting a quick transaction of no more than rudimentary 'experience' and that of wishing to make and savour a visit to a site of production or sale and with time no object can be overall catered to. In one mode a person will prefer one type of transaction and in another a different one. As has been said, according to type(s) of market being courted, a package of options, acting to complement and support each other, may need to be provided by the producer with or without intermediaries. Some consumers rather than only opting for one choice might deploy several over time, being stirred by one type to use another on another occasion and in another circumstance, for example when in everyday mode and then when in leisure mode.

Being Several-Faceted

Two examples of producers bearing more than one facet are Colman's Mustard and Bunalun 160 Organic Farm foods. Colman's is a very long established mustard producer in Norwich in East Anglia. It sells its items – in recent times extended beyond mustard – very widely through retail outlets such as supermarkets, grocers, corner stores etc. Its fame, profile and brand recognition, are, however, essentially still based on mustard. Some while ago recognizing this, Colman's opened a

Norwich city centre outlet, Colman's Mustard Shop. From the outset it was shaped as a visitor attraction and experience, to be an interesting public face of Colman's and its mustard to the viewer. It is essentially a gift shop and museum designed to show Colman's directly to the public and to be a PR vehicle. Colman's bulk of produce is not seen and remains sold through retail outlets as usual. A further feature of the Colman's sales initiative now is a mail order dimension offered through a Mustard by Mail catalogue and thus is also a direct consumer connection operation. So, Colman's is operating on three fronts.

Bunalun is a quite new firm having been launched in 1999. Its complete name of Bunalun 160 relates to the number of its organic certificate from the Organic Trust in Ireland. Its base is a farm in County Cork. Bunalun also has a 'strong mutual arrangement with an organic farm near Perpignan in France' (Geddes-Brown, 2000, p. 57) from whence some of the firm's produce derives. The couple owning Bunalun, the Chettles, both have an advertising background. In image the firm is upmarket and stylish. The Bunalun operation is through mail order, by the Internet, and from the department store Selfridges at its London and Manchester locations. Until 2002 Bunalun also had a shop in the small town of Skibbereen near to the Bunalun farm. Maybe the Skibbereen shop was a luxury and misplaced at an 'off map' location. However, any such appearances as these could have been both misleading and failing to recognize certain demensions. County Cork is a tourism venue, and moreover it is a favoured place to visit of Americans (these, in clichéd perception, always bearing the prefix 'rich'). The Bunalun Organic Farm shop provided the Chettles with a direct connection with consumers and allowed them to obtain feedback on their goods. Relationships were set up to be then followed through by mail order business and so new regular consumers obtained. In having had an interesting flagship venue of interest in a tourism location, the Chettles created a PR entity and public front offering a different consumer experience to go alongside mail order or sales through a department store.

Emphasizing that even a very small operation can develop more than one facet is the small crab shop, Cookies, in the north Norfolk part of England. The area is alongside the sea and is much part of the tourism trail. Its general timbre is of wholesomeness of style and the focus of its visitor activity is upon sailing, birdwatching, walking and admiring and purchasing craft items. Cookies Crab Shop, located in a small coastal village, proudly proclaims that has been open ever since 1956. It sells shellfish and samphire and through its simple yard garden has managed to create the other dimension of a café consisting of a few tables enabling customers to eat on the premises.

The Special Shop

A shop not connected to just one brand or product is, of course, the most usual type of food or drink shop encountered. To serve as not only a point of visit for those in 'everyday life position' but to be site of appeal to tourists it needs to have products and/or environment of speciality. Shops ranging from the wholefood or vegetarian produce outlet to those which retail items of a particular country or region produce, and which have an ambience in keeping, can deliver enough appeal of focus to bring a tourist's special visit and may well be offering more stimulation than the single product outlet finds possible. Probably, especially if they are newly-established, shops' danger in selling too much of the non-ordinary, obscure or old-fashioned – and whether the focus is single or multi-product – is that they can lapse into appearance of being a fake in the modern world – a museum exhibit, theme park presentation or piece of film set – rather than a real outside-world entity.

The Market

The market lends itself strongly to be attractive to tourists. It has attraction to the producer too. It has a particular culture of operation. It suits the tourist as much if not more than the everyday consumer. It suits a certain type of provider. One characteristic is of fleetingness, in that most types of market are not always at a site but rather are only present at certain times. Also their food and drink produce has a style of being temporary due to the seasonality of goods and by these being in small volume of number and so not always available. There is a sense generated in the impending purchaser that goods should bought *now* because to wait to another day would leave uncertainly about their re-appearance. There is a feel of 'impromptu' and 'unconstraint' to a market, albeit that for all but the most sudden or tiny market, structure and regulation will be there and underlying. The manner in which markets are used by both trader and consumer displays informality and less inhibition compared to a shop or supermarket. The style emitted is to encourage friendly chat and banter among all participants. Markets are ancient and traditional in concept, and on occasions and alongside buying the modern way in shop and supermarket, using a market can feel a pleasant and fundamental thing to do. They seem warm and vibrant. These overall features deliver an appeal to the tourist that they are 'connecting with the real heart, depth and authenticity' of a place. The characteristics particularly fit the profile of what is appealing to be done in leisure time. In that phase the tourist and visitor have more time available for adopting the slow, wandering and open style of shopping and encounter that is somewhat alien now among an everyday life in which the maximum efficiency, minimal hassle, purchasing style predominates. Meanwhile, for the provider whose produce and style suits them to sell through a market, and provided they attend the stall themselves rather than an intermediary operating the stall, they are put in an excellent and particular position of direct dialogue with the consumer.

The market serves the role of being an entity for gathering a variety of produce and often non-food or drink items too. Its purpose is making sales and generally its main flavour is commercial, and albeit that frequently its site, installation and administration is by a local government authority and so by the public sector. A larger market may represent 'the country come to town/city' and be a method for producers from a range of different locations to foregather as an entity, and to a particular ethos, and to make contact with a large amount of consumers, both locals and tourists. Close to Vinopolis, for example, is the twice-weekly Borough Food Market which gathers producers from throughout Britain (Boniface, 2001). In the farmers' market instance, these may have been helped financially, and in setting up, and in their promotional efforts by public sector agencies towards objectives of assisting farmers to have a livelihood, to help keep them working and conserving the land, to make better quality food available and for reducing long transportation of foodstuffs, and for other general society reasons. Their emphasis, as has been said, is on 'the local'. In tourism terms, as with all local markets, the tourist is travelling to the market, or choosing to visit it when already in an area, for its specialness of some kind and its distinctiveness to locale. As has been portrayed already, the market overall is a special type. The consumer can perceive it in the role of being old, traditional in concept, and historical, as in the position of delivering an alternative, more profound, and more distinctive and individual type of commodity than the supermarket. Also, it renders a general environment of particular and lively sociability, and frequently it is the stage of direct provider-consumer connection and communication. Often additionally a market's environment is the open-air and that delivers it a special dimension too for all participants. Annie Hubert describes the capacities of the market this way,

'To feel the pulse of a village, district, or city, there is no better place than the market. It's a place of exchange for material goods and intangible realities, a space and time in which human dynamics can take shape and become manifest. Markets also often draw out the visual, olfactory, and auditory aesthetics of a given population. Moreover, they offer the inquisitive visitor a marvelous [sic] opportunity for "getting inside" a different world' (Hubert, 2001, p. 98).

Of course, as has been indicated already, markets vary in type and size. As a huge scale market is the open-air Naschmarkt in Vienna, specifically dedicated to food, that is open six days a week and which carries items 'from all corners of Europe and beyond' (Leuker, 2001, p. 14). Markets may be held for particular occasions. They may be only at a particular time or period, as for example are Christmas Markets. As a distinct group, and with variation even among them, are farmers' markets. In the UK, there are those under the stipulation and aegis of the NAFM, which organization, as was said in Chapter 3, requires the local ingredient to its markets. This is that food has to be locally produced, food has to be the own produce of the seller, 'a principal producer' of the food must be attending to the market stall. The overall market must have an available policy that embodies and announces how stallholders are supporting more sustainable production (Green, 2001, pp. 114–115). Farmers' markets clearly have characteristics to be tourism products since 'shopping at farmers' markets is actually fun', and the consumer is 'actively encouraged to sample, to taste and to chat' (p. 166). They are *destinations*. Among general society benefits are that 'food miles' are reduced and a local economy is intended to be boosted and local jobs provided. The organization Friends of the Earth reports that its 'analysis of farmers' markets around the world [Bullock, 2000] … has found that farmers' markets can strengthen local economies and provide employment' (2001, p. 17).

Buying for Holiday Cooking and Consumption

A feature not mentioned so far, which all sites retailing food and drink and available to the consumer when on holiday have ability to be, is that these can be meeting tourist's needs for items to purchase while self-catering on holiday. To lessen the load on whomsoever is doing the cooking, probably some meals will be consumed at a restaurant, pub or café. Staying in to eat while on holiday is to be in danger of losing the essential differentness demanded of a holiday compared to daily life routine. So, shopping in a different way, or for a different style of ingredient – as many of the examples described here represent in one feature or another – delivers these described options with the demeanour to equip them to feature in tourism. The picnic is in the middle and happy position of offering a relatively non-routine experience anyway to the tourist – and this without the additional stimulation from being placed amid a fresh location to home – and which can be composed of food and drink obtained by the tourist from the holiday region.

A Different Experience Off-Site

This chapter has seen that there are altered type and experience present and to be obtained from sites of food and drink provision and information that are separated from the food and drink item's place of growth, production or processing. The essential disadvantage to be overcome and alternative benefit to be found for, is of loss of contact and interest for the consumer from not seeing production and environment of production. An off-production site however can remove difficulties for the producer of marrying production with visitation and can release greater opportunity to provide a facility or range of facilities entirely catering to the consumer, and to be entertaining and accessible. It has been shown in this chapter that options are not necessarily mutually exclusive and that some can be chosen to act together, and be supportive of each other towards objectives. Options overtly of the everyday can be deployed to capture interest, and to stimulate use of other options including those more overtly in the tourism realm. Also has been shown how much apparent everyday experiences can feature happily too in an alongside role as tourism entities. It has been noted too that tourism is not always 'pure' tourism in the sense of having completely separate and identifiable features not experienced at home. It has been displayed that self-catering holidays have a dimension of everyday to them and that, towards staying seen as tourism in the holidaymaker, buying and using food and drink of some different dimension to everyday, helps keep alive the sensation of having an 'other' and holiday experience. Particular events of outlets and markets have only been referred to in passing as they have received more attention in Chapter 10.

Visitors hooked on apples, at The National Trust's Hughenden Manor, UK

Bedroom breakfast at Michel Bras's hotel in the Aubrac, France

Pick Your Own fruit in Norfolk, UK

Currying the consumer's favour, London, UK

Cider and beer at The Ludlow Marches Food and Drink Festival, UK

A. Gold, a new traditional British food shopping experience, London, UK

Seeking travellers' attention: the Laguiole cheese factory, France

To meet the visitor, Wilkin's jam factory, Tiptree, UK

Visiting a pub near the waterfront, Maldon, UK

Viewing Côtes du Rhône, Avignon, France

Restaurant with a message, Stockholm, Sweden

Fresh fish 'shack' to visit, Aldeburgh, UK

Leading visitors to UK vineyards

Roadside force of feeling in the 'cattle country' of the Aubrac, France

Chapter 8

Accommodation

Types of Emphasis, and Ways of Invitation

This chapter considers places of accommodation whose food and drink are their point of focus. For these venues of residence, the motivation to travellers in making their choice is either in the kind and calibre of quality of the food and drink being made available along with facilities for sleeping or else that to a food and drink attraction has been added the convenience of accommodation.

Of course, the questions to be asked are: 'why should this focus exist, and in the two somewhat different types?'; 'why is the emphasis appealing to the tourist, and of which kind?'; and 'what is the appeal to providers to place this particular weight?'

It can be appreciated at once that if a tourist's object is a gourmandizing and imbibing experience of full intensity, then appealing to them is the provision of accommodation beside it because they can relax completely into the sensation and not need to travel to another place to sleep. Also they can have more enjoyment by consuming into another day. Of course, the very existence of accommodation may well encourage a consumer from being a day visitor for a meal or drink to becoming a holidaymaker and who stays a night or more. In accommodation being used, the stay on premises or in complex is extended, and with the new experience being added also, so altogether the provider is presented with opportunity for gaining more revenue from the consumer. The provider, knowing the predilection towards food and/or drink of a market, may decide to make these their main earning items and so provide accommodation of simplicity and of not too great cost to act merely as an encouragement to the consumer to visit and then to remain a longer time. Often it will be that, recognizing they have a particular market that is one of indulgence, and probably affluence too, the provider will know their sector as seeking an experience overall of commensurate quality to the food and drink portion of it. Therefore, in the instance the group will be content and happy to pay well for excellence of all dimensions. Nonetheless, to be remembered by the provider is that what is distinguishing them and bringing visitors to their door from the many others delivering accommodation is their *particular food or drink*. So, above all, the provider's food and drink must not disappoint and must maintain the standard and character that are acting to appeal to the relevant market.

For Gaining Familiarity with a Way of Life

As different to the gourmet who wants to submit to luxury and pampering when being accommodated, is the enthusiast for traditional and farm foods who wants to stay on the farm to learn and see more of way and ambience of production and to find out about the *culture of farming*. These latter, too, however, need to find what they envisage. The theme and style of their accommodation, whether in a farmhouse, farm cottage or converted farm building, or else on a campsite amid farmland, should fit expectation, should convey suitable aura, and should demonstrate quality even if not luxury. Of other groups among food and drink connoisseurs and enthusiasts are those who self-cater but in luxurious circumstances – a villa in Tuscany for example – and who are aiming to be installed for a while among the life-way of an Italian land- or vineyard-owner. The attraction of being accommodated in a food and drink milieu is to be able to taste and/or cook its distinct produce. As much part of the lure of staying amongst a foodie or imbibing ambience also is for the opportunity presented for 'playing' at being the person whose residence or working environment is being occupied, whether, as examples, they are fisherman, celebrity chef, orchard owner, shepherd, vigneron, or farmer.

The Range Available

Essentially, accommodation that can have a marked food or drink orientation is in these categories, and which can overlap and may inter-mix:

- a hotel where the restaurant is the prominent feature
- a farm stay of certain type or else a stay at some other food or drink producer's premises and either catered or self-catered
- a seaside stay and among a locale where fishing is the focus, and the holiday either being in a hotel, a boarding house or a bed and breakfast [B&B] establishment, or else self-catered
- camping among or alongside a landscape dedicated to the production of a kind of food or drink, whether through growing a plant crop or harvesting a fish crop, keeping a type of animal, engaging in a particular type of food or drink production and manufacture.

Of course, to any of the types of accommodation may be added other features to offer more facilities.

The Provider – Tourist Relationship and Satisfaction of Need

A stay on the farm may be offered by a farmer for more than the direct money-making motive. For the farmer, and their sectoral and development agency stakeholders, the agenda may be to show to the outsider, and most usually also an urban-dweller, the ways and priorities of the farmer and to generate appreciation of their perspective. Nowadays it is far from routine for a person to be raised amid the agricultural process. So, it is useful for all society that the tourist, as a member of the public in general, is learning more about the process of food and drink production through spending time among it, and with an amount and depth of experience being available by a stay in the context. The similar opportunity to explore the culture and process of producing a food or drink item is available from residing for a holiday anywhere where the activity is happening, and with perhaps as the other key comparable experience to staying in a farming arena being to have a holiday in the surroundings of a fishing community. Between these two, the essential differences for observing are between: a culture originating in deciding and *growing* a crop; a culture resting on *gathering* an item carefully harvested and rationed but not positively produced – though with the fish farm as the manifest exception.

A difficulty for the offer of the stay at the small establishment – as with other offers from that direction – is making it known and available to the potential customer. An SME directly in the tourist business, such as a Bed and Breakfast [B&B] operation, can put itself as part of alliances and co-operations, and most likely it will be a member of the regional local tourist board and so will have access to help and advice on marketing and it will be able have some promotion through the board's umbrella initiatives. Direct selling and marketing through a Web site is an option. Appearance in directories and guides for the relevant type of accommodation, campsites or country cottages as examples, is another method of marketing, as is featuring as part of the portfolio of a specialist operator. The challenge is more demanding for the provider whose first role is food or drink production, and who is using tourism and offering accommodation to the tourist as the means to diversify and bring in more income. In this instance neither time is easily to hand, nor expertise pre-existing, for the second activity and for the necessary new marketing and connecting required. The central figure this situation relates to is the farmer. Cartwheel, which will be mentioned again in Chapter 10, is a farmer-led company for the West Country of England, and which is an example of an initiative offering and promoting farm holidays. Its offer is 'a farm experience' and bringing the occasion to,

'Spend time together as family. Explore the unspoilt countryside, collect your own freshly laid eggs for breakfast, feed a newborn lamb – a million miles from the hectic pace of modern life. Rediscover what really matters. Return home invigorated'
(Cartwheel brochure, 2001, p. 5).

It is clear that this offer seeks to instil a feeling that farming is an elemental feature missed by dwelling in town which is an activity lacking what is really important and which has powers of restoration and stimulation.

Adults among impending holidaymakers are reminded that they will have the opportunity of 'warm hospitality and delicious home cooking', and to

'Tuck into hearty, wholesome, local dishes, cooked to perfection, before climbing into a four-poster bed and dreaming the night away beneath a starlit sky' (p. 6).

They are advised,

'Give your car a break too and explore on foot from the farm – coastal paths, woodland trails, quiet lanes to the village pub, paths off the beaten track; full of natural beauty. Or, simply potter around the farm'.

Among the activities described, they can:

> 'Pick mushrooms, blackberries, wild strawberries – or enjoy a picnic' (p. 8).

Farm restaurants and farm shops are also part of the Cartwheel promotion and farm attractions, such as Dairyland Farm World in Cornwall and The Big Sheep in Devon, are also included in it. B&B, self-catering, camping and caravanning are the types of accommodation included. The National Trust is a participant member of Cartwheel.

The Cartwheel enterprise, and with the brochure slogan 'Come to life on a Cartwheel farm', makes a clear offer with food and drink at its core, and which bears the message that farming is important, and that implies that farming is a culture and way of life of depth, fundamentalism and value, and which suggests that urban life has basic deficiency. More matter-of-fact and less polemical in stance is the Norfolk and Suffolk Farm Holiday Group in its 'Stay on a Farm' brochure that has the participation of the East of England Tourist Board. This simply is a directory with illustrations of participating B&B and self-catering opportunities on farms and these are overall promoted as bases for discovering the countryside. Not surprisingly, given the location, cycling and walking is an explicitly-suggested method of so doing. In message attuned to that of Cartwheel – though in manner more serious and in style more simple and 'laid back' – is the leaflet (in Polish and English) of the European Centre for Ecological Agriculture and Tourism [ECEAT] and which promotes overall 'Holiday on an Organic Farm in Poland'. It is trailing a full brochure of information available in Polish, Dutch, German, along with English. So, it must be assumed that domestic visitors along with tourists from the other three nations represent the target markets.

Ninety eco-farms are available, and the leaflet advises the tourist,

> 'Your visit will help us put our ideas about a sustainable future into practice. Real countryside, real food, real rest and people at their home'.

Poland's countryside is conveyed in the leaflet as at a relatively pre-industrial stage, and as being a cultural milieu and environment style different – and more happily and beneficially orientated – compared to that of England. It is explained and commented,

> 'ECEAT-Poland offers cosy camping and/or lodging on small organic farms…. In the most beautiful natural areas, especially in mountainous regions, visitors can meet with local people and learn both about the local culture and environmentally-friendly farms. These farms are well-suited for people who appreciate a quiet atmosphere, unspoiled nature, unchanged traditions and healthy food. And the farmers especially appreciate the cultural and informational exchange, as well as the increase in their income from eco-tourism, which they happily reinvest into organic agriculture'.

The Self-Catering Accommodation Position

Self-catered holiday accommodation – either a building, caravan or tent or similar – occupies a position of certain ambivalence of being set for tourism use but nonetheless needing certain everyday actions to operate. It sets out to deliver a tourism-type experience of difference to home while in basis it is a home. Because it represents a certain merging or linking between the holiday and the everyday, so a diminution of the 'otherness' of the holiday experience is being risked and needs attempting to be mitigated. For the self-catered accommodation unit to be taken into the realm of tourism, some clear feature to it, or its way of use, needs to be not as of home. The first method is in the type of accommodation. This needs to be different from that of home; and a tent, a caravan, or a conversion of artisan or industrial premises, will in most circumstances serve the role of contrast. Another way is in the style of running the accommodation; a cook, housekeeper or maid can be supplied to the holiday accommodation and so leaving the tourist with minimum household chores to do. Many tourists opt to consume main meals out, and so really only using the accommodation as a base for sleeping. The last main way is to deploy the opportunity of being in a non-everyday environment and to take time and pleasure in choosing and understanding and buying, and cooking at base, distinctively local ingredients.

The type of tourist, and the type of experience they require, will condition the way they 'play' the situation. A young adult attending a camp in a warm climate with friends, for example, may put emphasis on installing a camp fire and cooking only simple meals while giving considerable attention to obtaining and consuming lots of local wine; and all as part of having a general experience of conviviality, liberation, and the open air. As a multi-faceted camp experience was the One World Camp 2000 holistic event over a week, aiming to be 'a truly magical mid-summer festival' and in which, the publicity leaflet described 'Individuals and families come together from all over the world in this unique atmosphere of rest and activity, fund and freedom to choose what to do'. The Camp embraced 'over 200 workshops and lectures … with separate activity programmes for teens and children of all age groups'. There were evening 'Campfire activities'. Natural wholefood organic 'gourmet meals' were supplied thrice daily. A variety of accommodation was available both indoors (private rooms or dormitory-style) and outdoors (own tents). The emphasis was on the individual composing their own holiday from among the elements of 'natural lifestyle' on offer. A definite emphasis was food and cookery: with the type of meals provided; the 'macrobiotic educational programmes'; and that sponsors were The Natural Cookery School, the organic whole food shop Bushwhacker Wholefoods, organic and biodynamic food shop Cook's Delight, and organic and wholefood distributer Clearspring. Also involved were Soyfoods, a distributer of organic and vegan foods and Freshlands (now Fresh and Wild) which is a small chain of natural food stores.

Accommodation with Connections

Appropriate Linkages

As accommodation often provided in connection with learning, and of a direct and focused type, is that of the cooking school. The accommodation in connection provides the opportunity for reinforcing a message of cooking expertise and for delivering a rest and holiday in theme to learners. Cooking schools will be discussed in Chapter 10, and one to be mentioned is Ballymaloe in the south west of Ireland. Ballymaloe is a large and spread complex overall, and with as main features on one side the Country House Hotel and Restaurant and on the other the Cookery School. The core and starting point to all was Myrtle Allen opening Ballymaloe Country House (hotel) and Restaurant. Later her son and his wife opened the nearby Cookery School. Between them, the family have written a number of Ballymaloe books. The hotel-restaurant is a clear entity with pool, tennis court, golf course etc, and it has its own shop and café, but also it is 'feeding' off the School due to enabling guests to attend cookery demonstrations for a fee. Accommodation is too offered at the Cookery School – which is residential or non-residential – and this is in the form of self-catering cottages produced from converting farm buildings at the home of Myrtle's son and daughter in law.

The benefits of putting accommodation and other food or drink resources in close connection and association have been described already. Showing recognition of the potential of accommodation in connection with other facilities are two different types, these both putting wine establishments and hotels alongside each other. The first is Three Choirs Vineyards in Gloucestershire in the UK which began in 1978, and which in 2000 put a 'modern motel-style' hotel amid its winery. A restaurant was already present and it offers lunch and evening meals with a perspective over the vineyard (Duncan, 2001, p. 11). Apparently (Three Choirs English Vineyard Web site), the hotel was provided by popular request and so as to enjoy the vineyard setting and for the experience to be maximized of dining in the restaurant. The hotel offers both weekend and mid-week packages. In Australia the grounds of an existing historic house, Chirnside Mansion, have been used for providing a winery, Shadowfax, and a hotel named The Mansion Hotel. Also provided is a polo ground. Visitors are able to picnic in the grounds. For the winery building, the emphasis is on a state of the art style of architecture and which reflects the process of winemaking.

Linking Consumer Type with Style of Accommodation

It can be seen that markets for the various types of accommodation in association with food and drink can range considerably. The representation of extent can be between provisions:

- to meet a 'back to nature', roots and wholesomeness impulse in the consumer;
- to cater to consumer wishes drawing on connoisseurship and gourmet-ism;
- to feed a desire of consumers to use a facility that is up-market, stylish and fashionable, and which their peer group for impressing will recognize as such.

As generalizations, the following can be said. Camping and B&B facilities tend to be used by the first group. Self-catering facilities cater among all groups according to what are their type, cultural context, status and level of grandiosity. Foodie or designer establishments appeal to either the young person or the Third Ager, and to either of the aspirational or the well-off and comfortable. Accommodation in association with a teaching or demonstrating facility appeals to the lifelong learner by type according to best match with their differing social and cultural shade. Probably suiting them most will be modest mid-range accommodation of various types but the food and drink with which will be high quality but neither necessarily 'showy' or of very high cost.

Establishments Linked with Celebrity, and to Renown and Fashionability

Hotels, in offering a complete living experience to the tourist, are the accommodation option able to provide *a most total ambience* and so most equipped to support the tourist's cultural identity and chosen social position. As Gillespie opines discussing élite establishments of eating and drinking,

'design, fashion and semiotic carriers are deliberately devised to combine towards the influencing of purchasing behaviour, and the satisfaction of both the psychological and physiological needs of the guests. In this way, élite hotels and restaurants can actively create a form of life style accessory, which can provide a stage on which consumers can enact their carefully designed identities'.

He adds that facilities trying to cater to be seen as superior in contrast to routine mass entities are deliberately acting in the way and differently, saying 'This is a formal strategy, distinguishing these establishments [the élite ones] from the generally more formalistic focus on product and service of chain-owned brands' (2001, p. 106). Gillespie quotes his and Morrison's identified styles (2000) for use singly or as several together. These are 'Traditional timeless elegance', 'Exclusive fashionable minimalism', Exclusive dramatic and theatrical environment', 'Informal elegance and chic', and 'Unique luxury leisure'. Gillespie relates that establishments using a range of these devices are 'emitting semiotic carriers' and which 'are then translated into powerful sensory differentiators' (2001, p. 107). After summarizing that 'Élite establishments explicitly apply the concept of sensory differentiators to achieve significant competitive advantage within certain market niches', he goes on to conclude,

'All hotels and restaurants have the potential to provide consumers, either deliberately or through serendipity, with a wealth and depth of semiotic carriers and sensory differentiators that can be used to benefit business performance'.

Redman described that the British seaside, following a long down-turn, had fledgling re-positioning occurring in 2000 through some its hotels and which only lacked lacking good marketing for proper realization. He portrayed Cornwall as one area with the change. He said, 'The "up"-marketing isn't just hype – look no further than Padstow, where Rick Stein [a celebrity fish chef] puts the fashion into fish 'n' chips'. He describes also the revamped Hotel Tresanton whose 'cool good looks lure couture crowds year round' (2000, p. 69). The Tresanton possesses a sophisticated gourmet restaurant.

Hotels run by chef mega-stars draw guests from far and wide. Clearly, however compelling their other accoutrements, these hotels are being visited for food (and wine) reasons. Their essential offer is a gourmet experience of the highest level. Delivering a slight 'twist' to this is the innovatory Michel Guérard (Ypma, 2001). His activity extends over several food and drink matters and which now includes owning a Chateau vineyard in Tursan in France. As was described in Chapter 4, he has gained fame more than anything else from producing a cooking style, Cuisine Minceur, and which was followed by the more conventional Cuisine Gourmande. His hotel interest is among his group of activities at Eugénie les Bains, France. Accommodation there now ranges over four hotels, of different levels of luxury, from the original spa hotel to the Couvant des Herbes, La Ferme aux Grives, and La Maison Rose. For the restaurant Les Prés d'Eugénie, Guérard has three Michelin stars. These signify that it is worth a journey.

A compatriot of Guérard is famed chef Michel Bras (Ypma, 2001). He shows the 'pulling power' of good food to the ultimate in that his base is the remote area of France where he was brought up, the Aubrac. He has three Michelin stars for the food of his establishment. Bras's concept is individual, and extreme in a sense. The clientele attend at a futuristic hotel placed on an empty hill and which is 'designed on the principle of discovery and enjoyment of Aubrac'. They are accommodated in rooms set into the hillside, from which they can walk directly out in the countryside, and with the immediate vicinity in front of their rooms having been re-planted with wild flowers local to the area such as viola and gentian. Overall, Bras's aim is to help guests appreciate the country he loves, and this object is pursued by delivering a whole experience with the food and drink, and style of meals – hearty traditional 'Aubrac Breakfast' including wine can be consumed from 10 am, for example – at the centre. However his hospitality extends to suggesting activities such as, from the 'Indefinable Aubrac' leaflet, to gather bilberries which will be render into jam in the hotel kitchen, to 'pick the "tea" of the Aubrac, to gather meadowsweet, some of which Bras uses in desserts, and so on. Leaflets of activities are of other themes too, such as art and culture. Full information, and bearing Bras's personal comments, is made available for the discovery tour, 'thus opening doors and removing barriers'. For a picnic on the outing, bread, sausage, the local Laguiole cheese, and fruit and wine are obtainable, and provided in a backpack for their easy transportation. Local 'people to meet' and 'things to take back home' – of the latter, cheese and meat for instance – are listed for guest information. The overall aura to the experience of the Michel Bras hotel-restaurant is of sensual and special pleasure (Bras, 2002). Bras aims to give his guests a flavour of the Aubrac through all their senses, not just by those of taste.

Range and Portrayal

The aim of this chapter has been to demonstrate various kinds of accommodation establishment with food and drink features that are in some way special or else have connections to such particular dimensions, and to show how matters are being presented and are relating. The endeavour has been:

- to show different weightings and associations among features;
- to demonstrate how a format can be chosen by a provider according to circumstances;
- to portray what a likely type of market is;
- to depict who needs to benefit from the overall presentation;
- to regard whether all benefits are direct or whether other partners are participating and need to obtain gain.

It has been shown that a range of offer is possible, and how accommodation can act to bring a large and more extensive presentation to the tourist and with, as the objective, greater provider gain.

Chapter 9

Feeding and Drinking

Destination, and Neighbourhood, Establishments

This chapter will look at eating and drinking establishments. As in tune with what the book is centrally about, which is food and drink and related centres and outlets as objects to visit, its essential focus will be places to eat and drink that are so distinct and appealing that they act as destinations for tourists. Of course, too, such places can serve as merely features of support and fuel and with other attractions being pursued as a tourist's main objective. The main group for discussion is venues that are being destinations due to the food or drink that they serve. Mention too will be made, however, of the category of routine and neighbourhood establishments, and which are not such to act as lure from afar but which are necessary or tempting destinations to tourists once within an area. The main types to be considered are restaurants, tearooms, cafés, pubs [public houses] and inns, and bars.

Centres of Attention

It denotes considerable appeal and fame to a particular food or drink establishment if the visitor treats it as an attraction in itself. They may do so either in making the place as the whole object of a trip or else as the main feature of a day during a holiday. Important to this chapter will be to show what elements cause, and contribute to, certain establishments standing out as attractions from among the vast number in the world provided for consuming food and/or drink. The basic and obvious features are those of:

- having speciality and excellence of item;
- being known about and recognized.

These criteria, of course, are likely to relate to the other types of attraction among food and drink tourism too, and accommodation is an obvious example. To be emphasized, however, is that by the sheer amount of eating and drinking places in the world, and with often many to each tourism locale, competition between them all will be especially fierce. The context of being 'the only place in town' is a relatively unusual one. It is of course a very lucky situation for the provider, assuming that his/her overall locale is enough to draw the attention of the consumer. However, the outcome may be possibly less happy for the consumer. This is that complacency about style and quality of product could occur in an establishment – rather than good distinctiveness – in the instance of a provider being in position of sole supremacy.

The Modest Local Establishment

The asset that the restaurant, tearoom, café, diner, pub, inn, and bar of modest pretension, modest quality, and modest price have to offer as a destination is one of being accessible – mostly and theoretically. Its other feature, contrasting strongly with the site of prominence, is of being commonplace. This kind of locale can be the regular and appropriated haunt of the resident precisely due to its unspecialness and undemanding-ness, and its probable consequent style of homeliness, neighbourliness and localness. From this dimension, the place will have a certain home-from-home aura of familiarity; and – due to the home consumer being in mode of relaxation and of not working, cooking and doing chores – it may be delivering a more relaxed environment. The surroundings of conviviality, congeniality, homeliness, and community will appeal to the tourist for their local authenticity message. An appealing opportunity is being represented for the tourist of meeting local people, and depending that an atmosphere of welcome to outsiders – rather than of exclusion – is pertaining. It should be mentioned that 'localness' need not be represented through a neighbourhood restaurant that serves cuisine traditionally associated with an area, but also by ethnic, 'foreign', restaurants and which have become firmly implanted as part of a local community and showing its cultural diversity.

Level of Frequency of Eating and Drinking Out

There is an aspect too to eating out and drinking out while on holiday. This is that the tourist – unless they are either eating at their place of accommodation or are in the previously discussed 'midway between everyday and holiday mode' of being a self-caterer – *has* to eat and drink out. Therefore, while some gourmands or enthusiasts for a particular drink, might well go somewhere 'special' all the time for consuming, other tourists will be pursuing such establishments only sometimes or not at all. The commonplace and local food and drink location will be the most-days or daily destination of tourists on a budget and/or needing to eat meals out a lot.

Fast Food, and the Fish and Chip Shop

Here, two types of food supplier need mentioning: the fast food establishment and the fish and chip shop. The former usually epitomizes globalization in that it operates to a global style, and its food itself may also be 'global' even though maybe locally-sourced, but also it can be local in being a small, low cost outlet for purveying food from nearby. The fast-food chain will most likely offer 'eat-in' or 'take away' options, as does McDonald's, and so may even the 'small hut' or 'small stall' type of operation which will provide 'eat-in' with either a few indoor tables and chairs or else same outdoors. The fish and chip shop more normally only offers 'take away' food to eat but sometimes a restaurant is provided too. All of these places – and from the fish and chip shop queue to the tables of the hamburger establishment – act as local meeting places. This is, again, for the low cost of their food, their lack of pretension, and so their accessibility.

Consumer Types

The types of eating and drinking establishments offer different experiences for consumption and each type can have a different type of clientele among users – residents and tourists. The following are broad, stereotypical generalizations of some of these clients. The foodie may well be knowledgeable and interested about drink also, and most particularly this is likely to be the liquid that accompanies dining such as wine, and those of aperitif, digestif, liqueur, whisky and brandy which start or complete this eating experience. Some among wine 'buffs' can be relatively uninterested in food. The 'serious drinker' who consumes alcohol at a pub or inn or bar can devote their enthusiasm and connoisseurship in this direction and with no particular, or even-less-than-average, interest in the subject of food.

The Café

The café – in emanation from the historical position of the coffee house (Pendergrast, 2001) – appeals, and certainly currently is promoted as such, as a social space and which is denoted as 'third space' – another location for being between home and work and where the person can 'hang out'. The connotations from history of the coffee-house as location of radicalism seem meanwhile to have been 'pasteurized out'. In certain places – middle-Europe most especially, and Vienna is the classic example – has come to exist an embourgeoisized version of the coffee house. This is a genre which acts to be meeting place, location to read newspapers – as traditionally has been the instance of the coffee house, site to occupy long, and as space serving almost as being 'home from home'. The use is made of it by mainly an outwardly traditional, ageing market and whose representative probably is an apartment-dweller who will not have an extensive own residence. Such places, as being not very common to everyday, not being associated with young, very busy people, and having cakes of high calorific content, represent difference to routine to most people and so these serve as special destinations and treats to visit when on holiday or at leisure. In the eastern and southern Mediterranean, the coffee house is similar in terms of being a place to convene, talk and relax, but the substance consumed will be coffee of the distinct, concentrated and sweet type known as 'Turkish'.

The term café has come to be used to denote an establishment of wide-range and less distinct format than either of traditional or – Starbucks-kind – 'third space' model, though drawing on both of these in some ways. It has coffee certainly, and probably often light snacks and meals – as both the traditional and 'third space' type will do, but from thence it ventures into a lack of clarity of certain feature and in which individuality more reigns. The main essence of these places is their informality and lack of much structure of when, and what, to consume. They act as places to patronize informally and throughout the day, and for small- or large-scale consumption, and to imbibe coffee, soft drinks, and alcoholic beverages. As a modern example of the type and which is sited to be a small destination, is the Café Hiili in a large park in Helsinki, near Finlandia Hall of which Alvar Aalto was the architect. It is a simple cabin to the design of Kilo Sirola from winning an architectural competition among students of Helsinki Polytechnic and it was installed as part of Helsinki's being a Cultural Capital Year in 2000, in which year there were others such as Avignon. Café Hiili is essentially a bar and coffee outlet but of such good design as to offer an outdoor, semi-outdoor, and indoor experience.

Pubs and Inns

Of all types, perhaps because of the direct focus upon alcohol and with 'tongue-loosening' seen as an occurrence of consuming it, the pub and inn have the most connection with talk, conviviality and bonhomie. They are traditionally male domains. Games are often a feature of the activity of an inn and sport an element of its conversation. The bar can be like this too, in its regular and community focal point incarnation, but when of the type frequently attracting the prefix 'trendy' and with a young or aspirational user group, it becomes more outwardly mixed and wide-ranging and more 'glossy' and fashionable of appearance.

Categorization and Option

As can be seen, there are different ways to typify an eating or drinking establishment. Categorization can be by type of clientèle, broadly as in 'family' or 'male orientated' or 'female orientated', and in different or more detailed ways such as to arrive at 'under 30s', 'sports-lovers', and 'the metropolitan rich'. A restaurant or bar in a very tourist-frequented area can be in the category of being 'tourist haunt'. Differentiation can be by kind of food and drink delivered, e.g. fish restaurant or 'real ale' pub, or by calibre of food and cooking or drink provided, as in the stars of Michelin for restaurants of scale of quality. Unless they are very globalized in nature, the cultures of aura and way of operation of differing establishments are rooted in where they are and what they offer. These are evident to the consumer, and they feature as why a particular one is chosen and on a particular occasion. For the tourist, probably the essential choices they are making are among:

- the establishment characterized by 'colour', localness and authenticity;
- the place showing ease, friendliness and familiarity;
- the location manifesting great special-ness and distinction.

As represented by these options, is a selection between the unknown and the essentially familiar. Depending on the kind of consumer and upon the type of holiday, both options may well be pursued during the holiday's course.

Styles and Methods of Visibility and Encounter

For the provider and stakeholder, an important basic needed recognition is that the tourist needs to eat somewhere while on holiday, and that even when in a self-catering role the tourist is almost bound to be consuming some food and drink 'out'. This understanding leads to the panoply of food and drink provisions being put in association with attractions, and ranging from an independent ice-cream stand outside a historic monument to a café located in a museum. Similarly, making suitable establishments known to people touring on their own by giving information about them through such as TICs is helpful to the tourist and helps deliver business to the provider. The places with which the tourist are unfamiliar are likely to be of the unspectacular, 'not a destination in their own right' and 'part of local community life' category. A distinction is between those establishments needing promoting to the tourist before they set off to its place or area, and those that the tourist will 'trip over' when visiting an attraction and so in the latter instance the essential endeavour is promoting the attraction. However, a lot of attractions have noted the foodie and 'third space' inclination in the public, and are making an attractive and high-calibre restaurant, café or bar available as an entity to be used and enjoyed separately from the attraction, and by both a tourist and local sector.

As examples of stakeholder/provider recognition of the tourist's need and interest in eating and drink while touring, and of the usefulness to provider and consumer of refreshment sites being vaunted to the tourist are:

- the 'Eats and Treats along the Wall' article in the *News from Hadrian's Wall World Heritage Site* magazine of August 2001 and which represents English Heritage's and other sponsors' – such as The Countryside Agency and the Hadrian's Wall Tourism Partnership – promotion of private sector food and drink enterprises along Hadrian's Wall.
- the leaflet 'Tables Regional d'Auvergne' lists restaurants in the Auvergne who in 2000/2001 were offering regional cuisine and to allow its discovery. Their special regional dishes are mentioned. The Auvergne is depicted as giving its taste to France. The visitor can identify participating restaurants by the red chef's hat logo each is displaying. This promotion by the Regional Chamber of Agriculture of the Auvergne is described as being one of several under the overall title and initiative, 'Tables des Régions of France'. Other partipating regions are noted as Franche Comté, Picardie, Nord/Pas-de-Calais, and Champagne-Ardenne. To these and the Auvergne were to be more joining the scheme in the year following, the leaflet explains.

As reaction to a consumer strong food and drink enthusiasm, and acting to help build it too, are a range of guides, directories, publications and magazines. These serve as solid background and underpinning to the – usually passing – particularly focused promotions, brochures and leaflets of agencies and groups and whose message represents particular pleading about the appeal and interest of a food or drink type, its area or gathering of providers. The various guides stoke food and drink enthusiasm and interest in being present and visible during everyday life, helping keeping in mind making visits for food and drink, assisting in pre-planning them, and generally acting toward trips being engendered for the purpose of seeing and consuming food and drink and their processes. As examples of general guides are *The Good Food Guide* of long-standing, the relatively new Lonely Planet *World Food* series that has been mentioned previously, the very new Time Out *Eating and Drinking* series that has guides for Barcelona and for Rome. Special sector guides include those for pubs (Aird, 2002 (ed.)), pub food (Aird, 2002) cider (Mathews, 2000), beer (Protz, 2002), and curry (Chapman, 2000).

Cultures of Domain

It can reasonably be said that the focus of restaurants, pubs, inns, and the reason for their being chosen, is either particular items to consume or style and aura or special location, or else that they are convenient and inviting and unthreatening as opposed to being distinct. This is notwithstanding that each kind has a culture of type and sub-cultures within this.

Tea and Coffee Examples

The café and coffee house can be more diffuse, floating and complex as has been explained, and albeit that a very strong central culture is permeating them. The tea domain appears to act somewhat differently again. The tearoom in its British, or British-derived, style, in contrast to the café's most often relative raciness of association, has a reputation of being 'safe' and genteel and holds the tradition of being suited for, and patronized by, 'ladies'. In their colonization of tea, the British scooped it up and made it their own cultural entity.

Tea was introduced into England in about the mid 17th century and was initially a high-cost beverage. The appearance of pleasure gardens to replace coffee houses as fashionable locations at which to congregate by the mid 18th century, and, that the provision of tea and bread and butter was part of the admission fee of some gardens, helped tea 'arrive'. It role was raised, after urbanization had delivered pleasure gardens' decline in the early 19th century, with tea meetings being a feature of the temperance movement. The ABC [Aerated Bread Company] opened the first public tearoom in London in 1864 to provide a location for tea to be provided for customers purchasing its cakes. Others then appeared towards tearooms being well-established by 1900 (Pettigrew and Crocker, 2000, pp. 9 –11; Pettigrew, 2001).

The Executive Director of The Tea Council, which organization promotes tea in the UK, describes that, 'Today, afternoon tea is a major tourist attraction for visitors to our shores' (Lewis, 2000, p. 5). While tea as a drink is much in favour with UK residents, albeit that coffee is now frequently the preference from among the two, afternoon tea is a great draw and delight to them when they are tourists and visitors in the UK themselves. Much like the hotel breakfast, afternoon tea has come to occupy an almost sole role as a leisure, away from home, activity. Afternoon tea is an anachronism. It represents an experience that is essentially now entirely heritage, but it is a heritage much pursued and regarded with enthusiasm and affection. The tearoom can be a more wide and diffuse entity than that serving afternoon tea – frequently it is open all day and offers snacks and light lunches and coffee and others drinks – but its whole culture and aura derive from that seen as pertaining to afternoon tea. The setting has been described in another chapter and so will not be portrayed again fully here. The general expected ambience is of clutter, floral pattern and dark wood. Cakes, the centre of the production, are usually on prominent display and these will be 'home-made'. The type of food and the procedure and paraphernalia associated with the tearoom and its process, along with that the time of afternoon tea fits lengthily and awkwardly in the day when full-time work is the usual practice, has ensured that afternoon tea has become much the visitor's and holidaymaker's preserve. While tourism can be seen as its strong role, the tearoom nonetheless has considerable regular local patronage, and as a place of treat and meeting. Patrons from the community appear to be particularly women and of an age or disposition not to be in work or at least in full-time work, and to whom the essentially feminine aura of the tearoom seems to appeal most. To attract a wide local clientele the tearoom needs to be open suitable and sufficient hours to suit a general populace. Therefore, as with other types described in this chapter, the tearoom has a visitor and home market, though some examples in a tourist honeypot – a cathedral town for example – may have its consumers drawn very predominantly from the outsiders. The National Trust is an organization recognizing the strong position of food and drink in its overall visitor offer, and puts emphasis on generating an aura of home-made-ness and tradition to its comestibles and imbibables. As indication of 'the tea-following' is the Trust's explanation in its *Tourism and The National* Trust leaflet that in the year 1995 it served more that five million cups of tea in its tearooms.

Catering to the tearoom enthusiasm and helping to promote teashops (tearooms) and deliver consumers to their door are guidebooks of tea trails and teashop walks. These may be produced by county, such as those for Suffolk (Anderton, 1998) and 'Secret Sussex' (Ellis and Cherry, 1997), by areas such as East Anglia (Patefield, 1999), and with as a main presentation, The National Teapot Trail (The National Teapot Trail, 1999). This last embraces England, Scotland and Wales, but can only show a selection of the whole 800 that exist. The National Teapot Trail initiative was begun in 1989 with a small Trail of twenty Yorkshire Dale tearooms.

The tearoom traditional concept shows itself as extremely unprone to alteration, and doubtless it is the 'certainty' and distinctiveness and other-worldliness that it offers that renders its appeal. It is a clear example of the invitingness generated in the visitor of the 'sheer difference to the everyday'. The tearoom is not routine to quotidian existence but it conforms to a type very strongly and this combination of difference and assuredness seems be a 'winning' one. As an ultra-typical item in almost every respect is The Essex Rose tea house in Dedham, which village is in the heart of the area known as 'Constable Country' after the English landscape painter whose territory it was. It is, therefore, sited in a much tourist-frequented place – and this is the usual instance of tearooms. Its building is old – 16th century in origin, and there has been a tearoom operating for decades. Open daily except during the Christmas period when it closes, the tea house offers items such as 'a bowl of home-made soup, a nourishing snack or a delicious cream tea'. Indicating the style and ritual associated with afternoon tea itself, the brochure too states, 'Traditional English afternoon tea is always served in the finest china cups and from a warmed china tea pot'. The Essex Rose's interesting dimension is that since 2000, its owner has been the notable Essex jam firm of Wilkin and Sons. Wilkin's jam factory at Tiptree, some miles distant, has a museum, tearoom and Visitor Centre shop open to the public everyday in summer and six days a week in the winter. So, here is evidence of suitable connection being made between two complementary entities.

In East Anglia, further to the north, is a brave venture. It is in Cley, a village alongside the north Norfolk coast and which overall area is a tourists' venue and including to the discriminating and connoisseur type. The Café at Whalebone House while operating as a tearoom deliberately tried to break the traditional tearoom mould. Its two proprietors said about their aim and idea in their book of 'recipes and ruminations' (Meadows and Curtis, 2001),

'The twenty-first century has arrived, and we think it's time to break away from the rather old fashioned, twee tea room image: lots of dark wood, lace, flowery tablecloths and waitresses (always female!) in black skirts. Our focus instead is to blend the best of the English tea tradition – home-made cakes, high tea savouries and a good range of teas – with what's new and exciting in the café culture: good coffees, interesting food with a Mediterranean influence, newspapers and magazines to read, and great style … in other words, a cool place to be'.

They went on to explain what they believe are the unusual dimensions of their provision: being small, deliberately; encouraging a slow turnover – 'We like it best when you sit for ages over your coffee or your lunch, enjoying some peace and quiet or the chance to have that conversation you never quite manage to have at home'. Their sourcing is careful and very selective. They offer only what has been made by themselves on the premises – bread apart – and this not supplied elsewhere. Customers are treated as if visiting their home.

Meadows and Curtis are enthusiasts of Slow Food which is offered in their establishment. In their interpretation Slow Food is characterized – for suiting 21st century lifestyles and which demand food to be available quickly – as being a speed and attitude of the mind and spirit rather than necessarily pace of body against the clock.

The stance of the two is polemical. They ask such questions as 'Are you prepared to brave sight and smell of a real butcher's shop, or buy your vegetables dirty at the gate of the farm that grew them?' Their essential aim is to try to encourage their readers and consumers to think about their relationship and attitude to food. There is a Web site – www.thecafe.org.uk – which gives similar information to the *Slow Food* book, and also some expansion and update about the Café. The whole effort is interesting. It has the courage to be overt about its principles. Also, and remembering that their Café is located in a tourist area, it and its background which Meadows' and Curtis' book *Slow Food* and the Web site reveal, are an example to indicate one of this book's messages. This is that tourism delivers time/space to consider food and drink and its issues and for trying different types and new ways of approaching food and drink. The, interesting for interpretation, evolution of 2002 was that The Café at Whalebone House ceased serving tea. It provides lunch and dinner.

Cultures Among Eating and Drinking

This chapter has been considering types and examples of food and drink consuming establishments. It has not sought to be exhaustive in covering every possible category. The essential aim has been: evaluating certain kinds and examples for seeing what these are delivering and representing to the tourist, and most specifically in cultural terms; and along with this, revealing what provider activity, objects and cultural dimensions are pertaining. In process of survey it has been noted or implied that certain establishment types have come to be associated with a culture of group, gender or behaviour, and are communicating a subliminal message of, as examples: femininity, gentility and nostalgia, but its role of the past when in the USA as a vehicle for women's liberation should be noted too (Whittaker, 2002) – the tearoom; masculinity and machismo – the pub and old-style bar; trendiness – the new-style bar and the designer restaurant; wholesomeness and naturalness – the wholefood or vegetarian café; proletarianism – the fish and chip shop; pause, consideration, meeting and 'outside the box' talk – the coffee house and café. Throughout the gamut, an extensive cultural range is on offer for tempting the food and drink tourist.

Chapter 10

Special Events and Devices, and Resources for Education

Why the Need?

This chapter will consider events produced as special items and will look also at occasions and courses produced to deliver skill, learning and education.

The first questions to ask are why, as part of food and drink tourism, should occasions that are particular and extra be delivered, and why should situations for obtaining knowledge be offered? General answers to the questions are these. A special event can be a method to 'freshen-up' a resource. It can be the way to bring it overall back into the notice of the consumer, to render a place newly inviting to them, to encourage them to revisit. The particular occasion offers a point of focus, and entity of novelty, for making a promotion. It can act as a vehicle for informing the consumer about a site's existence or about a food and drink matter or subject. A certain event, or body of events, can be shaped to appeal especially to a particular audience, and therefore one type of deployment is for drawing in a *new market* that does not currently use a place. Another way to use a particular event is simply to bring in *more visitors*. A special occasion or festival can be provided tactically in time, and so, as examples, delivered at the end of the usual visitor season to extend it somewhat or in the middle of a low season for bringing in a greater number of visitors for that period. A further motivation for providing an event is to use it for *bringing socio-economic benefit* in association to a host community.

Of course, particular events can either be produced specially for motives, or else existing occasions that are in the cycle of a host community can be deployed for tourism. Already present events will have embodied meaning in that they are embraced among a society's culture and practice. Events related to the agricultural round, such as a festival of celebration of some particular crop having arrived in appearance, or of an overall harvest having been gathered, are examples. Another occasion can be for celebration of a food or drink special to an area. Other relevant events can be both other kinds of celebrations and any sort of community important moments, all of whose character is to have food and or drink as their heart of method of expression (Luard, 2001).

Mechanisms, Styles and Roles

The event and the festival are some entities used in tourism. The trail and route (Moulin and Boniface, 2001) on a food or drink type or subject are mechanisms to move tourists to new places and over wider areas. They carry the attendant expected outcomes of tourism's effects permeating more extensively than without them being used as devices. A trail – when fulfilling a role of offering an extra attraction and aiding the build up of critical mass of features to an event or situation to attract visitors and consumers – can be very local and immediate to the main thing. Its position is to help heighten invitingness and to offer diversification for widening market appeal. It does also, however, very much retain the basic roles of drawing items to consumer attention and of bringing visitors to places and outlets they might not otherwise know about to visit or feel strongly impelled enough to go and see.

As a distinct category of occasion is the learning event about food or drink and its care and preparation. This is likely to be experienced by the holidaymaker – as opposed to the student for a career in cookery, food and wine – over a quite short period such as a half-day, day, weekend or week. The supply of holiday courses, however, while maybe only during a particular season, can be continued on a more or less continuous basis. Since these occasions *are* holidays, albeit that two dimensions of learning and vacationing are being linked, their *ambiences* and *environments* will be salient to their level of attractiveness to the consumer along with the immediate aspects of what it being taught and by whom. The context of the learning event – the calibre of the landscape surrounding the venue, the amount of facilities and good restaurants especially, the level of desirability of climate, if weather appeal is affected according to season – is a conditioner. Of course very salient are the quality and appeal of the immediate base, the hotel or college where the event is held and any accommodation separate. Relevant too is likely to be how much a course goes out into its immediate area for field trips.

The educational type of event described above is of the overtly educational kind. There are myriad others provided that are present for informing and educating and for developing visitor interest and commitment but which wear their role more lightly and in which position they may be slotted in among a mixed programme of events or otherwise be delivered more dilutedly. In contrast, and at the other end of the scale and of another distinct kind, is the very focused event that is the food or drink trade show, conference, seminar or training session for professionals, intending professionals, stakeholders or academics. This entity is in the business tourism realm. It frequently looks to use an away-from-home location as a base of concentration to help knowledge be generated, ideas and opinions be exchanged, and expertise increased, among participants about the food and drink industry, its background and methods of operating.

Before or After Tourism

Food and drink events that involve tourism extend between:

- the occasions which existed before modern tourism occupied them and which possess an existing and central society, community and everyday function beyond and above tourism;
- the occasions created or recreated with tourism as the sole or partial objective for the action.

Range of Weight of Attention

Events with food and drink tourism as in occupation also range along a continuum between: those treating food and drink lightly and as means for delivering entertainment; those having the objective of serving an educational and informational role, and in a serious way. As about mid-way along this latter of these two mentioned stretches are directly food- and drink-related holidays. These are characterized by tourists occupying foodie accommodation and being led, or steered to act in self-guided way, to vineyards, food outlets, etc. Of course, some tourists, and the food and drink connoisseur among the whole category, may plan a holiday and its tour programme entirely individually and from their own knowledge.

The Matters of Age, Depth and Authenticity

Concerning events connected to food and drink and which are used in tourism, items for consideration are such as these. What is being attractive to the tourist? How much does it matter to the tourist for an event to be old and authentic – and whether in reality or simply in their perception? Might an impression of traditionalism and age to an event be the critical portion of its appeal to the tourist, and, therefore, why should this be? If an event is invented, rather than emanating from past and custom, and the tourist realizes an event is an invention, is it less inviting and rewarding to them than an event that has been held for long time and uninterruptedly? Are antiquity and cultural connection crucial dimensions affecting that the tourist opts for and enjoys an event, and if so why? Is, perhaps, something deep being touched? Is, maybe, part of the appeal of food and drink occasions their link with a profundity and elementality not much visible in modern life and industrialized, standardized and globalized systems and processes? In relation to the festival, Gardiner cites Lefebvre's belief 'that modernity represents the dissolution of genuine intersubjectivity, and the end of popular celebrations like the premodern festival' (2000, p. 83). Describing a viewpoint of Weber 'that as a result of rationalization the Western world has grown increasingly disenchanted', Ritzer says that 'Thus, instead of a world dominated by enchantment, magic, and mystery, we have one in which everything seems clear, cut-and-dried, logical, and routine'. He suggests, 'Consider how the dimensions of McDonaldization work against enchantment' (2000, p. 132). Concerning what manufactured new 'traditions' are produced for and what they mean to those producing them, Warde has this to say,

> 'Behind invented traditions lurks the imagined community, a site of social group membership that promises collective security and group identity'.

His continuation opines whom these are appealing to and so is suggested that traveller and tourist gain subsistence from them. The essential benefit is to meet fixedness and culture in common, and to obtain reassurance from the encounter. This is a contrast of appeal to a person on the move, 'alone', prominent and vulnerable, and in circumstances fresh and changing. Warde says:

'Acceptance of the authority of comparatively fixed and shared dispositions or customs of a social group is a comforting antidote to the uncertainties of personal adventure and innovation' (1997, p. 66).

Warde then moves on to make the telling but different, though related, point,

'Ironically, the prominence of localized identifications with food coincides with the general decline of spatial differences in consumption patterns' (p. 67).

This remark is to suggest that the very arrival of revived attention to local food is an outcome of, and reaction to, a globalized eating and consuming lifestyle.

That food has an important role in offering an affordable and available means to deliver authenticity to the tourist is the opinion of Reynolds, saying, 'Food … is perhaps one of the last areas of authenticity that is affordable on a regular basis by the tourist'. He adds the warning, however, about the inauthenticity to which food is potentially victim because of its essential quality of immediacy, temporariness and dynamism, in saying, 'Yet because it is perishable, cannot be transported, preserved or put in a gallery to be revered it is the easiest to copy and to degrade' (1993, p. 49).

Food and drink events where 'real old' or 'new old' is the dimension are some types. Other types make no pretence of being other than new occasions in both introduction and in style. The appeal of these latter to the tourists is by current merits and their strength of worth is in what they contain of present nature and relevance rather than for any connotation of age and tradition. It should be recognized, however, that an important group exists of completely overtly new events but whose role of interest to the tourist is that these fresh occasions are conveying information about and tapping into old ways. They meet a curiosity in the tourist to find out about old methods and styles, and with a possible view to adopting and using some of them, due to reaction against globalization, worry about quality and safety of food and drink delivered by the mass production method, and concern about processes and impacts of the industrialized procedure.

Added Value as Crucial

Probably the essential encapsulated role of food and drink events is that of delivering *added value*. Events, occasions, trails, courses provide something extra, whether to embellish and heighten a basic product, to extend it, to render more information about an item or process, to give wider benefit of more producers being included and visible, or to offer a further different dimension to the tourist. Another feature of food and drink events having tourism as an aim, is that, while they frequently occupy high season times of summer, they fit suitably and are to be found very much during autumn, a shoulder season. Cookery and training events, of course, have the particular benefit of being able to be offered at any times of the year in which the market would wish to use them.

Types of Events

Events are of these main types:

- festivals
- shows
- conferences
- tours and trails
- tastings
- demonstrations
- farm and other production venue visits
- educational schools and holidays
- multi-featured overall promotions.

The Multi-Featured Occasion

One example of category of the multi-featured overall promotion is Dorset Food Week in the UK. It occupies a mid-autumn slot of crops' particular ripeness and readiness, and with apples featuring particularly. It caters to the half-term school holidays. The Week acts to offer a highlight at a shoulder-season time and is a mechanism towards keeping more tourism happening for a larger portion of the whole year. Its provider is Dorset Food Links Ltd which is a company comprising local food producers and District Councils (local government). Along with offering Dorset Food Week, the company, whose aim is 'to help farmers, independent retailers and communities to work together to create a local food economy which generates economic, social and environmental benefits to the rural areas of Dorset' (Dorset Food Week 2001 brochure), delivers a local food directory and co-ordinates and manages eleven Farmers' Markets in Dorset. The programme of the Week embraces displays and tastings of produce, cookery and food production demonstrations, a guided tour of a smallholding, guided farm walks, treasure hunts relating to food, a 'Foraging for Wild Food' walk, a Harvest Home Festival, an Organic and Local Food Fair, an Appley Feast, markets ranging from Farmers' to Womens' Institutes, a Halloween Party, pea-sowing and a Hog Roast, apple bobbing, a Dorset Apple Cake Bake competition, and special tastings at shops and special meals at restaurants. The Week is supported by Dorset Health Authority, the Dorset Rural Enterprise Fund, and Dorset Community Action.

On a smaller scale, but of similar type is The Big Apple celebration in a parish, Marcle Ridge, whose whereabouts, interestingly, the promotional leaflet depicts as 'Herefordshire', the old location, rather than Hereford and Worcester as since 1974 has been the amalgamated single county. The event is described as representing 'a special opportunity to enjoy the autumn countryside in the Herefordshire parishes on the Marcle Ridge'. Among the features are 'The Common Core' of apple sales and cider sales and tastings and a fruit farm coffee shop, and then lunches and suppers at pubs and inns with apple and cider recipes manifest, cider making demonstrations, hearing 'Ciderlore ... true tales of cider making and cidermakers', an informational stroll on the subject of perry pears, a talk on the origin of the apple, a cycle ride and a dance display by Morris Men (traditional English folk-dancing).

These two examples communicate the types of essences such events are displaying and which are characterizing them. Tapping into depth and age and old cultures and ways, and trying to keep alive, revive or revisit old approaches and customs seem apparent. Reasons, both temporal and fundamental, why this might be have already been suggested.

Displaying realization of the opportunities available to it of autumn, as a time in which its properties have capacities making them appealing to visit and with particular seasonal dimensions, is The National Trust. In the season of what the poet Keats described as 'mists and mellow fruitfulness' (*To Autumn*), the domestic market, often having been satisfied earlier in the year and in high summer by exotic foreign travel, seems wanting and disposed to go back to roots and home country locale, to pursue native and deep tradition, and to re-explore and celebrate old home ways, customs and beliefs. This apparent motivation is tapped into by many providers in autumn, and highlighted by events relating to apples (Common Ground, 2000), fruits seen as particularly English in association and entity. The National Trust delivers as part of its autumn presentation: fungi forays; apple days with tastings and sales, an apple fair, an apple festival; pumpkin days; pruning workshops; learning hedge-laying; heavy horse ploughing demonstrations; wine tastings and lectures; (old fashioned) pudding weekends; lecture lunches on local cheesemaking, 'the picking garden', historical cookery; a tea party for considering the history of tea; and along with local and seasonal fare routinely available in its restaurants.

Small Enterprise Events

A scheme offering several events is that instigated by a sole apple farming couple. It was launched at The Ludlow Marches Food and Drink Festival 2001. It is called Cropsharers and – with the role to diversify – has the objective 'to encourage people to take an interest in how the fruit is grown and in the countryside' (The Countryside Agency, 2001b, p. 8). Cropsharers invite subscribing members, who then receive both fruit 'and invitations to four open weekends, seasonal celebrations such as the ancient cider apple orchard ceremony wassailing, Apple Day, barbecues, orchard walks and the opportunity to learn crafts'.

The Festival

Taking the actual name of event of festival are, as varying examples: the Ludlow Marches Food and Drink Festival; York Festival of Food and Drink which embraces ten days in September; Eastnor Castle Festival of Fine Food and Drink which is a early October weekend occasion of 'Celebrating the Region's Food and Drink'; the Highland Food and Drink Festival, sponsor of which is Tennent Caledonia Breweries; and the fledgling Liverpool International Food Festival which in its first year of 2001 was held during five days of October and one of whose supporters is the Liverpool Culture Company. The Ludlow occasion, held over three days in September, and centred in marquees located within historic Ludlow Castle's perimeter, is billed as '*the* weekend for food and drink lovers!' Its 2001 programme was a combination of items of displays, lectures and cake and pork pie competitions and demonstrations and talks, and a waiters' race and an ox-roast in the main arena, along with outreach events of markets, an ale trail, a sausage trail, a cake trail, a festival loaf trail for voting for bakers in a competition, a cheese tease quiz, a producers' market, a herb market, special food at retailers, outlets and inns and organic farm visit, and a gourmet weekend at a farm. The York Festival is along similar lines and is very large. As part of its 2001 programme it had days allocated to particular themes – 'World Food', 'Yorkshire Food', and 'History of Food' as examples – and each one with a special sponsor, such as the 'First Class Food Day' which has the railway company, GNER, as its sponsor. There are 'Roving Feasts' by theme and 'Festival Dinners' of various types. Also the Festival has a 'Fringe' of events amongst which were in 2001 'A Talk on the History of Bettys (a famous tea room) and 'An Audience with Starbucks' (the global coffee provider). Bettys as an ultra-establishment and traditional place is not the most likely contender for an 'alternative' slot, and Starbucks less still, but doubtless the latter allocation represents clever marketing by Starbucks.

The Show

The show is an event ranging from the smallest kind of a village-produce-related occasion to an agricultural or special-interest society manifestation, or a trade display. At the major scale and operating as a central event for visiting in England, not least due to its venue at the National Exhibition, is the BBC [British Broadcasting Company] Good Food Show, held in association with a national newspaper, the *Daily Express*. Its year 2000 occasion, held over five days at the end of November and the beginning of December, was billed as offering 'All the Ingredients for a Great Day Out'. Alongside the over 450 individual exhibitors were features of famous chef demonstrations, a wine tasting theatre sponsored by the Vinopolis wine visitor attraction, an Organic Pavilion that the Soil Association had supported, a 'gastronomic journey through time', and a Seasonal Christmas Market. In format it is not so dissimilar to the Festivals described above, but in character its emphasis is much less upon aiding and supporting the local, and local farmers and producers, and more on representing a direct commercial enterprise of offering visitor entertainment and promoting the BBC Good Food brand – including its dedicated magazine.

The Feast

The European Capital of Culture endeavour has a more social stance, varying somewhat in style and intensity according to the culture and way of the place being represented. It is made up of a range of component events and presentation, and as the title suggests, culture is to the foremost. The Gourmet Pavilion for Avignon was described in Chapter 7 and the Café Hiili in Helsinki in Chapter 9. Rotterdam as 2001 European Capital of Culture had the general aim of both outward display and inward 'dialogue with the city's residents and to make personal, sensory experiences possible'. Rotterdam has a diverse cultural mix of citizens and wished to generate in them experience of 'cultural cohesion in which differences do not have to pose a threat, and where confrontation should not be feared' (Rotterdam 2001 Cultural

Capital of Europe, 2001, p. 77). It provided 2001 World Flavours, a two-month presentation of cafés/restaurants of food from various parts of the world put in a central square and portrayed as an 'eating festival' (Rotterdam 2001 Cultural Capital of Europe leaflet). These were presented as giving 'concrete form to this fantasy: *by using a meal together, we get to know each other*' (Rotterdam 2001 Cultural Capital of Europe, 2001, p. 77).

The feast is a chameleon according to its purpose. Its type of manifestation will depend on how much the feast is established in advance of tourism and for a core purpose of host celebrating and ritual and remarking the benison of the earth, how much it is manufactured for attracting tourists, and how much it bears providers' and stakeholders' object of wanting its use for social engineering or bringing a commercial outcome. As a feast of firm and wide objective was the 2001 'Big Breakfast' staged by Cartwheel 'a farmer-led marketing company' for farm tourism in the West of England, and which has previously been discussed. The event was actually a series of breakfasts, composed of local produce, and with accompanying food stalls, staged at five places during the usual peak tourism time of August. Its role was to vaunt that the South West of England – an area whose livelihood has a strong tourism focus – was 'reopened' to visitors after closure due to the foot and mouth disease outbreak and to thank for public support 'during a difficult time'. The company has a system of 'Cartwheel Carrot' vouchers 'to encourage the sampling of local foods and activities'. Also, it provides information on Farmers' Markets in its area. As a contrasting example, a ubiquitous entity in England, is the 'medieval banquet' that is held in hotels and restaurants etc, and usually with waiting staff dressed in pseudo medieval dress. Its emphasis is on delivering to the consumer a rolicking good time and to the provider – he/she intends – a rollicking good profit.

The Fair

The fair puts emphasis on being an occasion for gathering together, for sale of goods, and usually it also has items aimed to be of fun, entertainment and information. Frequently too it is for celebrating or honouring someone or for showing something specific. It may have a specific calendar slot due to what is its subject or focus. It has a somewhat different face according to whether it is of ancient, or pseudo-ancient derivation, or else it is a revival, and provided for the general public, or if it is a trade fair in which instance it is essentially a trade show. As an example of a fair focused on a specific, and seasonal, type of food is the Alba Truffle Fair held over more than two weeks in October in Italy and the purpose of which is the sale and celebration of a special gourmet item. A recent revival of an old event, located around a church dedicated to a Christian saint and so connected to the Christian religious calendar, is the 'traditional' Bartholomew Fair which has been revived in London and which first new Fair in 2000 was begun by a sheep drive over London Bridge by a female celebrity chef. The Fair is medieval in origin, and it came to occupy two weeks at the end of August and beginning of September around St Bartholomew's Day. It was described as a 'phantasma' and was so rumbustuous as to be closed in the 19th century. There are single regular events of similar sort, for example in Ashburton in Devon, the 'Ancient Ale Tasting And

Bread Weighing Ceremony'. This is said to hail from a ceremonial event in the town, commencing in AD820, of quality control of ale and bread.

The Trail and Guide

Leading visitors to events, helping them to plan an itinerary, and showing them how to get to them is all part of the process of packaging and promoting them. Trails serve the aims already mentioned of helping deliver visitors to a breadth of area, and of showing routes and helping them find a way round to occasions and products. In 2001, The Taste of the West Food Trail Guides (www.foodtrails.co.uk) were launched by a UK Government Farming Minister, Lord Whitty, and who emphasized in his launching address the importance of food tourism to the south-west of England economy. The Guides are made available all year long at TICs, visitor attractions, and at farmers' markets, food shops, hotels and restaurants, etc. The 'Simply Appetising' leaflet offered by London Transport with help from the magazine *Time Out* naturally presupposes that London Transport's services will be used for visiting the items listed – 'Food for all tastes by Tube and bus'. These attractions include regular events such as markets; and the traveller is also directed towards a leading School of food and wine.

The Event Overtly for Learning

Holidays or trips away whose focus is learning about food and drink or else about their way of use or preparation or about methods of hospitality range in type as has been said already. Essentially, holidays either gather holidaymakers to learn on site, and maybe with side trips out, or else they are tours, guided or self-guided, to discover food and drink items, production centres and outlets. All are special events in the sense that they have discovery and learning as their particular type of focus. Eric Treuille's handbook *The Guide to Cookery Courses* (2000) conveys the range, which extends from cookery demonstrations and wine tasting at the Edinburgh deli cum restaurant Valvona and Crolla, through the Curry Club Curry Cook-In weekend courses of Indian cookery, to Sydney Seafood School's classes, Pata Negra gastronomic holidays in Andalucia, the Gritti Palace School of Fine Cooking at the Gritti Palace Hotel in Venice, Tasting Places's cooking holidays in Thailand and Italy, and Arblaster and Clarke's worldwide wine tours beginning from the UK. The American *Shaw Guides* deliver a guide on-line to recreational cooking schools over the world from Bhutan to Brazil. As companion to the *Eat Smart* series of guides are Eat Smart Culinary Tours to various countries such as Poland and Turkey. Among the 'empires' of celebrity chefs offering cookery courses are those of Raymond Blanc, Rick Stein, and Anne Willan and Roger Vergé. Under an overt heading of education, The National Trust offered a course in 2001 at its new Brancaster Millennium Centre on the north coast of Norfolk called 'From Sea to Saucepan: Fishy Tales' and which as well as explaining how to cook fish, talked about from where it derives, and included in the course was a harbour trip on a renovated whelk boat and a meeting with a local fisherman. The Ballymaloe Cookery School is part of a wide Ballymaloe complex of experience in Ireland under the aegis of its well-known chef proprietor Myrtle Allen, and as was described in Chapter 8. The group embraces a hotel, restaurant, café and craft and kitchenwareshop at Ballymaloe House, the Cookery School and its Gardens and a café and shop at Shanagarry House nearby, and of other elsewhere items, a gallery, and factory for chutneys and pickles. Ballymaloe displays the cross-fertilization and relationship that is possible between an event of a Cookery School and other items suitable. At the Cookery School itself, gardening and lifestyle courses are offered as well as those on cookery itself.

An example of a professional event and with an academic dimension was the 2001 'inaugural international wine tourism event' of the International Wine Tourism Conference at Margaret River, Western Australia. It was held at a winery, the Leewin Estate and included an expo along with the conference. The Conference overall was 'devoted to educating delegates how related businesses in wine tourism can co-operate to develop a regional product that can compete internationally for a significant share of the tourism market'.

Flavour of Occasion

This chapter has not sought to offer information on *how* to set up and run events and schools. Other books, such as Watt (1998) and Langford-Wood and Salter (1999), go into detail of all dimensions of establishing and operating events. The aim in this chapter has been to give a flavour of the types of events being offered and to show what their main character and components are. They exist, in essence, because an existing provision is not delivering all necessary dimensions, for acting as a medium to drawn attention or redrawing attention to a feature, and for bringing extra income to a provider and for producing a different experience and more or new value to the tourist. They serve well too in working as levers for the social aims of bringing communities into greater communication and integration amongst others and outsiders, and to be occasions for overt or subtle educating and informing. Outside events, such as a fair, show or market or feast, and taking place in public space, are those occasions that can especially occupy the role of bringing vibrancy and interpersonal dialogue.

Chapter 11

The Wine Dimension

Why Wine, Especially?

A selection of core products that are the focus for those food or drink enterprises which are present in tourism are to be discussed in Chapter 12. Another such core product, wine, is being allocated this separate chapter. Giving wine a whole chapter of discussion is not so much that it is an entity more prominent in tourism than other basic food or drink items – through it is certainly emerging as very strong feature (Boniface, 2001, p. 116) – but more for three other reasons. One is that wine tourism is an item appearing to reveal many entities indicative of wine and food tourism generally. The second, obverse, point is that wine tourism seems to be a rather encompassing type of tourism and so to address it is to consider a quite wide, and so informatively useful, feature. The third cause is that wine tourism seems to be emerging into an especial highlight of attention and to be much discussed, and as a part of this it is undergoing industry and academic debate (Dowling, 2001; Hall et al., 2000a (eds)), and so it seems that – as a consequence – it ought to have particular focus here. The considerable look at what is 'going on' in wine tourism and what has been said about it, is to view and evaluate this area itself. It is also too to find what extrapolations can be made and what implications may exist for any other part of food and drink tourism, or for food and drink tourism overall.

Culture, Locale, and Roots

Perhaps part of why wine tourism is becoming such a prominent element is that it maybe represents most overall and prominently what appears to be causing, generally, consumer enthusiasm to pursue food and drink tourism. Discussing holidaying with wine as the objective, Simon paints what is the appeal of the wine holiday but incidentally too is probably conveying why tourists are motivated to travel for food and drink overall. She says,

> 'there are plenty of places where vine-growing and wine-making are still a way of life, inextricably woven into the history and culture; places where, surrounded by his vineyards, the man who made the wine will shake you proudly by the hand and proudly pour you his past three vintages ...

> Dream holidays happen around wine because, it hardly needs saying, the product lends itself to enjoyment and relaxation. They also happen because wine regions usually have other assets. Enchanting landscape is an obvious one ...

Where vines flourish, McDonald's seldom does. Good authentic food is surely a prerequisite for any wine-orientated holiday, and wine and food grow up together in these [wine producing] regions'
(2001, p. 6).

What is being said here is that travel for wine is: for finding a specific lifestyle and culture; for it being a basis for meetings local people; because constituents expected of a holiday of pleasure and relaxation are rendered and in-built; due to scenery of appeal being provided; that being encountered is a natural arena for the real and rooted in food as well as in wine.

The Experience

Hall et al. draw attention to a central aspect of wine tourism to bring its consumer adherence, which is the nature of being experiental (Hall et al., 2000b, pp. 6–8). Mitchell et al. (2000, p. 130) commenting on the imagery in an article about visiting a vineyard, say that this

'suggests that there is more to wine and wine tourism than the simple consumption of a beverage or that this experience is limited to the senses and emotions associated with the wine alone. Wine tourism experiences (as with most tourism experiences) are much more than this, relying on the characteristics of the individual…, the setting in which they occur, socialization with the personalities of wine, and interaction with other elements of the experience such as food, accommodation and other visitors. It is the sum of these elements, not each individually, that make up the winery experience'.

This remark underlines that wine tourism is a good example for showing realities pertaining to many other types of tourism activity and which exist in the experiental realm.

What, Who and Where, and with Distinctive Own Culture?

The role of this chapter is to try to present tourism whose focus is wine. So, as well as trying to show why wine tourism is being considered particularly, it must define what wine tourism is, ask what purposes is serves, and evaluate who is the consumer of wine tourism. Also it needs to present where wine tourism activity is occurring. Important too is that it should consider whether wine tourism operates to its own culture, and if so what it is.

It has already been suggested that wine tourism is a particular operation, and is both quite encompassing but yet is distinctive. Part of the particularity must stem from that wine in its central existence, not in link to tourism, has a special following, and follower, 'the wine lover'. So a stage of specialness is set for wine tourism to occupy as connected entity. This leads to identifying who the wine tourist is. It is reasonable to assume that they are the wine lover and connoisseur, and who is using their holiday for further pursuing their existing interested. De Certeau et al. depict wine drinkers as joyous people compared to those who merely drink water, and they see wine itself as having the 'cultural function' of being 'the festive face of the meal' (1998, p. 90). Also it can be expected that travel by the wine-initiate through relevant regions, and so encountering wine growing and its landscape, will encourage a new member to the group of those appreciating wine. Is, however, wine tourism attracting other markets, and are there special and different entities catering to them and offering, or needing to offer, separate, differently composed experiences, to those consumed and preferred by the wine buff?

Interpreting Wine Tourism

Hall and Macionis offer, with their co-writers, their 1996 definition of wine tourism, that it is 'visitation to vineyards, wineries, wine festivals and wine shows for which grape wine tasting and/or experiencing the attributes of the grape wine region are the prime motivating factors for visitors' (Hall et al., 2000b, p. 3). To the European ears of this writer, this definition has a distinct New World cultural ring to it. A European way of attitude is perhaps more coloured by how wine has been viewed traditionally and over long time in Europe and also how tourism entities are in that part of the world. From a position in the UK, it is suggested that the following can be destinations and act as part of wine tourism: vineyards with their shops, cafés, restaurants, and in instances their hotels; wine shops and other retail outlets; wine trails; wine routes; wine holidays, tours and trips; wine themed attractions and museums; wine bars; wine related events and festivals; restaurants, hotels, pubs and inns whose focus and central item of appeal is wine. Of course, with this range of inclusion, a more wide range of market and appeal too is signified.

Citing Vinopolis, the wine attraction in the UK, as one among examples of cause, Cambourne et al. opine (2000, p. 303) that a broadening of a narrow concept of wine tourism may be needed. They say,

'it is perhaps appropriate to extend the definition of wine tourism beyond the location of vineyards and wineries, to encompass tourism activity influenced by, and occurring within the regional *terroir* or *appellation*. That is, wine tourism becomes tourism activity influenced by the physical, social and cultural dimensions of the winescape and its components'.

This opinion recognizes a cultural element, among others, to the procedure of wine tourism. The activity's extending in physical and geographical terms, however, goes not far, extending only from the immediate vineyard to its regional vicinity. Presenting what a widened definition could embrace in terms of activity and market, and which, essentially, represents wine tourism not being confined solely to operation within either a vineyard or its associated environment, they say

'Conceptualizing wine tourism in a non-wine specific context, such as simply purchasing a bottle of regional wine in a restaurant, cycling or walking through wine country, or eating regional cuisine, broadens both the market and the wine tourism practitioner base. In doing so, it not only expands backward economic linkages, but also recognizes the importance of social and environmental linkages ...'

These remarks lean in their portrayal towards what, from a European perspective seems a 'natural' definition of wine tourism and role for it, and which recognizes wine tourism as to be within a *socio-economic and cultural paradigm.*

It must be assumed that background and situation influence how wine tourism appears and is seen. Dowling and Getz, discussing 'Wine Tourism Futures', convey not only a certain picture of wine tourism but also show why it is coming to strength in contemporary times. They explain,

> 'A recent surge of interest in the formal planning, development and marketing of wine tourism reflects a major, late twentieth century mega-force, the intensification of global competition for tourism, leading destinations and the industry to seek competitive advantage through niche marketing. Also stemming from this force is the increasing linking of tourism to other industries, in this case agriculture and wine, for mutual benefit. This has resulted in many new partnerships and a growing emphasis on joint marketing efforts. A subset of this "partnership" trend is the linkage of various niche markets, such as wine, industrial, cultural and agritourism into more comprehensive, lifestyle packages' (2000, p. 49).

Why the Existence of Wine Tourism?

The elucidation above, though only actually relating to Western Australia, gives context to 'why wine tourism should exist', and in the style described which is of breadth and association. Their explanation could as easily read for why food and drink tourism overall has appeared in the particular formats manifest, and it demonstrates how wine tourism is a useful case to study for wider application among the food and drink tourism realm.

The essential message Dowling and Getz transmit, and if extrapolated onward and outward, is of food and drink tourism being a method with sub-methods, and these of relative freshness and newness, that enable tourism operators in a very competitive situation to connect with distinct markets. Furthermore, the activity of food and drink tourism allows mutual support partnerships to be built up and for helping associates outside tourism and who may be in a weak position and are no longer able to survive alone. In the light of many rural areas being unable to sustain themselves now from solely agriculture, and of certain post-industrial urban areas – and which are home to food and drink production plants – being similarly in a shaky position, and of backward or disadvantaged areas generally usually unable to fend for themselves without aid, it is no wonder that food and drink tourism represents such a mechanism of deployment and hope.

The Complexion of the Wine Tourist

The various cultural elements inputs to the arena of wine tourism have been alluded too somewhat. They range over the culture of vine growing and wine preparation itself and within it the influence of different soil, practice and practitioner. They cover where and how wine is sold and purveyed. In a role of delivering public information being drawn in, ways of dissemination and display are introduced. In delivering a distinct experience related to wine and which offers consumer enjoyment, tourism and its ways, methods and objectives are a specific inclusion. The last main dimension is cultures of the various consumers of wine tourism. From information 'mainly from Australasia' Mitchell et al. (2000, p. 121) portray the wine tourist as in the 30–50 age group, from the 'moderate to high income bracket', and from in or near the relevant wine region. They show that there is a strong similarity with Folwell and Grassel findings (1995, p. 14) of the late 1980s winery visitor in Washington State, USA, as 'middle-aged with an above average income'. Mitchell at al. warn that research being undergone in 1999 in New Zealand by Longo and Mitchell was leading to the indication 'that there are significant differences in winery visitors between regions let alone between countries' (2000, p. 23). They suggest that to identify the wine tourism consumer(s) more clearly attention can usefully focus on consumer lifestyles and values and they describe (pp. 125–126) the lifestyle types the Movimento del Turismo del Vino identifies which are 'The Professional: 30–45 years old', 'The Impassioned Neophyte: 25–30 years old', 'The Hanger-On: 40–50 years old', and 'The Drinker: 50–60 years old'. From the descriptions given, the first two types in degrees of level appear as 'the connoisseur', the third, and the second to a certain amount too, as 'the aspirational', and the fourth as 'the rather heavy and indiscriminate drinker'. It is maybe unwise to try to make an interpretation from these examples, but it could be said that despite that they represent different places and 'voices', there seems to be a certain common picture emanating from them. This is that there is a wine tourist who is enthusiastic for the whole taste, ambience and information of wine, and another wine tourist whose essential interest is in the effects of consuming wine. These two categories still seem to convey an overall audience base whose focus is wine in itself. Also to be taken account of and noticed as featuring are *tourist* types, who are looking for an experience in their various categories such as family group, day visitor, theme park visitor, entertainment seeker, walker, coach tourer etc and for whom wine is an interesting fresh subject to act to deliver new sensation, new focus of holiday, day outing, museum visit, and at bar or restaurant stop. The multi-faceted attraction, such as Vinopolis or Copia can cater to many of these, and just as the wine-emphasis bar, restaurant or hotel – the small Hotel du Vin chain in the UK is an example of the last – meets needs of some. Also to be remembered is that among wine tourists is the specialist wine tourist in the form of the wine purveyor, and the wine tourism industry person and equivalent academic, and whose wine tourism experience will focus upon a trade show or conference as well as on trips to vineyards and wineries etc. A conference embracing a simultaneous visit was the First New Zealand Wine Tourism Conference held in association with Air New Zealand which was staged *at* a winery, the Montana Brancott, and which was depicted as 'a wine tourism complex'.

Information

For wine tourism, as with other food and drink tourism, the stimulation, support and adjunct to tourism visits are pre-information and knowledge. The data needing to be known are both of wine, and of where to travel to find it and its landscape. Publicity material, courses, books, guides etc deliver information in a standard way. The Internet serves a strong function, and as examples of this are: VinoSearch which is a comprehensive database to world's wine regions; the champagne region of France Website which includes a suggested tour itinerary; the burgundy wine Website that is for professionals and amateurs and which embraces information on events and a database of 'over 600 enterprises offering public access'.

Old and New Cultural Shade of Wine Tourism?

In discussion and treatment of wine tourism, and as has been alluded to already, more than a hint exists of difference of flavour of cultural attitude and concept concerning wine and wine tourism between the new growing and freshly followed areas of the New World and those old established and pursued of the Old World. This may stem simply from the long existence of wine being grown in these latter areas and installed as part of their culture. France is probably pre-eminent in this respect. As Barthes comments, 'Wine is felt by the French nation to be a possession which is its very own, just like its three hundred and sixty types of cheese and its culture' (2000, p. 58). Wine is to France as tea is to England or Britain. In the Old World, its vine growing and wine imbibing is seen as a part of its heritage, and it is interesting to observe France delivering in 1999 the first wine-centred World Heritage Site (the Saint-Émilion area), and this was followed by the Alto Douro Wine Region of Portugal, which grows grapes for port wine, being designated a Site in 2001: these both are in the 'cultural landscape' category. In 2000 the Wachau district in Austria was designated a Site, in the group of cultural landscape, and in part due to the long-time activity of viticulture represented. Also, both France's champagne and its burgundy regions, a part of the Rhine valley in Germany, and the Tokaj sweet wine producing area located near Tokay in Hungary, were in early 2002 all at various stages of submission to become Sites on the basis of their grape-growing activity and cultures. That World Heritage Sites are featuring wine areas can only serve to increase their profile as tourism destinations. As indication of the depth and complicatedness of culture France manifests in relation to wine is Frochot's paper on French wine Brotherhoods and wine tourism (Frochot, 2001). France has various festive occasions relating to wine, for example a festival at Saint-Émilion for celebrating the grape harvest, and a party at Beaujeu for the arrival of Beaujolais Nouveau (O'Connor, 2001, p. 14).

Cause of a slight separation in slant, style and emphasis concerning wine tourism between the Old and New World is most likely attributable to the former's longevity of growing vines and producing wine and to its tradition and complacency of way of life. Noticeable is that centre of evaluation and analysis of wine tourism is the New World. Its viticulture and its wine tourism products demonstrate freshness and new-ness and have a character of directness to their style and manner. A comparison made by D'Arcy when discussing wine in South Africa, draws the intended distinction of approach. She says, 'In Europe, wine appreciation might all too often be an excuse for pretension, but in South Africa the gutsy grape is just a good excuse for a bit of fun'. She proceeds to describe a typical day's wine tasting which involves a morning at the beach, thereafter selecting a non-imbiber for the day to be driver, attendance for an inexpensive good lunch at a winery, and to 'then idle away the afternoon at tastings along one of the signposted tourist wine routes' (2001, p. 8). Instinctively this would sound too 'easy' and informal to the European who tends to seek for more of an experience of savour and depth and formality and based on pre-knowledge, planning and some struggle of effort.

The UK in Distinct Position?

Strangely and usually, in the particular instance of wine tourism, the UK seems rather in a position of straddling the Old-New World cultural difference that seems to be pertaining. Essentially, the nation used – a long while past – to grow vines (in climatically possible areas) and then did not do so again until quite recently. She has been mostly in historical times an imbiber rather than grower of wine, and so she has been in cultural environment contributed to by both activities, rather than only the one. The UK is, therefore, somewhat conditioned by an old grower's perspective, but on the whole not directly so. Now it is setting up vine-growing (in parts of the nation) and wine tourism anew, as if it were from the New World, but not in quite complete respect because of the background and context just described. So, 'a revival' is the accurate way to describe today's vine-growing in the UK. This makes the UK an interesting case to view. Along with the cause depicted to consider the UK wine tourism activity are the others referred to much in this book for looking at the UK in relation to food and drink tourism – such as need for diversification from agriculture, food scares bringing increasing preference for organic foods, etc. Also, there is the reason that the UK is a tourism-providing experienced and orientated country, not least due to being particularly far along the way from industrial to service industry and of which latter endeavour tourism is a strong element.

Wine tourism at crop sites in the UK, like wine growing itself, is a not an endeavour of great magnitude but it is burgeoning considerably. Most tourism providers who are vineyards are small, independent operations. However they understand well how to operate appropriately to their type and size. This comprehension shows both in what kind of presentations they are making on site, and in their acceptance of the benefits of promotion and marketing as part of a group as well as by individual effort. They are presenting themselves appropriately to suit their markets. These are, essentially: connoisseurs and knowledgeable persons: family groups looking for a few hours out in the countryside of pleasantness and relaxation and with some facilities of some shopping and simple eating and drinking and for whom wine is not the particular motivation for arrival. Some example of vineyards' tourist provision has provided before this, and so here will only be mentioned very few for being indicative. Frequently other supporting features to those concerning wine directly are delivered. Frome Valley Vineyard offers walks, a Tasting Room, wine purchase and modest refreshments and suggests in its leaflet that it represents a good outing for group visits from such as 'W.I.s [Womens' Institutes], gardening clubs or similar societies'. It offers mail order purchase of wines and it has a website. Carter's Vineyards provide a vineyard trail, a nature trail, an exhibition of renewable energy, wine tastings, a winery, and a tearoom. Wroxeter Roman Vineyard provides a vineyard stroll, wine sampling, lavender fields, 'Old Roman Walls' and rare breed animals all to view, and has a Farm Shop.

Sedlescombe's 'England's Premier Organic Vineyard' delivers a Vineyard and Woodland Nature Trail, a Wine Tasting Bar, Vineyard and Woodland Picnic Areas and a DIY [Do It Yourself] low energy house exhibit. It has Soil Association accreditation and it is 'A Taste of the South East' member.

As has been explained, cooperative promotion is well under way. As examples are the leaflets for East Anglian Vineyards, for Vineyards of the South East from the South East Vineyards Association, for The Vineyards of the West of England and of Wales from the South West Vineyard Association. English Wine Producers have a Web site. An independent endeavour is the UK vineyard Website which Oliver Richardson at Brunel University has set up from interest and which lists English and Welsh 'tourist-orientated vineyards' and which also delivers history of British wine production. Delivered in 1998 by compilation of Gerry Symons was *Jancis Robinson's Map of the Vineyards of England and Wales* (Symons, 1998) which displays in – handy for travellers – map form the vineyards of the United Kingdom Vineyards Association members. Jancis Robinson is a UK wine authority who edited *The Oxford Companion to Wine* (1999).

It can be seen that there is low key but well organized promotion of UK vineyards and these features generally characterize the vineyards' visitor presentations themselves. As has been already emphasized, there is not, as yet, a UK wine central visitor experience to equate to the USA's Copia. Nonetheless, in its fresh incarnation as a wine producing area, the UK can compare well – in certain respects – with somewhere approximately equivalent in duration of how long it has been growing vines and attempting wine tourism. This example of comparison is the Margaret River area of Western Australia of which expert opinion is 'that it "probably has, overall the greatest quality of any wine region in the world"' (Ottaway, 2000, p. 7) but which while possessing 'some great little hotels and restaurants', yet in 2001 had no guidebook available locally to its region.

What can be defined in the UK as wine tourism can encompass more than vineyards and their facilities and travels round them. Bars, inns, restaurants and hotels which have a wine focus, and wine merchants' shops and outlets, all of which are so special in the dimension of their wine and associated ambience for this to lead them to being a destination can be included. Wine tourism in the UK does not just embrace what is contained and grown there. As an affluent nation, and moreover which has a taste for wine, and which generates tourists to go overseas, it will regard as part of its wine tourism activity to visit places of vine growing, wine purchase and consumption in other countries. The firm Winetrails is indicative of a specialist operator catering to the need and which offers long haul destinations to independent travellers with wine as the object but which, as so often occurs in food and drink tourism, brings in other elements, in this instance cycling and walking (D'Arcy, 2001, p. 8).

Reviewing wine tourism across the world, it can be seen that, of countries and regions engaging in it, not all are at same stage in catering to tourists, or seeing it the same and displaying the same style and emphases. This appears much due to their culture and background. The New World seems most to interpret wine tourism as vineyard and winery visiting and it is delivering a tourism product of matter-of-factness and which is having considerable assessment of how the process is going which includes academic evaluation. The Old World – Europe essentially – seems more to be applying wine tourism as an extra item for attaching to a long everyday lifeway of wine production and wine imbibing and which colonizes and deploys the traditions and activities associated with wine-making. A dimension to wine tourism in some places of the Old World is that it is an activity being set among a context of rural disadvantage and agricultural crisis. Organic wine production is a feature too, and in the UK the emergence of this is linked to a general move to organic foodstuffs and encouraged by public worries about the quality of food and drink made by large industrial processes.

Culture and Ambience

Probably central to what is happening and to the success, touristically, is how much the wine industry is understanding how to move to operate in the field of tourism. In several places in this chapter the word 'ambience' has been used, and it seem clear that the wine tourist – above all among food and drink tourists – is drawn to and expects to 'buy into' total ambience and rich cultural association. A wine industry catering to tourists needs to appreciate this. Williams writes on how wine tourism destinations are evolving from presenting a visitor image of production and process to one that displays a recognition about tourists. This latter is that tourists are nowadays liable to require aesthetic and experiental features and to want items to deliver these around wine as the central focus (Williams, 2001). Much of this chapter points to what Cambourne et al. observe, that 'tourism and the wine industry are inexorably linked' (2000, p. 298). This coexistence, fully seen and recognized, should offer considerable potential to wine tourism, and for a shape of culture to it of distinctiveness and interest, and maybe to act as indicator and guide to other portions of food and drink tourism.

Chapter 12

From Among the Cornucopia

Indicative Choice

Wine as it features in food and drink tourism was discussed in Chapter 11. This was because it serves as a particular matter among food and drink tourism. This chapter will follow by discussing some from among the many other items to act as points of focus to food and drink tourism. They have been selected to serve as indicative of the wide cornucopia that is being used. This chapter, therefore, is about certain food and drink items that are being vehicles of food and drink tourism.

The Wholesome and the Exotic: the Different

It appears that the range in tourism use falls into two main characterizations in the tourist's mind, though one far from necessarily excluding the other – as will be shown. The perception may be overt or unconsciously present. The first type is food and drink that the tourist sees as traditional, wholesome, fundamental, real, authentic, and artisan-delivered, and 'true' in some way that food and drink from mass and large industrialized processes are seen as having lost. The items are regarded as having depth, and heritage and good cultural 'story'. They are identified with everyday consumption, but a style of a time gone by. Speciality and homemade bread, farmhouse cheese, beer, cider – and wine, of course – are examples of the category. The other type of food and drink is that which to the tourist is 'from abroad', and which in everyday life is only used very occasionally – such as for a special meal, or else is not obtainable at all without a journey to its source. It is distinctive to a place, and is rare and exotic to the tourist, albeit that among its home community it may be very 'everyday'. The very large tendency is that both groups of food and drink will bear the typification of being local and not obtainable anywhere in the world with equivalent efficacy to a McDonald's hamburger or a Starbucks latte, and albeit that in reality some items may be found fairly readily in many parts of the world. The matter is both consumer *perception* of specialness, and that food and drink obtained locally carries the connotation of greater freshness that that which has journeyed long 'food miles'. It appears too that added value, and including more status among home-base peers, accrues for the tourist in buying an item at its place of origin even if it can be, and is also, purchased by the tourist also on their home ground. Among the items in the group are honey – because though an everyday item in generic terms it conveys different flavours according to the nature of the environment of the bees providing it – and also jam, sweets such as Turkish Delight and Calissons d'Aix, condiments, herbs, special cakes, particular types of coffee and tea, and kinds of alcoholic drinks such as ouzo, raki, pastis, and aperitifs and liqueurs special to an area. If the tourist is merely visiting the locale of items, seeing how they are produced, and consuming them there, then that some goods are perishable is no difficulty, but if items are also for bringing home then the field is narrowed to those which will 'keep' and also that can be reasonably easily transported and which home regulations allow admittance to.

The second sector of goods takes on more obviously the categorization of 'exotica' because they are not routine in some way. However, the first category is as much exotic to the tourist because its goods, in the kind depicted, are unusual. The most same base food as that of home, unless of most truly globalized manifestation, will have a different culture of background and operation in a place that is not home. So, for the tourist – and importantly – both types depicted here are 'non-everyday'. Essentially, any item of food and drink encountered while travelling will have a different dimension and so will act to engender interest in the tourist and which they have time to pursue.

The discussion above focused mainly on the items themselves. However, when the circumstance delivered is that the object being pursued by the tourist is not merely the item itself but also, and often, more its production process and environment and/or its way of preparation for consumption, then a non-everyday matter is very easily the delivery. The feature then being offered is an overall *experience*.

This chapter is to look, therefore, at certain food and drink items which act as the focus of various entities to appeal to tourists. Some others, bread and jam, as examples, have been considered as part of the discussion of other chapters; and Chapter 11 addressed wine. To the food and drink tourist, an item very rare and/or distinct to an area is bound to act as a magnet to visit. Therefore for the purpose here, which is to see how food and drink items can be used to render tourism attractions, it has been regarded as appropriate to choose for discussion a greater proportion from those of core and common type. This is since these appear ostensibly as more of challenge to use for causing a tourist visit.

Foods

Honey

The appeal to the consumer of honey can be seen as: its connotation of age of use as a sweetener; that it is produced naturally by bees; that it displays the flavour of different environments from the different flowers from which the bees draw nectar to process.

The basic product is a honeycomb. Human intervention is required to create and manage the honey-making context of the hive, to gather the honeycomb, and to do processing to render liquid honey and of different extent according to whether clear or thick consistency is required. The culture to be viewed, therefore, is the human method of intervention in honey being produced – breeding and keeping bees is called apiculture – and the method and lifestyle delivering a particular honey's territory of context with its flora. A whole region of France, Lozére denotes itself as

'Honey's Land' that is 'safe from any local pollution, in a sane environment that is rich with an exceptional and wild flora' and 'skill [sic] bee-keepers'.

Farm gate promotion and sale of honey is a familiar entity and is frequently a very small and modest operation. It is, nonetheless, appealing to tourists in offering an experience of meeting the local apiarist or farmer and their environment together with purchasing a 'piece of a place' at very inexpensive cost. Chain Bridge Honey Farm, 'A Hive of Industry', operates on a larger, focused, scale at its location. It overtly caters for visitors, including parties, with a dedicated Visitor Centre giving information on the bee subject. Its apiaries are throughout north Northumberland and the Scottish Borders. Admission to the Farm is free, so income comes from a shop selling honey, beeswax candles and propolis (bee-gum) that has long-known antibiotic properties. As another example is Quince Honey Farm which produces considerable amount of honey, mainly clover honey, from hives round north Devon but with some heather honey due to hives being taken to Exmoor for a period in the summer each year. Quince Farm has 20 observation hives at its site at South Molton (Webster, 2000, p. 44). As a different style of enterprise in the UK is Berrow Honey, situated near Worcester, which puts particular focus on bee-breeding. It is a member of the Bee Improvement and Bee Breeding Association [BIBBA]. Berrow Honey and wax and candles are retailed through local Farmers' Markets, and shops and farms shops. In London is The Hive Honey Shop which, in addition to selling honey, has an observation hive – behind glass – and from which a tube allows the bees into the shop's back garden. The UK capital is also host to the National Honey Show (Webster, 2000, p. 44).

Meat

A long and central connotation of meat as food is with hunting, as opposed, for example, to growing which is the method of arrival of much food and drink. This is albeit that meat is now largely farmed, and that even game shooting is customarily a managed activity. Meat has, therefore, a culture concerning skill in animal capture and killing, and one of animals being bred and raised. Meat relates to cultural choices: with religion, belief, conscience, ethic, preference, value and interpretation, and availability, driving these. Some people are vegetarians and vegans and eat no meat of any kind. Some groups consume only certain types. Islam demands butchery of a certain style, called halal. The turkey is strong in North American culture party just due to presence but mostly because traditionally it is consumed at the family supper of Thanksgiving Day.

The dimensions briefly spoken of are in and among society and so they sit amid tourism. It can be seen that differing cultural ways with, and attitudes towards, meat will be displayed by countries and areas visited and by those visiting them.

Concerning the UK, Urry reports:

'Eating beef has been particularly significant within British culture. Roast beef and Yorkshire pudding signify middle-class suburban taste that has become generalised. Roast beef is normally consumed within the family: it stands for family life. It is thought that roast beef is good for one: to consume roast beef is a right of the British'
(Urry, 2000, p. 171).

He describes the scares of BSE and vCJD – each disease involving cattle – and implies the blow to their essence of being caused to the British. For the tourist to Britain, probably their two most possible encounters or visits in relation to beef will be the Tower of London's yeoman warder Beefeaters in their bright traditional garb and Simpsons in the Strand's dining-room baron of beef. Denhay Farms near Bridport in Dorset is an example of a farm which welcomes visitors to a farm shop and which has pork (air dried ham, gammon dry cured bacon, cured meat sausages) as focus, along with cheese. Denhay suggests suitable recipes for its products. A beef farm from which naturally-reared Aberdeen Angus beef can be purchased direct is Church Farm, Shrawley, north-west of Worcester and said as in 'Worcestershire' – the old pre-1974 county. It has the support facility of Farm House Flora that offers dried flowers, and in season, The Christmas Barn that provides Christmas decorations. As an example of a 'destination' butcher is F. E. Neave in the Suffolk village of Debenham and who deploys local free range stock, and whose speciality at its premises is 'curing and smoking, using old country recipes'. Its essential focus is pork – ham, bacon, pies and sausages. The firm is a member of both Tastes of Anglia and Food from Britain. Its activity draws attention to the culture of how meat is prepared.

Fish

Fish has particular cultural significance to Christians. Like meat, fish has an existence from of old as a food being caught rather than grown. Nowadays, it is farmed as a premeditated, and often, rather than rare, activity, and as well as being caught in the wild – and even this latter is usually now a managed endeavour. Unlike the production process of meat, which is not customarily appealing or visible – apart from animals being seen grazing – the process of catching fish is more appealing and fishing's culture and circumstance are more inviting and picturesque. Sea-water fishing has rendered a distinct cultural milieu and aura. It has delivered coastal and estuarine communities with people, boats, buildings and trappings particular to the endeavour. Even just to say 'fishing village' is to conjure the picture of bobbing boats, old nets and 'old-salts' and to deliver an image of tourist appeal. The general environmental appealing-ness apart, usually either or both of shop/market purchase and café/restaurant consumption of fresh fish is possible from waterfront or nearby premises. An added dimension of attraction to the circumstances of fishing is that visitor *participation* is possible. A fishing opportunity or lesson can be available on sea or river and a trip on sea or river can be made in an existing or erstwhile fishing boat.

The chance of fresh fish to eat will make people travel. Also, in being a special area of food, this acts as lure too. The 'empire' of restaurants, hotel and cooking school in Cornwall of Rick Stein (Ellis, 2001, pp. 200–201) is an example conveying the truth. The endeavour is helped and supported by Stein's amount of celebrity from books and television series'. A similar complex – quite some portion of which is operated by the one firm of The Whitstable Oyster Fishery Company – is at Whitstable, a town at the mouth of the Thames estuary in Kent which has been a special site for oysters since Roman times. There are converted fishermen's huts to rent as accommodation, a hotel, and seafood restaurants and bars (pp. 74–75, p. 243). The culture is permeated with 'London-ness' due to its relative proximity to the UK capital and especially by having – together with road – rail and river linking it to London (Wright, 1999, p. 11). At Abbotsbury Oyster Farm in Dorset, visitors are able to see the oyster farming process and eat at the seafood bar that overlooks 'Britain's oldest water reserve'. Rayner, praising the place, says, 'The Oyster Farm is not a pretty place, but it is lousy with authenticity' (2002). Not far inland from this, at Longbridge Deverill, is the Purely Organic Trout Farm and Shop. Soil Association criteria are met for trout whose water has arrived through beds of organic watercress. Watercress is a particular traditional item of this general area of England. The item is sold at the shop along with other organic vegetables and fruit, and together with local honey etc.

As a type of building concerning fish, and with a process of novelty and interest for the tourist, is the smoke-house. As operating examples of fish smoke-houses are those – whose main focus is the herring – on the Danish island of Bornholm in the Baltic Sea, and many of which have accompanying shops. At the smoke-house at Hasle is a museum devoted to the subject of the smoke-house and also some smoked fish can be consumed.

Cheese

For relevant countries and places, cheese is a way of displaying cultural distinctiveness. France overall presents – as General de Gaulle's famous remark about the impossibility of governing a nation of so considerable a number of different cheeses displays – an identity linked with cheese, albeit that, as de Gaulle's comment was clearly suggesting, that persona is composed of much individual difference within it. France's variety of cheese is at the core of the appeal to the tourist of the country in food terms. This is along with wine being the corresponding essential matter of appeal in the drink category. The example of France displays how cheese lends itself easily for showing variation and difference. So, cheese is a particularly suitable and obvious item for deploying for tourism because it provides a matter for showing distinctiveness of place and a cause to visit a site of production.

As France's 'king' cheese, Roquefort has this special position to encourage visitors to go to its centre in the town of Roquefort sur Soulzon in south-western France. Producers such as Societé and Papillon offer free tours of the natural caves, the traditional sites for maturing the cheese that has been already made elsewhere. Farm tours in 'Roquefort country' are also on offer. The catchment area for the ewe's milk to provide Roquefort covers a large portion of nearby countryside, including the low-population-density limestone Causses [plateaux] to the east-north-east of the town of Roquefort, and so the cheese is a major contribution to local livelihood of this remote and disadvantaged area. Roquefort also has high-profile and symbolism from being the French global product suffering from 'tit for tat' of increased import tax to the USA after France had banned import of USA hormone-injected beef, and to bring the anti-junk food cause celèbre incident – of repercussion and anti-globalization activism on the world stage – of José Bové's assault on his local McDonald's at Millau, a town not far distant from Roquefort sur Soulzon. On one Causse, Méjean, and in a village catering to tourists is a cheese factory, employing 17 people and using milk from sheep of 14 local producers, described as representing 'a taste of life' on the Causse Méjean. It has an accompanying café-restaurant and retail outlet from which are obtainable free recipes for using local produce. From further north than the Causses comes the Bleud'Auvergne, an AOC [Appellation d'Origine Contrôlée] cheese, which acts as the focus of a whole festival in tourist season.

The Cheese Market at Alkmaar in The Netherlands which dates from 1622, albeit that the town has a longer tradition of connection with cheese, is described by Solazzi as 'one of Holland's major tourist attractions' and which is 'visited every year by more than three hundred thousand people from all over the world' (2001, p. 106). It has a ritual of procedure. She says it is now 'possibly more a matter of folklore than business. The vendors are not small producers' (p. 107), and with the huge majority of produce being that of the cheesemakers' association of Noord-Hollandse. But even with this outcome the cheese is nonetheless local and almost all of it young Gouda, with Edam and herb cheeses being the rest.

In the UK, a festival for British cheese overall is held at the end of September, and which encompasses: the announcement of the British Cheese Awards; a cheese market; cheesemaking demonstrations; tastings and workshops; special lunches and dinners. The event, held at a location in or near the tourist area of the Cotswolds, is sponsored by a major supermarket and the BBC [British Broadcasting Company] *Good Food* magazine. Among handmade cheesemakers in the UK acting as tourism features is Monkland Cheese Dairy that has revived a century-old cheese, Little Hereford. Visitors can see the stages of producing cheese and there is a café, which serves 'Little Hereford' ploughman's lunch along with homemade cakes, tea, coffee, ciders, wine and soft drinks. There is also a shop selling a range of farmhouse cheeses. As a smaller visitor entity in the same county of Hereford and Worcester is Mars Goats at St Michael's Farm which produces goats' cheese and milk and is open to visitors to its door. In the tourist and foodie centre of Ludlow (Moss, 2002, pp. 28–35), a town in Shropshire not far from either of these two, is Ludlow's a shop offering cheese and speciality food and which has a Cheese Café. At England's north eastern end is the Northumberland Cheese Company that has a fromagerie, tea room, and offers tastings of its prize-winning cheeses, and which invites visits with the slogan 'Come and Savour the Real Taste of Northumberland'. It has too a farm shop offering a wider range of produce. Part of the cause of re-emergence and new introduction of British farmhouse cheese can be attributed to the presence and promotion of the shop Neal's Yard Diary whose outlet in Covent Garden has become a tourist stopping point. It also purveys other special British Isles produce such as oatcakes, and, in season, apples from Brogdale Horticultural Trust (see below and Chapter 6). Food from Britain has nonetheless noticed (2000) that the 450 cheeses produced in the UK are yet neither well-known to the home market or people overseas.

The Apple

It can be seen how much cheese – even when a type has become a global entity – can serve to portray and represent place, localness, and distinctiveness. Like beef, regarded by the British (or is it only the English?) as especially their own, and as part of their identity and way, is the apple. Twiss says, 'The apple is more firmly rooted in our history and culture than any other fruit' (1999, p. 4). The Chairman of

Brogdale Horticultural Trust, Earl Selborne explains the feature and the further range of extent, saying,

> 'Apples and apple orchards are part of our cultural heritage. They have helped to shape not only our landscape, our economy and our taste in food and drink, but our mythology, religious beliefs, art and language' (2001, p. 7).

Brogdale, which is in Kent – a main apple-growing area, is open to visitors. It is the home of the National Apple Collection and its heritage is as a former Ministry of Agriculture Research Station. Now funding is also from Wye Agricultural College which is part of the University of London and by revenue from visitors who can partake of tours, can patronize the tearoom and shop, and can buy or order rootstocks of a variety of soft and top fruits from the plant centre. In October they can attend the annual Apple Festival during which time an exhibit of a huge variety and tradition is displayed and with many types available to buy and some for tasting concurrently, and a number of workshops and lectures being provided.

The presence of the apple in Britain is thought to be attributable to the arrival by invasion of the Romans, and with the crab apple being already native to Britain. The apple features in Classical and Celtic religion and in these cultures and those of Persia, and too in legends of Scandinavia (Morgan and Richards, 2001). The apple had revived interest in Western Europe through the Cistercians and their culture of 'manual labour and cultivation of abbey lands' (p. 25). In England, the fruiterer of Henry VII established a major fruit collection in Kent that helped plant the country as an apple area. Cider (see below) was the product of the large part of apples in Europe in the Middle Ages. The arrival of Protestantism in the 17th century delivered a boost to the apple and apple orchards as they had the right character of attraction. Morgan and Richards say 'of all the tree fruits, it was the apple that appealed to Protestant sensibilities most. Apple trees were neither greedy nor temperamental' (p. 56). English varieties of apple number 6,000 and 'Most are extremely localised' (Coward, 2000, p. 9). Coward depicts that the apple is the focus of a project of the organization Common Ground to 'revitalize orchards' and which she reports the Director of Common Ground as saying, is for reason of this:

> 'Underneath the economic argument, there are also cultural and ecological arguments.... If you pull out an orchard it's not just losing a few trees but a way of life. Apples and apple orchards have the same symbolic importance for the English landscape and culture as olive groves for the Italians or vineyards for the French. They are a traditional food source, whose cultivation shapes local landscapes, imagination, diets and wildlife. If there is no place for English apples it would destroy more than livelihoods'.

Common Ground has given the lead in bringing about a whole range of Apple Days and events at the time of the apple harvest's completion and of schoolchildrens' half-term holiday. These embrace apple games, displays, tastings, pruning demonstrations, orchard walks, and special apple foods and menus, etc. Common Ground describes Apple Day as 'an annual celebration of apple orchards and local distinctiveness'. A major provider of apple events as part of the promotion is The National Trust. It should be remembered that Common Ground has shown its attention to apples and orchards to the extent of producing a whole book on orchards (2000). It was called upon in an earlier chapter.

With the apple as a ubiquitous product, perhaps the main challenges for the UK small-scale apple producer and who wishes to be a visitor venue, are how to create sufficient interest in the consumer to venture to their site and how to encourage the consume to choose their place from another. Norbury's Norrest Farm is a farm for pears and cherries in addition to apples – though these last act as the central type featuring. Its feature is to be a PIY [Pick Your Own] location and so it is only open in the picking season that extends from June/July to October. Available on site during this time are Norbury's Cider, Perry and Fruit Wines but which all year round can be obtained at a nearby garden centre. Jus tries to make itself stand out by its product being single variety apple juice and a selection of which are obtainable from its home base, Glebe Farm in 'Herefordshire' (a county abolished in 1974 – when it merged with Worcestershire to become Hereford and Worcester – as has been said already) or else the product is found at a retailer. Jus' promotional leaflet speaks to the tourist, saying,

> 'Looking for something different to take home? Apples are one of Herefordshire's treasures but they are seasonal and not always available. However their flavours can be found in single variety apple juices. So take home a memory of Herefordshire's orchards in a bottle. It makes a good present for friends as well'.

As a last example, also self-depicted as in 'Herefordshire', is Dragon Orchard, which reveals itself as 'a small traditional fruit farm'. The owners have produced the concept of 'Dragon Orchard Cropsharers' which 'offers … the unique opportunity to share in the life and abundance of the orchard.' It is asking for help for this orchard to be preserved. Its events were described in Chapter 10. For a subscription a member of the public is offered – as well as four Open Weekend visits a year, guided walks, seasonal celebrations – quarterly newsletters, and a share of the autumn crop of apples, pears, single variety apple juice, cider and preserves (jams). The promotional leaflet for the scheme provides the quote 'The apple we eat is the landscape we create'. It gives too to an extract vaunting the speciality and importance of the orchard from *The Common Ground Book of Orchards*.

Drinks

Cider

Following considering apples, it is a rather obvious next step to turn to cider. It goes naturally alongside cider in development and custom. As an example of the latter in the UK is 'Wassailing the orchards on the eve of Twelfth Night – the practice of thanking or appeasing the deity of apple trees to ensure next year's crop – [which] became one of the most important events of the year in cider counties' (Morgan and Richards, 2001, p. 145). Cider counties were those where the climate and the soil suited the cider endeavour best, essentially the west of England – Herefordshire, Somerset and Devon particularly but Worcestershire also – and with Norfolk and

Kent and Sussex as outlier sites (Foot, 1999, p. 11). That Britain was invaded in the 11th century by people from Normandy – an area with a strong apple focus – and production of cider in monasteries assisted cider's strong role in Britain. Morgan and Richards depict that 'By the end of the 17th century, cider and cider making had become part of the fabric of English rural life' (Morgan and Richards, 2001, p. 145). Its main connotation has tended to be as drink which is 'rough' (Foot, 1999, p. 10) and of the people, albeit that a 'smooth' persona and regal and aristocratic use existed too. Cider's basic link has been with agriculture and its way of life. Foot says that 'Bulmers, based in Herefordshire, are the biggest producers in the world' (p. 11). Bulmers offers tours of its plant in Hereford by appointment, and there is a shop, and snacks are available. Cider can be seen as being culturally a special British/English item in association with the apple so being. As has been listed earlier, CAMRA publishes a separate guide to good cider (Mathews, 2000). The following are representatives of small-scale 'Herefordshire' cidermakers, and differing considerably lot from Bulmers as the most large in scale. One firm is Gwatkin Cider and Perry – the latter beverage made from pears – and which drinks the firm describes are 'a long farmhouse tradition' and which has produced a CAMRA 'National Cider of the Year'. It chooses to sell through local outlets and with mail order on offer. By contrast Dunkertons Cider Mill, producing 'essentially sophisticated farmhouse cider' offers tours of the Mills by appointment and for a fee and with the pressing area open to visitors 'whenever possible' and without charge. Access to orchards depends on whether cattle that may be grazing the orchards are in presence. There is a shop and Cider House Restaurant. Weston's is a cider maker who has an award-winning organic cider. Weston's 'original mill and press can both be seen ... in the garden of the farmhouse at the mill' (Winslade, 2001, p. 75) and in the museum other machinery is on view. There is a restaurant at the mill called The Scrumpy House. As is befitting, Hereford, as the old county town of Herefordshire, is home to a Cider Museum that explains how cider has been made over time.

For a comparison with these items in the old Herefordshire is The Somerset Distillery and Burrow Hill Cider Farm. Visitors to the centre site, Pass Vale Farm, can purchase draught and bottled cider and also apple juice and cider vinegar. Both cider and cider brandy can be sampled. On view in the ciderhouse is 'all the paraphernalia associated with 150 years of cidermaking'. The copper stills located in a new distillery can be admired through armoured glass. The brandy is available at London outlets such as A.Gold in Spitalfields – whose stock is English traditional produce – as well as from local outlets and certain cider farms over western England. Orders can be made through the firm's Web site.

Beer

Beer and ale are seen as synonymous but originally they differed in that ale was made without hops. Beer is another item seen by the British/English as especially theirs and a part of their culture. Germany and north west Europe similarly see beer as mainstream in their culture. Beer's particular strongness as a feature of the British/English cultural landscape is probably as much due to that it has a distinct place allocated for it to be especially imbibed in the pub as for its intrinsic features. In the UK, beer and ale have associations of being proletarian rather than grand and which stems from them being drinks of agricultural and factory workers. The very ubiquity of beer and pubs in the UK mean that they are unlikely to serve as tourist features – except as parts of absorbing a neighbourhood or community experience – without some distinctiveness being offered. The pub is made able to show itself as different from others through style of operation and facilities and add-ons, but beer can only do so in showing distinctiveness of self and preparation compared with mass-produced and large type and brand varieties. Ireland by contrast, though having other beers, is defined by beer of this latter kind and nationally, and which is by Guinness. In the UK, beer was early off the ground as a representative of a consumer backlash against mass production and commodification in food and drink and towards what was perceived as 'real'. Individual, small-producer brewed, and draught (in bulk, and from a beer cask or keg) as more preference than bottled, beers arrived as a considerable sector of choice. The formation of CAMRA resulted from, and encouraged, the overall impulse. The essential likely beer-related options to visit for the tourist can be categorized as: pubs, inns and bars; breweries; festivals.

The St Peter's Brewery Group is an encompassing example of a kind portraying itself as special and innovative. The Group's home location is St Peter's Hall in Suffolk and in whose former agricultural buildings the Brewery is located. The Hall itself is a restaurant and bar and which offers brewery tours. Beers are distributed around the UK in casks and also in distinctive bottles, and in these latter they go overseas too. They can be found in hotels, restaurants, pubs etc and in supermarkets, food stores and off-licences. As other parts of the St Peter's Brewery Group are: the de La Pole Arms which is a country pub with restaurant in a 16th century building; the Jerusalem Tavern in London which – though in name dates from the 12th century – is now in occupation of a building dating from 1720. A brewery of comparison is 'Britain's only thatched Brewery' (though in actuality only a portion is thatched), Palmers, at Bridport, Dorset. The Brewery has been in continuous production on its site since 1794. It offers tours three days a week in tourist season, and has a Wine Store.

As an event concerning beer is the beer festival. Peterborough Beer Festival is one such, and which has been running since 1978. In 2001, it ran over six days, featuring different draught real ales numbering over three hundred, and emanating from over a hundred independent breweries across Britain. Too, traditional cider and perry featured: Gwatkins, mentioned above, were displaying. Exhibits of unpasteurized bottled beer from Europe were also present. Noticeable is that while the drink was featuring and real and traditional, the food on offer was unremarkable and of the international junk-food type, though French crepes and German sausages maybe could be regarded as exceptions.

Whisky

While it is made in other parts of the world such as the USA, whisky/whiskey is pre-eminently a drink from Scotland, but with Ireland's whiskey to the fore and as a close UK competitor. In both countries the drink is a focus of tourist enthusiasm, and has many individual distillers in the style of the individual small brewers of beer. It is thought possible that Irish monks brought whisky to Scotland. It was first noted in writing as present in 1494 (Brown, 2000, p. 10) and probably with monasteries as one main production centre. Whisky became a part of the Scottish home in the area called the Highlands – 'whisky making was associated with the home much as baking a cake is today' – and apparently it was consumed thrice daily for medicinal purposes and as focus of a break. Farmers sold whisky 'on a part-time basis' along with their crops. Whisky in Scotland is either Malt, Grain or Blended, the first with barley as its only cereal and subdividing into being single or vatted (a blend), the second being a mixture of barley with other and cereals, and the third being Malt and Grain in combination (p. 15). Its areas are Highland, Lowland, Islay and Campbeltown (pp. 16–17). Whisky trails and visits are a strong and established feature of the Scottish tourism offer. Among distilleries of well-known whiskies is the Glenlivet Distillery in Banffshire. It is open to the public in tourist season and explains its production process in several languages. It has a shop and coffee shop. Many, but not all distilleries are open to the public but often visits need to be by appointment. An event with whisky focus, and serving as a vehicle of information and for promoting distillery visits, is the Spirit of Speyside Whisky Festival held in early May which conveys a generally strong Scottish Highland and/or Celtic cultural flavour through music and ceilidhs (dancing, singing and story-telling gatherings).

Other Drinks

The examples above are of well-known drinks that show cultural distinctiveness and which are acting as subject of items of tourist visit. Many other types could be called upon, and from both alcoholic beverages and soft drinks. Drinks range from the famous branded and global type to the ultra-local and distinctive. Of the latter – and along with wines – aperitifs, digestifs, liqueurs, brandies and whiskies, offer a particular opportunity for showing local and cultural flavour of distinctiveness, much as cheese does so as a food. As an example of representation are the drinks of the small firm on the Causse du Larzac in France – where José Bové resides – called D'Homs. This firm produces a Pastis of aniseed along with plants familiar to the region, Chantelune which uses the gentiane of the hills of the Cévennes or the Aubrac, and finally the Eglantine des Causses which uses a traditional recipe and whose base is the sweetbrier or wild rose. In tune with its main tourist season and its place among a nation whose countrymen tend to take their holidays at once and mostly in high summer, D'Homs shop is only open in July and August but it can be visited by arrangement the rest of the year.

Food and Drink Acting as Subjects of Tourism, and as Cultural Conveyors

The particular examples in this chapter have been used to demonstrate how types of food and drink are acting as the subject of features to which tourists are drawn and led. They serve to reveal how a gamut of foods and drink are, or can be used, in among tourism. They have revealed how much custom, belief, ritual and tradition – folklore and myth even – can be held and conveyed in a food in its process of production and method of preparation. It has been shown in this chapter that for a food and drink to act well in tourism it needs to have some sort of feature of not being 'everyday'.

The 'Home-Made' Difference

Ironically, one obvious way for this difference to routine being delivered is in a product being 'home-made' since many food and drink items are not grown or prepared from start and totally on home premises nowadays – due to amount of time and intensity of labour needed and not being available – and rather often meals being merely heated and consumed, or just only the last. Within this 'home-made' category can come such as cakes, jams, and pickles and alongside it is the 'home-grown' section of vegetables, herbs and fruits. As close relative of this kind is the sector that is rendering special, non-everyday types of a usual item: bread is an example from among these.

The Difference of Specialness and Unusualness

Then, extending out from this certain sort of entity is the whole wide realm of the what is deemed the speciality product, and which is not usual to everyday because it is foreign, is not easily obtainable, or is 'foreign' as in 'not often used' – Tabasco sauce for example.

The Object of Fame and Global Notoriety

The quite different type of food and drink item to appeal to tourists and whose production and home they will be interested to see is the famous product – the global entity. An example of this is Cadbury's chocolate, and which item has alongside its factory has a theme park type attraction 'Cadbury World' catering to visitors – this has already been mentioned – and to which has now been added 'Cadbury Land' among other new features.

Matters for Recognition

The important matters for recognition in relation to food and drink items as tourism subjects and objects are these: how much food and drink carries information and cultural signification and which can interest the tourist; how necessary it is that the relevant food and drink should communicate and represent enough not of 'everyday' to render it of appeal for holiday time and experience. To the tourist, the foods and drink to form attractions to them when on holiday must represent speciality foods in some way or another or if they do not then, instead, their circumstances and context must be special.

Chapter 13

The Crop Now, and For Sowing in Future

The Crop, and the Cultural Input

This book has shown food and drink as entities that convey culture and which are used culturally. The **way** that food and drink's raw materials are produced, collected, used, prepared and consumed; the differing **peoples** making the deployment of food and drink; the **place** that is context to food and drink and the type of land rendering them; the situation, **occurrence** and **belief** with which individual items of food and drink, or food and drink overall, are associated; these all manifest and provide distinct group cultures of manner of treatment and perception of attitude towards food and drink. Culture has been demonstrated as bringing influence from the past and making input to our contemporary food and drink ways, practices and attitudes. As one position to have emerged currently is for society – or groups among it – to treat food and drink as objects of tourism. Threads and instincts from history pertaining and relevant now; society's current flavour and composition; today's social contexts, and which deliver demands for food and drink tourism on grounds of economics, development, and politics, as well as by cause of culture; are influencing the arrival of food and drink tourism as a distinct and directly pursued entity.

The preceding chapters have sought to portray what is happening in food and drink tourism, for what reasons, by what derivation, and who are consumers, providers, and stakeholders, and to show culture's integral presence in the endeavour. This chapter will summarize and define the main entities relating to food and drink tourism and its emergence and will demonstrate where culture has been the cause of them and how culture is sitting. From this assessment it is hoped that sufficient clear characterization will have been provided of what has been produced and achieved, and the reasons for this, to indicate and suggest a likely future shape of activity and to portray what in cultural terms will be its conditioning influences. In essence this chapter's purpose is to state what drives food and drink tourism and, using this information, to suggest what can be opportunities, emphases, and steps for its onward path. This chapter will show today's crop of outcome and portray the potential – and hazard – of what could next be sown.

The Complexity of Cultural Realm Participating

This book's discussion and example has revealed that three different areas need view when food and drink tourism is considered. They are: the food and drink domain and its practices; the tourism industry and its wants and style; society's flavour and need. An inter-connection of these is present in food and drink tourism and correspondingly inter-relation occurs between their associated general, and many distinct within, cultures. Over these are the cross-strata of the different approaches and attitudes existing between those consuming, those providing, those enabling, and those having wider way influence. Initiative itself is layered as Hall, Mitchell and Sharples define, saying, 'Strategies to integrate tourism and cuisine in order to promote economic development and the creation of sustainable food systems occur at national, regional and local levels'. They stress that the ideal is that these layers should to be integrated for obtaining 'policy success' (2003). Hall, Mitchell and Sharples' remarks draw attention to the cultural dimensions present in food and drink tourism of local, regional and national – among the other cultural inputs. The situation of food and drink tourism, therefore, can be seen as very complex. This very complexity, however, is what is rendering its richness and probable power to fascinate.

Influences and Identity

Food and drink consumption, of course, has always been with us. The matter this book is trying to address is why food and drink *tourism* should occur. What forces are driving food and drink tourism to appear? Why is it happening now? The impellents bringing food and drink tourism can be divided under two categories:

- social and cultural influences
- practical requirements.

In broad generalization, these two can be characterized as the first centring in the mind, and the second being situated in matter. It has been shown in the progress of this book that features of these two dimensions are causing food and drink's appearance and bringing its now heightening and likely further development. Certain among the causes are fundamental needs being satisfied, others are basic needs deploying food and drink tourism as today's outlet rather than another; others are contemporary manifestations and uprisings and which find fit, realization and fulfilment in or through food and drink tourism.

Food and drink tourism has an identity, therefore, of social and cultural impositions met and melded with practical needs. Now will be summarized what are these various features of input. This should be noted concerning the elements: some have been present in the past and have come forward from it or are currently having a reappearance; others are old in derivation but are manifested in new way; further others are new introductions emanating from how society and groups have developed now to be.

To begin, the following are characterizations and purposes of sectors that have concern to food and drink tourism.

- Food and drink equates to: the everyday and routine
- Tourism equates to: leisure and the non-routine
- Providers want: income; agricultural or industrial diversification; community regeneration and development

- Society as a whole wants: safe and quality food and drink; environmental conservation and protection; means for collective and individual expression; a balanced, peaceable and sustainable world.

As has been explained, a particular and interesting feature to food and drink tourism, and making it rather different from other types of tourism, is that its subject – food and drink – is an entity located in everyday and core existence. It has been shown that this aspect brings the demand on providers to put and manifest enough character of difference from routine, sufficient excitement and alluringness, in their product to place it to be a tourism and special entity in the tourist's cognition.

For reason of the basic item, and its practices in association such as growing and cooking, having an everyday dimension, more than usual focus for a tourism entity needs to be put by the provider on product **ambience** as this aspect can frequently be the main element satisfying the requirement to demonstrate specialness. The **relationship to everyday** which food and drink tourism possesses is a factor continually showing and which renders particular challenges to the provider but also delivers special opportunities and potential likely benefits.

Causes of Existence

It is suggested in this book that contemporary features to society, the provider, and the tourist are combining to cause food and drink tourism's appearance and its espousal. Each among these motivators will be looked at.

From Society in General

First to be viewed will be the reasons coming from society and which act as an external general circumstance producing a need for response, and as one facet of which reaction food and drink tourism has the capabilities to be. Depicted above are the certain main forces of contribution to the scene. An advantaged world/ disadvantaged, First World/Third World, imbalance is generally accepted as for working for being avoided and as not helping the world community overall. It delivers separate areas of affluence and poverty in financial, quality of life, and health terms. Also too, but with the weight frequently allocated in opposite way, there are variations in landscape quality and cultural depth. Environmental damage, wherever emanating from, frequently affects all, as in the global warming, ozone layer outcomes. The obvious outcome of the general approach of seeing the world as one entity, whether in social, environmental, economic and commercial and cultural terms, is an increasingly-developed universal way of thought and action. As contributing to the world being looked at overall, and in overall way, are speedy communications, of information and transport. The particular outcomes relevant to food and drink tourism are: **globalization**, and as part of which is **time-space compression**.

The elision of time and space delivers the greater capacity of tourism. It delivers the experience of being able to move from same feature to same feature, hotel room or meal, as examples, in most places of the world. It makes a gathering or fusion, a global platter and drinking glass, attainable and as a usual norm. It can exacerbate global disparity through distant low-cost labour and resources being used and exploited for providing global brand goods. It can deliver a local product to travel many miles for consumption globally rather than only immediately as before. But this depends on mass amounts being obtainable: products of small-scale quantity will be left behind as not enough for satisfying the global appetite. Also, however, it 'throws up' and makes more pronounced by contrast, places unconnected to and left out from, global communication pathways. The pockets of difference have a distinct dimension – environmental, cultural etc – at home locale and in special measure, for offering to others if wished.

Global applications and scientific and technological innovations, and seeing distance as no obstacle, have delivered ready, and much inexpensive, food. Global food of ubiquity has been produced, whether in the forms of the McDonald's hamburger or Starbucks latte on every street corner or else the mango that is available to any table all year round, but at a high price – in several senses. Genetic Modification of food and by large-scale business interest and corporation has appeared. Questionable or inadequately-careful food practice have threatened food safety or has appeared so to do. There has been delivered in certain animals, BSE, vCJD, and – in the UK – foot and mouth disease. In the instance of the foot and mouth outbreak in the UK, the customary movement of livestock over long distances helped exacerbate the disease's spread and enormity. All these features too, revealing global or large and industrialized way of culture and action, have produced a contra-reaction, and which is a backlash of consumers querying food safety and in some number patronizing foods of local and known derivation and produced to organic or old-style and traditional method. Talking of Britain and before the impetus in the direction of the UK appearance of foot and mouth disease and discovery of reason for its quick escalation, Warde notes that, 'Ironically, the prominence of localized identifications with food coincides with the general decline of spatial differences in consumption patterns' (1997, p. 67).

Added to worries about safety of food and drink, and to those about the amount of quality of the atmosphere and living environment, the global citizenry is experiencing extra **safety concerns** and with each person worrying about their individual security, most distinctly after the events of '9/11' (11 September 2001). The globalized viewpoint is to be rather fearful about immediate circumstances and about the future. Manifestations of the feelings may be either the approach of seeking extra **comfort** or else the attitude of 'eat, drink, and be merry, for tomorrow we (may) die'.

As a counterforce to, and outcome of, globalization – a global method and lifeway – is the human urge to identify with place and community to make expression individually and noticeably. This need relates directly to culture. As this book communicates, activity concerning food and drink is routine and quotidian. Traditionally, food and drink have taken practice according to: soil, water, climate and landscape from whence they come; due to use and occasion associated with them; from method of preparation; by style of consumption chosen for them, and by whom is doing the activity. Globalization's essence is to be a global culture. It, therefore, has taken away from these old dimensions, the first especially; and albeit that the rest of the features continue, they do so in modern replacement format and in more standard kind of shape. Along with the other mentioned reasons for standing out against globalization, therefore, is to allow expression and make statement against uniformity; and keeping or reverting to local or individual ways of obtaining, producing, treating and regarding an item of food and drink acts as an **accessible** method to do this. Of course, some types of differentiation may actually cause difficulties if tourism is being hosted. A tourist of globalized, or different, cultural upbringing to the resident may, in encountering the latter's ways and rituals, find some unacceptable by the tourist's culture and insight, for example, the local community eating types of animals or birds that the tourist would not. A range of **cultural and ethical viewpoints** exist as to what is **appropriate** and need understanding concerning food and drink tourism's activity.

Consumerism is part of globalized (Westernized) procedure. Tourism features as part of this. Consumption – and shopping prominent among it – is at the heart of food and drink tourism. As the appearance of global environmental summits attests, the requirement to protect and conserve the environment for universal welfare and survival is another general impulse, though frequently, but not entirely, it is most strong from the most developed and consuming nations. A response is, Cha states, 'A brilliant concept turned worldview, Ecologically Correct' [EC] (Cha, 2001, p. 305) which promotes more spending as more saving. He says,

'The ideology of ecological correctness is increasingly a determining force behind almost every aspect of shopping, both physically and psychologically. From the food we eat, to the clothes and cosmetics we wear, to the malls where we shop, even to the hotels and resorts where we attempt to get away from it all, ecological awareness will be present. Ecological correctness has rapidly become one of the main organizing devices for the consciousness of consumption. By merging consumption and conservation, EC forms an endless landscape of enviroentrepreneurial shopping eco-topia. Leaving behind the greed-or-green dichotomy, companies have realized that this alliance – often times strategic, other times genuine – will produce highly sustainable profits. Very soon, whatever isn't EC will be in trouble, and this trouble means both the loss of an ecosystem and the loss of big money' (p. 306).

These comments suggest that globalization's impulses of making money and sustaining the environment are combining, to produce a new super-globalization culture of expediency and self-interest. This is another culture for the smaller-sized entities of particular groups, places and individuals to show difference from regarding food and drink consuming, if they want to display, and deploy as their item for tourism, a distinct culture concerning food and drink.

From Tourism and the Tourist; and from the Realms of Consumption and Food and Drink

The next matter is to summarize tourism in its now timbre and in its sector and aspects concerning food and drink. Tourism, to its consumer, represents a leisure activity and a non-routine happening. It serves frequently as an escape (from the everyday and routine). To draw tourists towards it, it devolves to show and offer different dimensions such as activity, relaxation, stimulation etc. The tourist has been described as having the seven longings of, 'paradise, the longing for childhood's fairy tale-land, the longing for the world of arts, the longing for rest, the longing for exploration and adventure, the eternal longing for the right one and the responsibility to meet one's death whilst still living'.

And the depiction is that

'these longings make a tourist move, to search for fulfilment in her/his life' (Tapaninen (ed), 1999, p. 82).

The comment further continues,

'The tourist's motive to travel is born of the need to satisfy the realities that live deep down in his/her soul, black holes: longing, passions, subconscious obligations and dream landscapes. When one leaves on a voyage, one travels a strange map.

Paradise is one of tourism's oldest stereotypes. People long for the happy garden of innocence where they can meet another one, completely naked' (p. 83).

Albeit that this overall portrayal is putting its interpretation of tourism romantically, it highlights tourism's level of depth and profundity and calibre of import for the tourist. Motivations are attributed to the tourist, certain of which food and drink tourism is well equipped to meet. It offers discovery and **sensory** dimension, stimulation and pleasure. It has features of meeting and it encompasses **conviviality**. Good food and drink engender a feeling of relaxation and the latter in alcoholic form has the capacity even to deliver a feeling of abandon. It has been shown that food and drink, as part of its long connection with ritual, has a strong aspect to be associated with celebration, in part through a fragility of dependability of appearance because of its basic connection with nature's cycle and imponderability. Celebration concerning food and drink is often connected to the agricultural cycle, to honouring gods seen as having influence over the process of agriculture and food preparation (fire for heat and cooking), as well as to honouring earthly leaders and influencers and to marking key joyous events in the human cycle such as birth and marriage.

The consumer following for 'real' and traditional food and drink, and which is manifestly **rooted** and which can be seen and identified as fresh due to localness, is perhaps part of a longing – and of most fundamental **nostalgia** – for an Eden unsullied and which when as tourist there is enough moment to pursue with fruitfulness and in concentrated and focused manner. It can be seen that in human attention to food and drink lies honour and respect for the properties of sustaining life of these. This lends to them, and their ways of being obtained, cultivated, and treated towards consumption, as significant. The dimension of **spirituality** is obvious to be attached to food and drink for a first elemental reason that the raw materials of it depend for appearance upon nature's uncontrollables and upon some serendipity. Awe of this and trying to find ways to bring influence to bear upon it all, leads to religiosity in connection with food and drink. They bear character of being **fundamental** items, and a sector now is seeking to connect with this dimension to food and drink more strongly due to believing that the modern scientific world is not giving the feature enough attendance and recognition.

Focus has been given to the importance of the holiday offering **time to give attention to food and drink** and in a different way and more meaningful way than usual life permits. Witzel, introducing the American drive-in, nostalgically remembers visits out along 'flavorful roadways' with his father to 'sample the best junk food that ever tickled our taste buds'. He describes 'the addictive lure of road-food', saying, 'the magic that it promised to add to our vehicular adventures were an addiction we couldn't resist' (1994, p. 9). They used to watched the 'pizza master' in full action and Witzel remarks that later on 'the trials of growing up and the demands of everyday living edged out the leisure time once used to watch the pizza man work' (p. 11).

Other descriptions similar to this below have been called upon already, but this here is included as a reminder and reinforcement of certain dimensions – such as soulfulness, magic, dreaminess, sensuality, addiction – that food and drink are able to bring to, or generate in, a holiday and which the operator clearly recognizes and is using towards their ends. Conveyed too is the significance and importance to generating appeal in providing and communicating ambience. This feature was mentioned earlier as helpful for adding to a basic food and drink item to make it become special and as among the domain of tourism rather than that just as part of quotidian existence.

'The montepulciano in our glasses glinted as red as any ruby in the soft rays of the autumn sunset. The aromatic fragrance of the Tuscan hillside hung in the still evening air. We dined on the terrace, watching the purple hills fade into night. The truffles were culinary poetry. Italy had worked its usual magic on body and soul. We were content with the world. The week had flown by. We would be back ...'
(Abercrombie and Kent, 2002, *Weekends and Beyond* brochure).

That this quote comes from the brochure of a tourism operator catering to up-market clientèle can be no coincidence. Underlined is that a considerable portion of food and drink tourism caters to the **connoisseur** and **aspirational** sectors.

The focus in the world of food and drink, as in the universe beyond, upon **celebrity** seems to represent a want to aspire and a feeling of personal insecurity and lack of self-esteem. Patronizing restaurants, hotels and schools and demonstrations of celebrity chefs is one method of associated with celebrity; another is visiting places associated with celebrities such as the bars in Cuba, El Floridita and Le Bodeguita del Medio, at which famous writer Ernest Hemingway was a regular and now which tourists attend in throngs (Geddes, 2001, pp. 212–213). Insecurity is perhaps partly what fuels the need to participate and to *show* participation. An element offered by many food and drink events, the cooking school for example, is not merely one of observation but of **participation**. Use can be made of food and drink and its events for showing distinctiveness as has been demonstrated, and often aspiration and insecurity are elements pushing a person's desire to display him or her self as different from others. Certain items are deployed for displaying refinement, knowledge, fashionability or rarified taste. Events such as festivals, street-food stalls, fast-food outlets, some bars and cafés, communicate and deliver **informality** and allow easy portrayal of **belonging** 'among the crowd'.

Mitchell and Hall consider in some detail consumer behaviour in food tourism itself and directly (2003). Characterizations of consumer types demanding seaside holidays are included in an ETC report *Sea Changes: Creating world class resorts in England* (ETC, 2001). These contain encapsulations of different kinds and emphases of food and drink use by the various categories of tourist identified. This matter is thought worth alluding to here for interest, and there may be relevance to the general scene, but it must of course be warned that no certainties can come from extrapolating from this research about markets of English seaside resorts and attempting the interpretation of the full domain. The segments identified are these:

- 'Conformists': who 'seek sameness and familiarity' and these favour restaurants, pubs, tea rooms and cafés;
- 'Sentimentals': who 'like expensive hotels and bed and breakfasts, have high expectations of hospitality and service and are prepared to pay more for better service'. 'They generally eat in more traditional restaurants offering a traditional menu.'
- 'Seekers': who 'are image driven' but on a limited budget and who 'are highly likely to stay in camp sites, hostels and self-catering accommodation.'
- 'Radicals': who 'are free spirits and big travellers' and whose presence at a destination 'acts to raise standards, set trends and stimulate the market.' 'They want distinctive restaurants, pubs, bars, clubs and nightlife' but prefer budget accommodation.
- 'Independents': who 'seek out different cultural experiences away from the crowd' and who 'prefer mid-standard independent hotel and bed and breakfast accommodation types to chain groups. They seek gourmet, relaxed restaurants serving local specialities.'
- 'Pragmatists': who 'are highly cultured and artisan', but 'frugal' and for whom, among other things, 'Ambience...accommodation... restaurants, cafés ... outdoor activities, traditional pubs, local shops and cultural interest' are important.
(ETC, 2001, pp. 23–25)

Tourists characterized through the material and example of this book as regarding food and drink and objects or highlights of travel appear as a main sector to be in the category of the educated, socially- and environmentally-aware or concerned, the tourism-experienced, the quite health-conscious, and the quite affluent, and the mid-to-late middle-aged. A younger, more fun-loving sector can also be identified and with a 'live for today' attitude prominent among it, and so its emphasis will be more on the hedonism properties of a food and drink product than its health-benefit properties. In line with demographics, all of these people will be increasingly likely to be urban-dwelling. In line with tourism's shape, all of them will most likely be drawn from the Westernized, developed, globalized, world. In line with being members of society they will all – albeit to differing extent – share its concerns and priorities described and one dimension of which, as has been depicted, will be to feel on a collective and individual basis, insecurity.

The food and drink tourism market can be seen as having core attributes and whose objectives food and drink tourism can satisfy, and which has two main subdivisions. The 'fit' between their overall feature and need and what food and drink tourism can provide is a reason for its emerging prominence, together with food and drink tourism's match of suitability to provider and society features and aims. The essential elements that food and drink tourism is able to offer the tourist are: means of showing distinctiveness and individuality; comfort – we speak, after all, of 'comfort food', and sensation of security; contrast with *and* connection to daily life; reconnection to roots and profundity, 'real' food and drink, and supposed better safety of food and drink; interesting ambience; enjoyment, stimulation and sensory pleasure.

An overall feature of food and drink, stemming from these being essential items, is their accessibility and approachability. In their fundamental entity they are **democratic**. Theoretically, they represent a device universally available to tourism.

From the Provider of Food and Drink Tourism

The key features to the background to food and drink tourism have been summarized. It has been seen what elements are crucially important about food and drink to the consumer and what food and drink tourism needs to represent to the tourist. Now it will be selected what food and drink tourism offers to the direct provider and to the stakeholder. The basic need that food and drink tourism should satisfy in a provider is that of earning. This immediately leads to a distinguishing feature to food and drink and which lends food and drink tourism as appealing to stakeholders, with politicians among them. Food and drink is frequently obtained from areas and circumstances now of disadvantage and which are in need of assistance. Food and drink's raw materials are grown or are nourished in a countryside environment, or they are gathered from off the coastline. Production sites are also often rural; otherwise they are industrial sites in town and city. For reasons of political edicts, such as those concerning prices allowed to be charged for goods; from legal impositions of practices to be followed on such grounds as health and safety; by too small size and lack of critical mass in context of globalization and multi-nationalism and being victim of these entities; many of old-established or traditional food and drink providers are not any more in a position able to survive financially. They are at peril to be in a socially- and culturally-impoverished position also. In essence, their way of life is at risk. A further dimension is that production plants may be technically obsolete or be obsolete through having insufficient capacity for competing with large providers and for economies of scale to be rendered. The situation of suffering and lack of money due to globalization and modern practice is not confined to the Western world: disadvantaged areas are anywhere throughout the globe where globalization either avoids them altogether or else exploits their need and disadvantage. Ironically, it is often pockets of the Western world that are suffering most – compared to their former level of livelihood – because they cannot compete with overseas products that are less expensive than theirs due to the lower – wage – costs in foreign production. Of course, as huge contrast to all this are the types of providers – of gourmet hotels and restaurant establishments, fashionable city bars etc – who are appealing and quality enough – and whose prominence media appearances of chefs, TV cookery shows etc, bolster – for them to be obtaining a fine livelihood in a general circumstance of consumer affluence.

Much reason for espousal of food and drink tourism and encouraging and helping its adoption is that – as has been demonstrated in this book – it can serve an important and wide role as a method of **diversification** for farmers who cannot subsist by direct agriculture alone. There has now been occurrence of a beneficial situation for all food and drink suppliers, but especially for those in the small-scale/ specialist/traditional style/organic categories. A 'silver lining' situation has happened in that the appearance of **food scares** – concerning GM food, vCJD, BSE – has put artisan, old-style and organic ways of production into much general favour, and with a sector among society attaching so much importance to food and drink quality as to be willing to pay the price necessary for increased likelihood of it. This has meant that a market opportunity exists to make a change, or shift of emphasis, in style of farming. As has been shown, diversification, moves towards organic production, efforts towards the provider being in more and direct consumer contact, have been supported and led by public sector initiatives and agencies. These have assisted in the delivery of necessary sites and the provision of correct types of outlet, and they have provided help in promotion with the objective to make the consumer better aware of what is on offer and how to find and obtain it.

A significant sector of suppliers should also be noted, often representing the most vibrant and appealing and interesting food-and-drink-concerned entities in a place the tourist visits and which act in conveying its full cultural identity. This sector is the 'ethnic' food and drink location – restaurant, street food stall etc. It acts to convey that a place is not mono-cultural and it represents 'otherness' against the conforming and dominant culture of a locale. It may seem especially approachable to the tourist, both by being an 'outsider – as the tourist is, and due to being low-cost – not least by favourable comparison with a 'home' culture, long established, very customer-frequented, competitor. Of course, most interesting to see and watch is how much the place displays its vaunted culture 'purely' and to what extent it represents a hybrid of its stated and original culture and that of its place of situation. Fort notes that in delivering a list recommending inexpensive restaurants in the UK in 2001, he is presenting a myriad portrait of which each one it includes is 'representing a community and culture that have made this country the most diverse, pleasurable and stimulating country of the world in which to eat' (2001, p. 4).

So, what does food and drink tourism represent for the provider and stakeholder, and what do they need to do to obtain benefit from it? It has been shown that there is a market to tap for country products. The rural provider's needs are: ensuring the tourist knows of their offer; enabling them to make contact with the product available. The provider in urban areas, many of which of these act as tourists' arrival point or as places they will be attending for other reasons, has a less uphill effort to get the tourist's awareness of their product – the restaurant, hotel, brewery or factory, as examples – and has less likely difficulty in bringing the tourist to encounter with it. Also, many urban products, through their context and association, have a fundamentally different kind of appeal and market to those of the countryside. Between the rural and urban area, the latter is more liable to be home of the industrial food and drink plant, and these in this 'modern' circumstance – however old, traditional, or picturesque they are – can need somewhat different style of presentational treatment to rural ones. When a site is in disuse it has the opportunity through tourism to emerge out of decay and obsolescence and have a total role as a tourist site. The difference of urban food and drink features to those of rural areas is due to the former's generally-accepted connotation being as *industrial* and *man-delivered*. In contrast, food production in the countryside has a different and aura in common perception; this is of being a process to ancient natural rhythms of delivery by *bounty of nature*. Essentially, the one kind of entity has purpose *to process*, whereas the other's is *to grow*, and one embeds in a culture associated with mass and united endeavour and the other sits in a culture that connects with small and independent effort.

Concerning food and drink tourism, having general thrust of appeal, to tourists, providers and stakeholders, is **'the countryside product'**. Largely, the metropolitan and urban areas take care of themselves, with individual providers able to make a living from a combination of locals and visitors. As has been shown, however, there are plenty of pockets of disadvantage in towns and cities, and some need initiative and agency help to get food and drink tourism operating and with success. Often what is needed is a collective theme or banner, and which allows small operators to join in and be promoted with it. Possessing a range of food and drink facilities, cities are able to attract both a young market and the more-mature connoisseur market. This leaves most attention on the countryside or on bringing its products to the consumer's view in the town by method of use of a retail outlet or a farmers' market. From the provider and stakeholder perspective, more effort is usually needed for a disadvantaged countryside than for a city equivalent. The likely causes of the countryside's propensity to being more requiring of initiative and help are:

- social isolation, paucity of facilities, and lack of many visitors;
- being victim to agricultural circumstances and impositions and that make the core rural livelihood of farming not adequate alone;
- its essential culture related to agriculture being undermined and being under threat.

As has been explained, rural food and drink tourism has the opportunity to turn these situations round, or to ameliorate them by adding another dimension. To support its potential to effect change, to bring socio-economic benefit, to reinforce or revive a culture etc, it has two dimensions of advantages: one is spectacular and major; the other is much more modest but nonetheless useful. The latter, alluded to earlier in the book, is that the growing cycle reaches its peak in a shoulder season, and so food and drink tourism focusing on agriculture and its products has an in-built capacity for an extended season compared with some other types of tourism. And, of course as a year-round cycle, agriculture, theoretically, always has something 'going on' albeit that at times it is either invisible or all-but-static.

This book's main thrust has been portraying the other, and central, advantage that rural food and drink tourism possesses. This is that the consumer – influenced by concern and satiety with the whole gamut of globalization, scares about food, the cult of foodie-ism, insecurity, nostalgia and lack of community from being most frequently not a rural resident, pressure of modern way and culture – is ready to consider and espouse, at least for a holiday's duration, **pre-industrial culture** and its elements. Their patronage is desirous and willing to be given to **the local** in the shape of food and drink for connotations of freshness and wholesomeness and for attendant cultural history. Humphrys, reporting the British farming industry's crisis of many years and the massive switch occurring to organic farming practice, remarks that 'the only way to make money is to sell at a premium price' (2001, p. 243). A substantial consumer band is prepared to pay this for increased feeling of well-being and security. With the usual way of the tourist being to be disposed to indulge themselves when on holiday, at that time of leisure they should represent leaders among a list of consumers likely to pay top prices for food and drink.

As a motivation of association of tourists to espouse countryside and seaside food and drink tourism is to assist and show sympathy to a wide provider group they see to be suffering – and whose lifestyle is under threat – due to imposition of complex and heavy regulations or by effect of animal disease outbreak and spread. On its front page, the newspaper *Suffolk Coast & Heaths* explained to tourists in spring/ summer of 2001 such a need for help that would be required from them once the foot and mouth disease outbreak, with its essential 'closure' of the countryside, would be over saying,

> 'The effects of foot and mouth are already hitting local businesses as well as farming. As restrictions allow, or are lifted, it will be vitally important to support rural businesses and local establishments and buy local produce'.

Of relevance to the whole wide circumstance of rural tourism and notable for its inference about the lack of total efficacy of unoverall and unconcerted effort, is that as part of UK Government's effort in relation to the foot and mouth disease outbreak, its Department of Culture, Media and Sport [DCMS] reported in October 2001 concerning tourism in relation to the year's epidemic, saying

> 'We recommend the immediate creation of a National Tourism Corporation for England, operating on the model of Urban Development Corporations …. This Corporation would be able to develop and implement a tourist strategy. It would have direct powers to distribute funds to areas in most need, in consultation with but not through the English Tourism Council, Regional Tourist Boards and Regional Development Agencies'
> (DCMS, 2001, p. 10).

A UK 'real food' membership campaign initiative which has been led from the provider direction – an inn-proprietor was its founder, and celebrity chef Antony Worrall Thompson has since become its President – is The Campaign for Real Food, already mentioned in this book, and which has aims such as

> 'to encourage restaurants, pubs and hotels to serve real food, prepared from fresh ingredients'

> 'to support the teaching of cookery in all schools'

> 'to provide a powerful voice for the public and to use the view of our members to lobby "decision makers"'.

As has been described, The National Trust has a large portfolio of properties, many of which are open to the public and are visited extensively. The Trust's Director-General perceives that 'it is in a unique position to make a real difference' in 'creating a thriving rural economy' (The National Trust, 2001a, p. 8). She reports that the Trust tries to 'buy local and seasonal food', describing

> 'Our restaurants and tea-rooms purchase more than 60 per cent of their food products locally, buying seasonal fresh ingredients wherever possible. At least two local butchers provide us with meat from our own tenant farmers, and we support local distinctiveness by serving for example, Kentish Hills water in Kent and Devon Spring water in Devon. Meanwhile, Jacob sheepskins from the herd at Charlecote [a NT historic property open to the public] and fruit and vegetables from Upton House [another NT historic property open to the public], both in Warwickshire, are successfully sold at the farmers' market in Stratford-upon-Avon. This experience has led to the planned creation of a farm shop at Charlecote in 2002' (p. 9).

That in 2002 the National Trust opened its first farm shop at one of its properties open to the public, Wallington Hall, has already been described.

It can be seen that food and drink tourism represents a valuable opportunity to providers and stakeholders, of which they have need, and which society and tourists want to exist. The demand to providers, many of whom are small operators, and some of whom are only entering a new arena of activity out of need or desperation rather than preference, and/or whom are diversifying from their prime and already full-time activity, is to give enough time and attention to considering and understanding how to act in the food and drink tourism arena of opportunity and potential bounty.

It has been identified that wine tourism is showing some lead, understanding and foresightedness of endeavour, and that it has features of application to, and encompassment of, food and drink tourism throughout. This extract, below, from the leaflet promoting the 2nd New Zealand Food and Wine Tourism Conference and the 1st Australasian Gastronomy Tourism Seminar perhaps delivers why, and explains – albeit somewhat over-romantically – what providers and stakeholders require to see and appreciate about the overall food and tourism domain, saying,

> 'Wine tourism is more than just a visit to a winery. Today and tomorrow it will embrace food as a key driver of the reason to visit a region. The title [of the Conference] 'Food and Wine Tourism' has been chosen to best describe what it is all about – the integration of the food and wine attributes of a region with its culture, heritage and lifestyle attractions.
>
> It is also about creating enduring memories for the visitor, especially to satisfy the expectations of tomorrow's discerning lifestyle consumer. Where food, wine and tourism are well developed, the visitor receives a sensational experience and spending increases dramatically. That is our opportunity but we will need to be world class to realise it'.

The exposition above encapsulates many of the matters and themes this book has sought to identify and embrace, and it includes or implies many of food and drink tourism's key words.

Food and Drink Tourism, and Culture: in a Nutshell

Appearing as the leitmotiv throughout food and drink tourism is the word 'local'. From the matter of this book, it seems that the associated word and concept of **IMMEDIACY** is what, above all, is being needed and represented in the food and drink tourism domain. Immediacy seems as an essential concept now appealing to society and to the food and drink consumer and so to the tourist, and to which is being attached importance also – for varied reasons – by the immediate provider and by their stakeholder helpers.

The immediacy needed by the food and drink tourist seems to be:

- that of **localness and freshness**
- that of **immediacy of gratification** – as is a general requirement of contemporary society.

Alongside the want for immediacy can be seen a need for the feature likely as ensuing from immediacy in its interpretation of localness, which is **distinctiveness**. Along with localness itself, distinctiveness is what culture delivers.

　　The general response portrayed appears caused by globalization as a culture and way of life. It seems partly produced by considerable fear of various kinds and among which are of loss of freedom, security, identity and individuality, and of reduction of quality and difference of food and drink due to mass-production processes. It seems partially delivered too by a wish for enjoying varied, rather than mono-cultural, ambience and experience. Also a fuelling aspect is a part of the modern globalized lifestyle being catered to, which is the craving for, and expectation of, instant pleasure and satisfaction. Food and drink represent very fast and accessible ways of indulgence.

　　The challenge for food and drink tourism is to use the dimension of immediacy within the context of the world as a whole and complex entity, and to do so creatively and freshly and far-seeingly, rather than parochially, unimaginatively and retrogressively. It has been the intention of this book to provide input towards this objective. More overall, this book has had the aim to portray cause, demeanour, and use, and set out a suggested future flavour, of that particular and wide endeavour, Tasting Tourism.

Bibliography

Aird, A. (2003) (ed), *The Good Pub Guide 2003*, Ebury Press, London.

Aird, A. (2002) (ed), *Great Food Pubs*, Ebury Press, London.

Alland Jr, A. with Alland, S. (2001), *Crisis and Commitment: The Life History of a Social French Movement*, Harwood Academic Publishers, Amsterdam.

Anderton, M. (1998), *Best Tea Shop Walks in Suffolk*, Sigma Leisure, Wilmslow.

Augé, M. (1995), *Non-Places: Introduction to an Anthropology of Supermodernity*, Verso, London.

Augé, M. (1999), *The War of Dreams: Exercises in Ethno-Fiction*, Pluto Press, London.

Barthes, R. (2000), selection and translation of Barthes, R., *Mythologies* (1957) by Lavers, A., *Mythologies*, Vintage, London.

Bauman, Z. (1998), *Globalization: The Human Consequences*, Polity Press, Cambridge.

Bayley, S. (2000), *General Knowledge*, Booth-Clibborn Editions, London.

Beardsworth, A. and Keil, T. (1997), *Sociology on the Menu: An Invitation to the Study of Food and Society*, Routledge, London and New York.

Birkett, D. (2002), 'Re-Branding the Tourist', in *Ethical Tourism: Who Benefits?*, Hodder and Stoughton, London.

Blythe, R. (1972), *Akenfield*, Penguin Books, Harmondsworth.

Boniface, P. (1998a), 'Are Museums Putting Heritage Under the Domination of the Tourism Industry?', *Nordisk Museologi*, No. 1.

Boniface, P. (1998b), 'Tourism Culture', *Annals of Tourism Research*, Vol. 25 No. 3.

Boniface, P. (2001), *Dynamic Tourism: Journeying with Change*, Channel View, Clevedon.

Boniface, P. (2002), 'Information Technology, Tourism and Biodiversity: in Society and in Relationship', in Di Castri, F. and Balaji, V. (eds), *Tourism, Biodiversity and Information*, Backhuys Publishers, Leiden.

Bourdieu, P. (1986), *Distinction: a social critique of the judgement of taste*, Routledge, London and New York.

Bové, J. and Dufour, F. (2001), *The World is Not for Sale: Farmers Against Junk Food*, Verso, London and New York.

Boyd, I. (2001), 'Isle of Wight "BIODIVERSITY" USE IT OR LOSE IT!"', *Insula: International Journal of Island Affairs*, Year 10 No. 2, September.

Bras, M. (2002), *Essential Cuisine: Michel Bras – Laguiole – Aubrac – France*, Ici la Press, Woodbury.

Brown, G. (2000) 2nd rev (ed), *The Whisky Trails: A Traveller's Guide to Scotch Whisky*, Prion Books Ltd, London.

Brown, J. (2001), *Spirits of Place: Five Famous Lives in Their English Landscape*, Viking, London.

Bullock, S. (2000), *The economic benefits of farmers' markets*, Friends of the Earth, London.

Burns, P.M. (1999), *An Introduction to Tourism and Anthropology*, Routledge, London and New York.

Cambourne, B., Macionis, N., Hall, C.M. and Sharples, L. (2000), 'The future of wine tourism', in Hall, C.M. Sharples, L., Cambourne, B. and Macionis, N. (2000b) (eds), *Wine Tourism Around the World: Development, management and markets*, Butterworth-Heinemann, Oxford.

Cha, T.-W. (2001), 'Ecologically Correct', in Chung, C.J., Inaba, J., Koolhaas, R. and Leong, S.T. (2001) (eds), *Project on the City 2: Harvard Design School Guide to Shopping*, Taschen, Köln.

Chapman, P. (2000), *The 2001 Good Curry Guide*, Simon & Schuster, London.

Chesser, J.W. (2000), Entry on food, in Jafari, J. (2000) (Ch ed), *Encyclopedia of Tourism*, Routledge, London and New York.

Chung, C.J., Inaba, J., Koolhaas, R. and Leong, S.T. (2001) (eds), *Project on the City 2: Harvard Design School Guide to Shopping*, Taschen, Köln.

Coe, S.D. and Coe, M.D. (1996), *The True History of Chocolate*, Thames and Hudson, London.

Cohan, T. (2000), *On Mexican Time: A New Life in San Miguel*, Bloomsbury Publishing Plc, London.

Common Ground (2000), *the common ground book of orchards: conservation, culture and community*, Common Ground, London.

Connaissance des Arts (2000), *la beauté in Avignon* exhibition guide, Guide No. 3, Connaissance des Arts, Paris.

The Countryside Agency (July 2000), *Eat the view: Promoting sustainable, local produce*, The Countryside Agency leaflet CAX 34.

The Countryside Agency (August 2001), *Eat the view: Promoting sustainable, local produce*, The Countryside Agency leaflet CAX 34.

The Countryside Agency (2001a), *Countryside Focus* Issue 15, August/September.

The Countryside Agency (2001b), *Countryside Focus* Issue 16, October/November.

Coward, R. (2000), 'Harvesting the forbidden fruit', *The Guardian*, Society section, 25 October.

Dalby, A. (2000), *Dangerous Tastes: The Story of Spices*, British Museum Press, London.

D'Arcy, S. (2001), ' What makes a great wine', *The Sunday Times* 8 April, Section 6.

Davidson, A. (1999), *The Oxford Companion to Food*, Oxford University Press, Oxford.

De Botton, A. (2002), *The Art of Travel*, Hamish Hamilton, London.

De Certeau, M., Giard, L. and Mayol, P. (1998), *The Practice of Everyday Life Vol 2: Living and Cooking*, University of Minnesota Press, Minneapolis and London.

DCMS (2001), *Tourism – The Hidden Giant – and Foot and Mouth* Government Response to the Fourth Report from the Culture, Media and Sport Select Committee, Commons Session 2000–2001, Cm 5279, October.

Donoughue, R. (1998), 'Foreword', in *Success with a small food business*, MAFF Publications [now DEFRA], London.

Dowling, R.K. (2001) (ed), 'Introduction', Wine Tourism theme edition of *Tourism Recreation Research* Vol. 26 No. 2.

Dowling, R. and Getz, D. (2000), 'Wine Tourism Futures', in Faulkner, B, Moscardo, G and Laws, E (2000) (eds), *Tourism in the 21st Century*, Continuum, London and New York.

Drysdale, H. (2001), *Mother Tongues: Travels Through Tribal Europe*, Picador, London.

Duncan, J. (2001), 'Beaujolais Britain', *The Observer* escape, 9 September.

Ellis, H. (2001), *Eating England*, Mitchell Beazley, London.

Ellis, J. and Cherry, P. (1997), *Secret Sussex Tea Trail: A Guide to the Tea Shops of East and West Sussex*, S. B. Publications, Seaford.

ETC (2000), *NewsETCetera*, May.

ETC (2001), *Sea Changes: Creating world-class resorts in England*, ETC, London.

ETC and The Countryside Agency (2001), *Working for the Countryside: A strategy for rural tourism in England 2001–2005*, ETC, London.

Enteleca Research and Consultancy Ltd (for the MAFF and The Countryside Agency) (2001), *Tourists' Attitudes towards Regional and Local Foods*.

The European Task Force on Culture and Development (1997), *In from the margins: A contribution to the debate on Culture and Development in Europe*, Council of Europe, Strasbourg.

Fernández-Armesto, F. (2001), *Food: a history*, London: Macmillan.

Fields, K. (2002), 'Demand for the gastronomy product: motivational factors', in Hjalager, A.-M. and Richards, G. (2002) (eds), *Tourism and Gastronomy*, Routledge, London and New York.

Fine, B. and Wright J. (1995), *Consumption in the age of affluence: the world of food*, Routledge, London and New York.

Flandrin, J.L. and Montanari, M. (2000) (eds), *Food: A Culinary History from Antiquity to the Present (European Perspectives)*, Penguin Books, London.

Flyvbjerg, K. (2001), 'Power Flour', *Copenhagen Living*, Summer/Fall issue.

Folwell, R.J. and Grassel, M.A. (1995), 'How tasting rooms can help sell wine', in *Direct Farm Marketing and Tourism Handbook*, University of Arizona.

Food from Britain (2000), *Cheese Report*. Food from Britain, London.

Foot, M. (1999), *Cider's Story: Rough and Smooth*, Mark Foot, Nailsea.

Fort, M. (2001), 'Fort's 40', *The Guardian*, 4 May.

Friends of the Earth (2001), *Get real about food and farming: Friends of the Earth's vision for the future of farming in the UK*, Friends of the Earth, London.

Frochot, I. (2001), 'French Wine Brotherhoods and Wine Tourism: A Complex Relationship', *Tourism Recreation Research* Vol. 26 No. 2.

Food and Travel magazine (Fox Publishing Ltd).

Gardiner, M.E. (2000), *Critiques of Everyday Life*, Routledge, London and New York.

Geddes, B. (2001), *World Food: Caribbean* Lonely Planet, Hawthorn, Australia.

Geddes-Brown, L. 'Taste of fresh Eire', *The Mail on Sunday* YOU magazine, 8 October.

Gillespie, C. (2001), with Cousins. J. (contributing ed), *European Gastronomy into the 21st Century*, Butterworth-Heinemann, Oxford.

Gillespie, C. and Morrison, A. (2000), 'Symbol, sign and senses; a challenge to traditional market communication?', *The Hospitality Review* 4.

Goldstein, D. (2001), 'Celebrating American Food', *Gastronomica: The Journal of Food and Culture*, Vol. 1. No 4.

Green, H. (2001), *farmers' market cookbook*, Kyle Cathie Limited, London.

Hall, C.M., Johnson, G., Cambourne, B., Macionis, N., Mitchell, R. and Sharples, L. (2000b), 'Wine tourism: an introduction', in Hall, C.M, Sharples, L, Cambourne, B and Macionis, N (2000a) (eds), *Wine Tourism Around the World: Development, management and markets*, Butterworth-Heinemann, Oxford.

Hall, C.M., Mitchell, R. and Sharples, L. (2003), 'Consuming Places: The Role of Food, Wine and Tourism in Regional Development' in Hall, C.M., Sharples, L., Mitchell, R., Cambourne, B. and Macionis, N. (2003) (eds), *Food Tourism Around the World: Development, Management and Markets*, Butterworth-Neinemann, Oxford.

Hall, C.M., Sharples, L., Cambourne, B. and Macionis, N. (2000a) (eds), *Wine Tourism Around the World: Development, management and markets*, Butterworth-Heinemann, Oxford.

Hall, C.M., Sharples, L., Mitchell, R., Cambourne, B. and Macionis, N. (2003) (eds), *Food Tourism Around the World: Development, Management and Markets*, Butterworth-Heinemann, Oxford.

Harris, D.R. (1996), 'Preface', in Harris, D.R. (1966) (ed), *The Origins and Spread of Agriculture and Pastoralism in Eurasia*, UCL Press Limited, London.

Harvey, G. (2001), 'Reinventing Agriculture', in Sissons, M (2001) (ed), *A Countryside for All: The Future of Rural Britain*, Vintage, London.

The Heart of England Tourist Board (2001), *Taster* The Food and Drink in Tourism Bulletin, August.

Heritage Hotels (2000), *Heritage: A Taste of Britain*, West One (Trade) Publishing Ltd, Marlow.

Hjalager, A.-M., and Corigliano, M.A. (2000), 'Food for Tourists – Determinants of an Image', *International Journal of Tourism Research* No. 2.

Hjalager, A.-M. (2002), 'A typology of gastronomy tourism', in Hjagler, A-M. and Richards, G. (2002) (eds), *Tourism and Gastronomy*, Routledge, London and New York.

Hjagler, A.-M. and Richards, G. (2002) (eds), *Tourism and Gastronomy*, Routledge, London and New York.

Honigsbaum, M. (2001), 'McGuggenheim?', *The Guardian*, 27 January.

Hubert, A. (2001), 'Sunday Morning in Limogne', in Petrini, C. with Watson, B. and Slow Food Editore (2001), *Slow Food: Collected Thoughts on Taste, Tradition, and the Honest Pleasures of Food*, Chelsea Green Publishing, White River Junction.

Humphrys, J. (2001), *The Great Food Gamble*, Hodder and Stoughton, London.

Inglis, F. (2000), *The Delicious History of the Holiday*, Routledge, London and New York.

Jeffries, S (2001), 'Bové relishes a second bite', *The Observer*, 12 August.

Kiple, K.F. and Ornelas, K.C. (2000) (eds), *The Cambridge World History of Food* Vols. 1 & 2, Cambridge University Press, Cambridge.

Klein, N. (2000), *No Logo*, Flamingo, London.

Klein, N. (2002), *Fences and Windows: Dispatches from the Front Lines of the Globalization Debate*, Flamingo, London.

Kurlansky, M. (2002), *Salt: A World History*, Jonathan Cape, London.

Langdon, P. (1994), 'Foreword', in Witzel, M.K. (1994) *The American Drive-In*, MBI Publishing Company, Osceola.

Langford-Wood, N. and Salter, B. (1999), *Event Management*, Hodder and Stoughton, London.

Leuker, A. (2001), 'Where There's Fizz In the Sauerkraut', *Time*, 19 March.

Lewis, I. (2000), 'Foreword', in Pettigrew, J. and Crocker, A. (2000), *The Tea Council's Best Tea Places*, The Tea Council Ltd, London.

Lovegrove, K. (2000), *Airline: identity, design and culture*, Laurence King Publishing, London.

Luard, E. (2001), *Sacred Food: cooking for spiritual nourishment*, MQ Publications Limited, London.

MacLaurin, T.L. (2001), 'Food Safety in Travel and Tourism', *Journal of Travel Research* Vol. 39, February.

McIntosh, R.W., Goeldner, C.R. and Ritchie, J.R., (1995), *Tourism: Principles, Practices, Philosophies* (7th Edn), John Wiley, Chichester.

MAFF (1998), *Success with a small food business*, MAFF Publications [now DEFRA], London.

MAFF 2000, *England Rural Development Programme*, MAFF Publications [now DEFRA], London.

Mason, L. with Brown, C. (1999) (for GEIE/Euroterroirs), *Traditional Foods of Britain: An Inventory*, Prospect Books, Totnes.

Mathews, D. (2000), *CAMRA's Good Cider Guide*, CAMRA, St Albans.

Mayes, F. (1998), *Under the Tuscan Sun: At Home in Italy*, Bantam, London.

Mayle, P. (2000), *A Year In Provence*, Penguin Books, Harmondsworth.

Mayle, P. (2001), *Bon Appetit! : Travels Through France With Knife, Fork And Corkscrew*, Little, Brown and Company, London.

Meadows, K. and Curtis, J. (2001), *Slow food*, thecafé@whalebonehouse, Cley.

Meethan, K. (2001), *Tourism in Global Society: Place, Culture, Consumption*, Palgrave, Basingstoke.

Michelin (2000), *The Green Guide: The West Country of England*, Michelin Travel Publications, Watford.

Mitchell, R., Hall, C.M. and McIntosh, A. (2000), 'Wine tourism and consumer behaviour', in Hall, C.M., Sharples, L., Cambourne, B. and Macionis, N. (2000a) (eds) *Wine Tourism Around the World: Development, management and markets*, Butterworth-Heinemann, Oxford.

Morgan, J. and Richards, A. (2001), *The Book of Apples*, Ebury Press in association with Brogdale Horticultural Trust, London.

Moss, G. (2002), There's this little place I know...', *The Observer Food Magazine*, August.

Moulin, C. and Boniface, P. (2001), 'Routeing Heritage for Tourism: making heritage and cultural tourism networks for socio-economic development', *International Journal of Heritage Studies* Vol. 7 No. 3, September.

Mudd, T. (2002), *Tip-top Fish and Chip Shops*, Studio Cactus Limited, Winchester.

The National Teapot Trail (1999), *The National Teapot Trail: The Guide to Teashops of Great Britain*, The National Teapot Trail.

The National Trust (2000), booklet *Farm Foods and Crafts from National Trust Tenants*, The National Trust, London.

The National Trust (2001a), 'The Director-General's Review of the Year', in *The National Trust Annual Report & Accounts 2000/2001*, The National Trust, London.

The National Trust (2001b), booklet *Farming Forward*, The National Trust, London.

The National Trust (2002a), booklet *Farm Foods and Crafts from National Trust Tenants*, The National Trust, London.

The National Trust (2002b), 'What's New', *The National Trust Magazine*, No. 97, Autumn 2002.

The National Trust (2002c), 'Serving up a double helping', *The National Trust Magazine*, No. 96, Summer 2002.

Nettleton, P. (2000), 'Why city children can't crack the country code', *The Evening Standard*, 11 October, p. 11.

O'Connor, J. (2001), 'Right time, right place', *The Observer*, 4 February.

Offitzer, K. (1997), *Diners*, Metro Books, New York.

O'Hagan, A. (2001), *The End of British Farming*, Profile Books Ltd with London Review of Books, London.

Ottoway, M. (2000), 'Vintage Australia', *The Sunday Times*, 16 July, Section 6.

Pascoe, D. (2001), *Airspaces*, Reaktion Books Ltd, London.

Patefield, J. (1999), *East Anglia Teashop Walks*, Countryside Books, Newbury.

Paxman, J, (1999), *The English: A Portrait of a People*, Penguin Books, London.

Peckham, S. (1998), 'Consuming nations', in Griffiths, S. and Wallace, J. (1998) (eds), *Consuming passions: Food in the age of anxiety*, Mandolin, Manchester and New York.

Pendergrast, M. (2001), *Uncommon Grounds: The History of Coffee and How it Transformed the World*, Texere Publishing, London and New York.

Petrini, C. with Watson, B. and Slow Food Editore (2001), *Slow Food: Collected Thoughts on Taste, Tradition, and the Honest Pleasures of Food*, Chelsea Green Publishing, White River Junction.

Pettigrew, J. (2001), *A Social History of Tea*, The National Trust, London.

Pettigrew, J. and Crocker, A. (2000), *The Tea Council's Best Tea Places*, The Tea Council Ltd, London.

Protz, R. (2002) (ed), *The Good Beer Guide 2003*, CAMRA, St Albans.

Rayner, J. (2002), 'Pearls of wisdom', *The Observer*, 15 September.

Redman, N. (2000), 'Britain needs a New Wave coast', *Evening Standard*, 15 March.

Reynolds, P.C. (1993), 'Food and Tourism: Towards an Understanding of Sustainable Culture', *Journal of Sustainable Tourism* 1 (1).

Ritzer, G. (2000), *The McDonaldization of Society*, Pine Forge Press, Thousand Oaks.

Ritzer, G. (2001a), *Explorations in the Sociology of Consumption: Fast Food, Credit Cards and Casinos*, Sage Publications, London.

Ritzer, G. (2001b), 'Slow Food Versus McDonald's', in Petrini, C. with Watson, B. and Slow Food Editore (2001), *Slow Food: Collected Thoughts on Taste, Tradition, and the Honest Pleasures of Food*, Chelsea Green Publishing, White River Junction.

Robinson, J. (1999) (ed), *The Oxford Companion to Wine*, Oxford University Press, Oxford.

Rojek, C. (2000), *Leisure and Culture*, Palgrave, Basingstoke.

Rotterdam 2001 Cultural Capital of Europe (2001), *Programme 2001* yearbook, BIS, Amsterdam.

Schlosser, E. (2001), *Fast Food Nation: What the All-American Meal is Doing to the World*, Allen Lane The Penguin Press, London.

Scruton, R. (2000), *England: an elegy*, Chatto and Windus, London.

Selborne, the Earl of (2001), 'Foreword', in Morgan, J. and Richards, A. (2001), *The Book of Apples*, Ebury Press in association with Brogdale Horticultural Trust, London.

Simon, J. (2001), 'Treading the true grape trail', in *The Sunday Times*, December 23, Section 4.

Sissons, M. (2001) (ed), *A Countryside for All: The Future of Rural Britain*, Vintage, London.

Solazzi, G. (2001), 'Alkmaar: The Cheese Market', in Petrini, C. with Watson, B. and Slow Food Editore (2001), *Slow Food: Collected Thoughts on Taste, Tradition, and the Honest Pleasures of Food*, Chelsea Green Publishing, White River Junction.

Symons, G. (1998) (compiler), *Jancis Robinson's Map of the Vineyards of England and Wales*, United Kingdom Vineyards Association, Saxmundham.

Tannahill, R. (Revised edition 2002), *Food in History*, Headline Book Publishing, London.

Tapaninen, J. (1999) (ed), *Finland: The Northern Experience, New Europe and the Next Millennium*, Tammi Publishers, Helsinki.

Time Out (2002), *Barcelona: Eating and Drinking*, Penguin, London.

Time Out (2002), *Rome: Eating and Drinking*, Penguin, London.

Toussaint-Samat, M. (translated Bell, A.) (1994), *History of Food*, Blackwell Publishers, Oxford.

Tregear, A. (2001), 'What is a 'Typical Local Food'? An Examination of Territorial Identity in Foods Based on Development Initiatives in the Agrifood and Rural Sectors', Centre for Rural Economy Working Paper 58, University of Newcastle upon Tyne.

Treuille, E. (2000) 2nd ed, *The Guide to Cookery Courses: Cooking & Wine Schools, Courses & Holidays Throughout The British Isles & Further Afield*, Metro Publications, London.

Twiss, S. (1999), *Apples: A Social History*, The National Trust, London.

University of Newcastle upon Tyne (2002), *Update*, Issue 147, 2 May, p. 2.

Urry, J. (2000), *Sociology Beyond Societies: mobilities for the twenty-first century*, Routledge, London and New York.

Veblen, T. (1899), *The Theory of the Leisure Class: An Economic Study of Institutions*, Allen & Unwin, London.

Walton, J.K. (2000), *Fish & Chips and the British Working Class, 1870–1940*, Continuum International Publishing Group, London.

Warde, A. (1997), *Consumption, Food and Taste: Culinary Antinomies and Commodity Culture*, Sage, London.

Warde, A. and Martens, L. (2000), *Eating Out: Social Differentiation, Consumption and Pleasure*, Cambridge University Press, Cambridge.

Watt, D. (1998), *Event Management in Leisure and Tourism*, Longman, London.

Webster, S. (2000), 'Five of the best', *The Observer Magazine*, 13 August.

Whittaker, J. (2002), *Tea at the Blue Mountain Inn: A Social History of the Tea Room Craze in America*, St Martins Press, New York.

Williams, P. (2001), 'The Evolving Images of Wine Tourism Destinations', *Tourism Recreation Research* Vol. 26 No. 2.

Winslade, R. (2001), 'Autumn Gold', *Organic Life*, October/November.

Witzel, M.K. (1994), *The American Drive-In*, MBI Publishing Company, Osceola.

Wright, P. (1999), *The River: The Thames in Our Time*, BBC Worldwide Ltd, London.

WTO (1999), Global Code of Ethics for Tourism, WTO, Madrid.

Ypma, H. (2001), *Hip Hotels: France*, Thames and Hudson Ltd, London.

Index